The Survivors Speak

A Report of the
Truth and Reconciliation
Commission of Canada

Truth and
Reconciliation
Commission of Canada

The Survivors Speak

**The Truth and Reconciliation
Commission of Canada**

2015

Truth and Reconciliation Commission of Canada

Website: www.trc.ca

Library and Archives Canada Cataloguing in Publication

Truth and Reconciliation Commission of Canada

The survivors speak : a report of the Truth and Reconciliation Commission of Canada.

Issued also in French under title: Les survivants s'expriment, un rapport de la Commission de vérité et réconciliation au Canada.

Available also on the Internet.

Includes bibliographical references.

Cat. no.: IR4-5/2015E

1. Native peoples--Canada--Residential schools. 2. Native peoples—Canada--History.
3. Native peoples--Canada--Social conditions. 4. Native peoples—Canada--Government relations.
5. Truth and Reconciliation Commission of Canada. 6. Truth commissions--Canada.
I. Title. II. Title: Report of the Truth and Reconciliation Commission of Canada.

E96.5 T78 2015   971.004'97   C2015-980020-X

Contents

Preface

On June 11, 2008, Prime Minister Stephen Harper issued an apology to the former students of Canada's Indian residential school system, calling it a "sad chapter in our history." That chapter is part of a broader story: one in which the Canadian government gained control over Aboriginal land and peoples, disrupted Aboriginal governments and economies, and sought to repress Aboriginal cultures and spiritual practices. The government, often in partnership with the country's major religious bodies, sought to 'civilize' and Christianize, and, ultimately, assimilate Aboriginal people into Canadian society. The deputy minister of Indian Affairs predicted in 1920 that in a century, thanks to the work of these schools, Aboriginal people would cease to exist as an identifiable cultural group in Canada.

Residential schools were seen as a central element in this project. For their part, Aboriginal people saw the value in schooling. It was at their insistence, for example, that many Treaties required government to provide teachers and establish reserve schools.

The decision to invest in residential schools was based on a belief that the cultural and spiritual transformation that the government and churches sought to bring about in Aboriginal people could be most effectively accomplished in institutions that broke the bonds between parent and child.

Ojibway woman with child in carrier basket. 1858. Library and Archives Canada/Credit: Humphrey Lloyd Hime/National Archives of Canada fonds/C-000728.

The Roman Catholic mission and residential school in Beauval, Saskatchewan. Deschâtelets Archives.

When Canada was created in 1867, the churches were already operating a small number of boarding schools for Aboriginal people. In the coming years, Roman Catholic and Protestant missionaries established missions and small boarding schools throughout the West. The relationship between the government and the churches was formalized in 1883 when the federal government decided to establish three large residential schools in western Canada.

According to the Indian Affairs annual report for 1930, there were eighty residential schools in operation across the country.[1] The Indian Residential Schools Settlement Agreement of 2006 provided compensation to students who attended 139 residential schools and residences.[2] The federal government has estimated that at least 150,000 First Nation, Métis, and Inuit students passed through these schools.[3]

The assault on Aboriginal identity usually began the moment the child took the first step across the school's threshold. Braided hair (which often had spiritual significance) was cut, homemade traditional clothing was exchanged for a school uniform, Aboriginal names were replaced with Euro-Canadian ones (and a number), and the freedom of life in their own communities was foregone for the regimen of an institution in which every activity

Students at the Roman Catholic school in Fort George, Québec, 1939. Deschâtelets Archives.

from morning to night was scheduled. Males and females, and siblings, were separated, and, with some exceptions, parental visits were discouraged and controlled.

Hastily and cheaply built schools often had poor or non-existent sanitation and ventilation systems. With few infirmaries in which students with contagious diseases could be isolated, epidemics could quickly spread through a school with deadly results. Because schools were funded on a per capita basis, administrators often violated health guidelines and admitted children who were infected with such deadly and contagious diseases as tuberculosis. Often, parents were not informed if their children became sick, died, or ran away.

For the first half of the twentieth century, the schools were on what was termed the "half-day system," under which half a day was spent in the classroom and the other half in vocational training. For the boys, this was largely restricted to farming and the crafts that a farmer might have need of, while the girls were trained in the domestic sciences. In reality, this was not so much training as child labour, undertaken to subsidize the ongoing operation of the schools.

Boys cutting wood at the Fort Resolution, Northwest Territories, school. Canada, Department of Interior, Library and Archives Canada, PA-048021.

The government mandated that English (or in Québec, French) be the language of instruction. And, although some missionaries had learned Aboriginal languages and provided religious instruction in those languages, in many schools, students were punished for speaking their language.

For most of the system's history, the federal government had no clear policy on discipline. Students were not only strapped and humiliated, but in some schools, they were also handcuffed, manacled, beaten, locked in cellars and other makeshift jails, or displayed in stocks. Overcrowding and a high student–staff ratio meant that even those children who were not subject to physical discipline grew up in an atmosphere of neglect.

From the beginning, many Aboriginal people were resistant to the residential school system. Missionaries found it difficult to convince parents to send their children to residential schools, and children ran away, often at great personal risk and with tragic outcome.

Students and staff working in the kitchen in the Edmonton, Alberta, school. The United Church of Canada Archives, 93.049P885N.

Although the issue of sexual abuse was largely unreported during the years in which the schools were in operation, over the past twenty-five years, it has become clear that this was a serious problem in some schools.

For most of the history of residential schools, teachers' wages in those schools were far below those offered to other teachers, making the recruitment and retention of teachers an ongoing issue. Although many remarkable people devoted their lives to these institutions, the churches did not require the same level of teacher training as was expected by the Canadian public school system.

Many students have positive memories of their experiences of residential schools and acknowledge the skills they acquired, the beneficial impacts of the recreational and sporting activities in which they engaged, and the friendships they made. Some students went to public schools so they could graduate and attend post-secondary institutions and develop distinguished careers. But, for most students, academic success was elusive and

One of the most northerly schools was at Coppermine in the Northwest Territories. General Synod Archives, Anglican Church of Canada P2004-09-404.

they left as soon as they could. On return to their home communities, they often felt isolated from their families and their culture. They had lost their language and had not been provided with the skills to follow traditional economic pursuits, or with the skills needed to succeed in the Euro-Canadian economy. Worst of all, they did not have any experience of family life or parenting.

By the 1940s, federal officials concluded that the system was both expensive and ineffective. As a result, the federal government began to substantially increase the number of on-reserve day schools and, in the 1950s, to enter into agreements with provincial governments and local school boards to have Aboriginal students educated in public schools. This policy of slowly winding down the residential school system was coupled with an expansion of the system in the Canadian North from 1955 onwards. Once again, children were separated from families for lengthy periods, taught by people who had no understanding of their language or culture, and housed in crowded and makeshift facilities.

Williams Lake, British Columbia, school hockey team. Museum of the Cariboo Chilcotin.

The partnership with the churches remained in place until 1969 and, although most of the schools had closed by the 1980s, the last federally supported residential schools remained in operation until the late 1990s.

In the 1980s, various members of Canadian society began to undertake a reassessment of the residential school experience. Starting in 1986, Canadian churches began to issue apologies for attempting to impose European culture and values on Aboriginal people. Apologies specific to the residential schools were to follow in the 1990s. Former students began to speak out publicly about their experiences, leading to both criminal charges against some sexual abusers and the launching of class-action lawsuits against the churches and the federal government. The cases were eventually resolved in the Indian Residential Schools Settlement Agreement, the largest class-action settlement in Canadian history, which was reached in 2006 and came into effect in 2007.

That agreement provided for a payment to all former students who resided in federally supported residential schools, additional compensation for those who suffered serious personal harm, a contribution to the Aboriginal Healing Foundation, support for commemoration projects, the establishment of the Truth and Reconciliation Commission of Canada, and the provision of mental-health supports for all participants in Settlement Agreement initiatives.

As part of its work, the Truth and Reconciliation Commission of Canada provided former students—the Survivors of residential schools—with an opportunity to provide a statement on their experience of residential schooling. This volume of excerpts from those statements is being published as a part of the Commission's final report.

At the beginning of the Commission's work, we questioned the use of the word "Survivor." It seemed to be a limiting, almost pejorative word. We saw it as referring to someone who was "just getting by," or "beaten down." We endeavoured to find an alternative, more suitable, word to ascribe to those who came out of the Indian residential schools.

However, over time, we have developed a whole new respect for the word. In "Invictus" (the title means "invincible" or "undefeated" in Latin), the English poet William Ernest Henley (1849–1903) wrote these words:

> Out of the night that covers me,
> Black as the pit from pole to pole,
> I thank whatever gods may be
> For my unconquerable soul.
>
> In the fell clutch of circumstance
> I have not winced nor cried aloud.
> Under the bludgeonings of chance
> My head is bloody, but unbowed.
>
> Beyond this place of wrath and tears
> Looms but the Horror of the shade,
> And yet the menace of the years
> Finds and shall find me unafraid.
>
> It matters not how strait the gate,
> How charged with punishments the scroll,
> I am the master of my fate,
> I am the captain of my soul.

A Survivor is not just someone who "made it through" the schools, or "got by" or was "making do." A Survivor is a person who persevered against and overcame adversity. The word came to mean someone who emerged victorious, though not unscathed, whose head was "bloody but unbowed." It referred to someone who had taken all that could be thrown at them and remained standing at the end. It came to mean someone who could legitimately say "I am still here!" For that achievement, Survivors deserve our highest respect. But, for that achievement, we also owe them the debt of doing the right thing. Reconciliation is the right thing to do, coming out of this history.

In this volume, Survivors speak of their pain, loneliness, and suffering, and of their accomplishments. While this is a difficult story, it is also a story of courage and endurance. The first step in any process of national reconciliation requires us all to attend to these voices, which have been silenced for far too long. We encourage all Canadians to do so.

Justice Murray Sinclair
CHAIR, TRUTH AND RECONCILIATION COMMISSION OF CANADA

Chief Wilton Littlechild
COMMISSIONER

Dr. Marie Wilson
COMMISSIONER

Introduction

Before the Survivor-initiated court case that led to the creation of the Truth and Reconciliation Commission of Canada, the Canadian residential school story has largely been told, to the extent that it has been told at all, through the documents and reports of the people who organized and ran the system. These documents describe the goals and methods of the federal government that founded and funded the schools, and of the religious organizations that operated them. Their written records contain the rationales for continued residential school operation, as well as internal, and occasionally public, criticisms of the schools. These have provided the basis for valuable histories.

Over the past thirty years, a growing number of former students have published their memoirs. In addition, Aboriginal organizations and individual academics have conducted research, and, in some cases, compiled and published transcripts of interviews and writings by former students, often with a focus on a specific school.

The Truth and Reconciliation Commission of Canada was mandated "to receive statements and documents from former students, their families, community and all other interested participants" and to recognize "the unique experiences" of all former students.

Over 6,750 people have given recorded statements to the Truth and Reconciliation Commission of Canada. Most of these were given in private settings. Others were given at the national, regional, and community events; sharing circles; and hearings organized by the Commission. These private and public statements form a key part of the Commission's legacy.

The Commission recognizes that the essential voice of the former students must be given a central place in any history of the schools. Since statement gathering has been an ongoing process throughout the Commission's mandate, it has not been possible to undertake a complete assessment and analysis of all the statements. This volume is based on a survey of the statements gathered from all parts of the country between 2009 and 2014. Almost all the statements come from individuals who attended schools after 1940. The volume begins with the students' lives prior to attending residential school, and then describes their arrival at the schools, and their experiences studying, working, and living in the schools.

Commentary and interpretation have been kept to a minimum to allow the students to speak for themselves.

Life before residential school
"We were loved by our parents."

When I think back to my childhood, it brings back memories, really nice memories of how life was as Anishinaabe, as you know, how we, how we lived before, before we were sent to school. And the things that I remember, the legends at night that my dad used to tell us, stories, and how he used to show us how to trap and funny things that happened. You know there's a lot of things that are really, that are still in my thoughts of how we were loved by our parents. They really cared for us. And it was such a good life, you know. It, it's doing the things, like, it was free, we were free I guess is the word I'm looking for, is a real free environment of us. I'm not saying that we didn't get disciplined if we got, if we did something wrong, we, you know. There was that, but not, but it was a friendly, friendly, like a loving discipline, if you will.

Bob Baxter.

— Bob Baxter, Statement to the Truth and
  Reconciliation Commission of Canada,
  Thunder Bay, Ontario, 24 November 2010.[1]

I'm come from a long way, I came a long way. I'm from Great Lake Mistissini. That's where I was born in the bush. It was a pride for me to say that because I was born in the bush in a tent. It's something that remains in my heart going to the woods, living in the woods. It's in my heart. Before going to the boarding school, my parents often told me what they were doing in the woods when I was born. What they were doing, we were in camp with other families. The stories my father told us, my mother, too.

— Louise Bossum, Statement to the Truth and Reconciliation Commission
  of Canada, La Tuque, Québec, 6 March 2013.[2]

Many former students spoke of what their lives were like prior to going to residential school. These recollections describe the ways in which cultural and spiritual practices and values had been transmitted from one generation to the next before life in the schools interfered with that process. They are also a reminder that these practices—and the languages in which they were embedded—are not things of the ancient past, but, rather, are vibrant elements of the childhoods of people who are still alive. Whether the governmental goal was assimilation, as initially stated, or, as the government later claimed, integration, the cultural practices described in the following section were under attack.

Before she was enrolled in residential school in Québec in the 1960s, Thérese Niquay lived on what she described as "the family territory." She had very positive memories of that part of her life.

> I remember especially the winter landscapes, fall landscapes too. I remember very well I often looked at my father, hunting beaver especially. I admired my father a lot. And I remember at one point I was looking at him, I think I was on the small hill, and he was below, he had made a hole in the ice, and he was hunting beaver with a, with a harpoon, and I was there, I was looking at him and I was singing. And I remember when I was kid I sang a lot, very often. And I also remember that we lived or my, my paternal grandmother was most often with us, my, my father's mother, and we lived in a large family also, an extended family in the bush. Those are great memories.[3]

Jeannette Coo Coo, who attended the La Tuque, Québec, school in the 1960s, said she was a member of what might be the last generation of Aboriginal people who were raised in the forest.

> In the forest, what I remember of my childhood was bearskin, which I liked. I was there, and it was the bearskin that my father put for us to sit on, that was it. That is why I'm pleased to see that here. And what I remember in my childhood also was the, my mother's songs, because we lived in tents, and there was young children, and my mother sang for the youngest, and at the same time this helped us to fall asleep. It was beneficial to everyone, my mother's songs, and that is what I remember, that is what I am happy to say that it was what was, I was raised with what was instilled in me, so to speak.[4]

Albert Elias grew up in the Northwest Territories near the community of Tuktoyaktuk.

> Yeah, when I first opened, like, when I first saw the world, I guess, we were outdoors and when I opened my eyes and started to, you know, and I was just a baby, I guess, and I, we were out in the land. The land was all around me, the snow, the sky, the sun, and I had my parents. And we had a dog team. We were travelling, I think it was on Banks Island, and I was amazed at what I saw, just the environment, the peace, the strength, the love, the smile on my dad's face. And when I wake up he's singing a short song to me of love.[5]

In the 1940s, Paul Stanley grew up speaking Kootenai (Ktunaxa) in the interior of British Columbia. As he told the Commission, he learned the language from his father. "When you're in bed with Papa, and he tells you about your first story, and it's about how the chipmunk got his stripes, and it was so funny to me, you know that I asked him every night to say it again."[6]

Eva Lapage was born in Ivujivik, in northern Québec, in 1951.

When I was a little girl, 'cause we live in igloo and we live in nomadic life and there was no white people and we move around from camp to camp, depending on the season. And we live with nature and our family and everybody looks after each other. And it was very, very simple, living, just survival in the way, looking for food and moving around.[7]

Bob Baxter was born on the Albany River in northern Ontario.

So, that's how I, that's how I grew up, you know, and knowing all that stuff where listening to the familiar sounds of my dad's snowshoes in the winter when he came to, when he came back from trapping late in the afternoon, towards, when it's already dark, and waiting for him to come home and tell us the legends, because no TV back then.

Eva Lapage.

So, it was great. My mom was great, too. She really looked after us, made sure that we were clothed and fed. That was good times.

I remember eating wild game all the time. And 'cause we had our grandparents that really looked after us, too, that I have good memories of, until, 'til that day that we were taken from there, taken away to school.[8]

Prior to attending the Roman Catholic school in Kenora, Ontario, Lynda Pahpasay McDonald lived with her family near Sydney Lake in northwestern Ontario in the 1950s.

We spent most of our time in the trapline, in the cabin, and we'd play outside and it was really good. There was no drinking. There was, it was, like, it was a small sized cabin, and my parents took good care of us. And they were really, I remember those happy days, like there was no violence. We had a little bit of food, but we always had a meal, like we ate, the beaver meat or moose meat if my dad got a moose, and deer meat, and, and fish.

She could not recall being physically disciplined during this time. "They more or less just told me, you know, don't do this, you know you'll hurt yourself and what not, but it was all in Ojibway, all spoken in

Lynda Pahpasay McDonald.

Ojibway. And I spoke Ojibway when I was a child, and there was a lot of fun." Her mother would harvest plants to be used as medicine.

And we would, my parents would take us out blueberry picking, and my grandparents would always take us blueberry picking, or we'd go in the canoe, and we'd go, you know, or my grandmother would always be gathering traditional medicines. She had picked the wild ginger, and I would go with her, and we'd go pick all the medicines that we needed.

And I also remember my mom picking up this medicine. It would, like, if we had any cut, or open wound, she would use this, like a ball, like, sort of a fungus ball, and she would open it, and she would put it on our wounds and whatever, and would heal, you know, real fast. And, and she knew all her traditional medicines.

And at the time, I remember my, my grandpa and my dad, they used to have a drum, and they would, you know, drum and they would sing, during certain time of the year.[9]

Mabel Brown had similar memories of her life growing up in the Northwest Territories.

You know life in the bush is really good. And when, when we were growing up we went, when my dad was alive, him and my mom brought us out into the bush. And we, we went as a family together. They taught us, when they'd teach us they taught us how to do things. They'd tell us first, they'd show us, and then we'd do it and then that's how we learned that. And that's how so many people now know when, when we see a snare or how to set it or set traps because my grandmother showed me how to set traps.

And how to tell what kind of trees are what and what the different kind of things you take off the gum, and things like that; what it's used for and you know, chew and my mom and dad used to dig up roots from the ground and I used to just love that roots. Chew on it and all those things are medicine for our bodies too. And I still, I still, can't eat just store-bought foods. I have to have caribou or fish or moose meat or something like that and to, to feel full; to feel satisfied.[10]

Emily Kematch was born in 1953 in York Factory, Manitoba, and grew up in York Landing.

My family is Cree in origin. My mom and dad spoke Cree and that's my Native language is Cree and that's the only language I spoke at home. And when I was six years old, I only understood basic, really like from my brothers and sisters when they came back from residential school. Like, "What is your name?" And I knew to say, "Emily" and not very much English. And I was very close to my mother. Her and I were, I was just attached to her like, I loved my mother and I knew she loved me. Same with my father, he showed it in different ways.

He was a very quiet man, but his actions spoke volumes. He hunted, he was a hunter, a trapper, a fisherman and that's how we survived, my family because he didn't work, he didn't have a job and my father was a, what they call a lay reader in the Anglican faith. He led church services in my community and my family was Anglican in faith. My father ran the services in my hometown of York Landing. He did the services in Cree and that's what I miss about our community right now, is that aspect is the Cree singing, 'cause it's not around anymore.[11]

Piita Irniq was born near Repulse Bay, in what is now Nunavut.

Piita Irniq.

> I lived in an igloo in the wintertime. A very happy upbringing with my family, and both my mother and father were very good storytellers, and they would tell legends, and they would sing songs, traditional, sing traditional Inuit songs. They would, my father in particular, would talk about hunting stories.
>
> My mother would sew all of the clothes that we had, you know, caribou clothing and things like that, sealskin clothing. I still wear sealskin clothing today, particularly my boots, you know, when I'm, I'm dancing, for example. So, my mother would sew, teaching my sister how to sew, so that she could become a very good seamstress when she grows up, or older.
>
> And in the meantime, I was apparently being trained to be a good Inuk, and be able to hunt animals for survival, caribou, seals, a square flipper, bearded seal, Arctic char, you know, these kinds of things, including birds. And I was also being told, or being taught how to build an igloo, a snow house.
>
> When I was a little boy, growing up to be a young boy at that time, my other memories included walking on the land with my father. My father was my mentor. He, he was a great hunter. So, I would go out with him on the land, walking in search of caribou, and I would watch him each time he caught a caribou, and I would learn by observing. As Inuit, I learned a long, long time ago that you learn by observation, and that's what I was doing as a little boy becoming a young man at that particular period of time.
>
> So, in the wintertime, we would travel by dog team. I remember travelling by dog team as early as three or four years old. Hunting, again, you know, hunting is a way of life that I remember when I was growing up for survival, and caribou hunting, and seal hunting, and fishing. And, and my, my father also did some trapping, foxes.[12]

Anthony Henry was born in Swan Lake, Ontario. "I was born in a tent in the woods so I was brought to the world in a very harsh environment, which I guess is a good thing because it made me the tough guy I am." He said he was raised in a traditional lifestyle based on

> trapping, hunting, fishing and harvesting of edible plants, such as wild rice and other edible materials. Total, total traditional style is what I call it. My parents were extraordinary people. They prepared me to be an independent individual. They taught me a lot of things that I've used throughout my life as a traditional person. They taught me how to survive.[13]

As Albert Fiddler was growing up in Saskatchewan, his father taught him how to live off the land.

> I remember my dad teaching me how to hunt, and learn how to snare rabbits, learn how to take care of horses. I was riding horses already on, four years old, and I'm riding with a bareback, and I enjoy that thing. I still remember that because I was a fairly decent cowboy, you know, like little beaver, as they used to call him in the comic books. I used to hang on onto just the mane. I didn't, I didn't even have a bridle.

His father also taught him to hunt.

> And it's funny sometimes, you know, and some of it was fun. Some of it was kind of patience, and pretty chilly sometimes when he was telling me when, how to snare chickens out of the, out of the willows. We're using this, a little wire, and a long stick, and standing on the dark side of, and waiting for the chickens to come and feed on the willows, and now we'd snare them down, yeah.[14]

Doris Young attended residential schools in Manitoba and Saskatchewan. Her early childhood was spent in northern Manitoba.

> The family that I had, my mother and father, and my brothers and sisters, and my grandparents, and my aunties and uncles. The community that I lived in was a safe one. It was a place where we were cared for, and loved by our parents, and our grandparents, and that community that I lived at we were safe. We were, we were well taken care of. We lived off the land, and off the water, meaning by fishing. My dad was a chief, but he was also what we would call a labourer in those days, but he was also a hunter, trapper, and fisherman, and that's how he supported us. And my mother spoke only Cree, and that's the language that we spoke in our household, and she thought it was very important for us to, to have that language because, it was the basis of our culture, as I came to understand it later in life. And she was the one that enforced that, that language that we spoke in our house.[15]

Delores Adolph was born in 1951 and grew up in a self-sufficient Aboriginal family in British Columbia.

Delores Adolph.

> Before I came to residential school, our, our families fished and hunted for our food. Our mother, she grew our own vegetables, because we were quite a ways from the stores, and because we lived in the remote area where, where there is no stores. And you know there was, our means of travel was canoes, so that's how we travelled.

> And our, our home life, it was not the greatest, but what our parents were trying to teach us how to, how to be, to keep busy, and then, and for us not to say there's nothing to do.

So, we, we packed water, and we packed, we packed our wood. Sometimes we had to roll our wood up, up the dike, and then roll it down the other side, and, and we had to learn how to cut our, our wood, and make kindling for the fire, and that was our way of life.

And, and my grandfather was busy trying to teach us how to build canoes. Build, make paddles. Build a bailer, to bail water out of our canoe. And, and then they were trying to teach us how to, how to race on those old fishing canoes, and we always beat the boys. And they didn't like that, because we, we beat them all the time. So, that meant that we were, that we were strong at that point, before we came to residential school. And my life has been upside down since I came to residential school.[16]

Rosalie Webber, who later attended a boarding school in Newfoundland, spent her early childhood with her parents in Labrador in the 1940s.

My father was a fisherman and my mother also worked with him and they worked together. He was a trapper and my mom trapped with him. Also my mom made all of our clothes and all of his clothing. And they knitted and they cooked and my mom was a midwife.

Rosalie Webber.

It was very happy. We were always busy with the family. Everything was a family thing, you know. I remember gathering water from the one little brook that ran through Spotted Islands, where I was born. I remember, you know, the dogs. I remember my brothers and I had one sister and, I had another sister, a step-sister, but she lived in Newfoundland and I didn't know her.

We were quite happy, you know, and my mother was a hunter like my dad. They'd go out in partridge season and, and always in competition and with a single .22 she'd come in with about 150 and he'd be lucky to make the 100. [laughter] And then the community would take it and it would be bottled and canned for winter provisions, 'cause being, being a trapper in the winter time, they all had their own trapping areas. So they, many of them went in their own traplines and as we did and my father trapped in Porcupine Bay. And so we would journey there when fishing season was over.

I was just a small child so I remember happy days.[17]

Martha Loon was born in 1972 in northwestern Ontario and attended the Poplar Hill, Ontario, school in the 1980s. Stories were a large part of the education she received from her parents.

They were stories that, you know, they, they taught us how, how to behave. You know they taught us our values. We even just, you know how, you know you hear stories about the beaver, and I always used to wonder why my mom would every time she was skinning beaver, she'd always set aside the, the kneecaps separately. She'd put those aside. And then afterwards she'd go, she'd go, either paddle out to the water somewhere, like a deep part, and that's where she threw them in. And, and I always know, wondered why she would do that. I've never questioned. It wasn't until I was older I asked her, like, "Why do you do that?" She says, you know, "This is what we're supposed to do, to respect and honour the beaver, to thank the beaver for giving its life so that we could eat it, use its pelt. This is what the beaver wants us to do." The same thing as you treat a duck, a duck, the duck bones a certain way. You know all that's got, got purpose and a reason for it.[18]

Grandparents played an important role in raising children in many communities. Richard Hall, who went to the Alberni, British Columbia, school, recalled with deep affection his pre-residential school upbringing and the role that his grandparents played.

Richard Hall.

And my grandmother she taught us to be orderly. She taught us to go to church. She dressed us to go to church. She loved the church. My playground was my friends, with my friends was the mountains, streams, the ocean, and we're raised in the ocean because we went fishing all summer long and we travelled to the communities, the fishing grounds because at the mountains where ... the places where we spend our days, times, the rivers, from in playing in the river, no fear and that was normal. With my grandfather, he took me with him at the young age, he took me, he taught me to work in the boats with him. He taught me how to repair boats. He will take me to talk to his friends and all I did was to speak their language and speak their Native tongue while they prepared fish around the fire. He took me wherever he went and I later learned that he was my lifeline. He helped me and guided me the best he could.[19]

Before going to the Qu'Appelle, Saskatchewan, school, Noel Starblanket was raised by his grandparents.

I attended ceremonies, I went to Sun Dances. I picked medicines with them. We did medicine ceremonies. We did pipe ceremonies. We did feasts. We did all of those things with my grandparents, and I spent time with my grandfather in those ceremonies, and I worked with my grandfather. He made me work at a very tender age. I was cutting wood, cutting pickets, cutting hay, hauling hay, all of that kind of stuff, looking after animals, horses and cattle. So, I spent a lot of good times with my grandparents, my, and the love that I had from them, and the kindness, and the very deep spirituality that they had. And so my formative years were with them.

I would spend time with my parents, but not a whole lot. So, mostly my grandparents raised me. My parents never hit me, my grandparents. I didn't know what, what it meant to be hit, physically abused. All I needed was one stare, or one look from my dad, or my grandfather, and my grandmother or my mother would always say *"wâpam awa"*[20] [look at that one], then I would stop what I was doing, because I knew how to respect my grandfather and my dad, didn't have to hit us, just, just took one look. [laughs] And so I grew up with that. And if we were acting foolish, or anything like that, or misbehaving, or whatever, they, they would just, they would just tell us in a good, kind way not to behave like that, and or if we were acting too silly, or whatever, they would tell us to calm down. They would always tell us that if you're gonna hit a high like that, you're gonna hit low, and I'll always remember that teaching, 'cause I tell my grandchil-

Noel Starblanket.

dren the same thing. When they get too excited, or too animated, or laughing too hard, or tickling, or whatever on an emotional high, I'll just tell them what my grandparents said, and I'll never forget that.[21]

Patrick James Hall was born in 1960 and grew up in what is now called the Dakota Tipi First Nation.

And, I remember, I remember a lot of times, I guess, with my grandfather, my grandmother. One of them in my mind, I remember. My grandfather used to haul wood on a sleigh. He had horses. And, so, my older brothers would go with him, too, and we just, he'd take us for horse rides. And, he used to talk with us all the time in Dakota. I mean, we used to, we used to remember what he said because we'd always be laughing, having fun, and.... My grandpa was very, very active guy. He, he always made sure, you know, he made sure that we had everything for the family. We used to go hunting, deer hunting and fishing, trapping. And, my mother, too, she was a very hard worker 'cause she used to be hauling water, cutting wood. And that was just during the winters. It was very hard 'cause we have to cut wood, and break the ice for water, and heat it up for the stove.[22]

Growing up in Sandy Lake, Saskatchewan, Leona Martin learned how to live off the land.

But my granny taught us some valuable lessons on, I didn't really know what they were until I got older, that she would. And my dad too, used to wake us up at 5:00 in the morning and we used to go snaring rabbits. He told us, "You have to get up before the animals," he said, "and you'll, otherwise they'll take your whatever you snared the rabbits or hogs ... the prairie chickens," that, "you had to get up early, don't be lazy."

And then we'd go back to bed and my mom would make the breakfast and we'd go off to school. My granny taught us to go picking berries and then she would can them for the winter, and she would give us some at wintertime.[23]

Andre Tautu, one of the first students to attend the Chesterfield Inlet school on the Hudson Bay coast, said,

In 1949, we started being told we had to go to school in Chesterfield Inlet. I came from a happy home and we had a good life when we were living on the land with my mother, my father, my grandfather, my grandmother, and my siblings of which I was the eldest. When I first went to school, I didn't know one word in English.[24]

Some students had very different memories. By the 1940s, decades of poverty, poor health, and social marginalization had disrupted many Aboriginal communities and families. Disrupted family life is, in fact, part of the continuing legacy of the residential schools themselves, and some families were already living with the impacts of the schools on older siblings or other family members who had gone to school before them. Many of the former students identify themselves both as "Survivors" of the schools, and as "Intergenerational Survivors," the children of parents who were also former student Survivors.

One former student, who attended residential school in the Northwest Territories, recalled that her home life was violent and frightening.

There was a lot of violence. There was a lot of, we were very afraid of my father. He was a very angry man. And, and my mother used to run away on him and he used to come home to us kids and then, just really verbally abuse us and make us really scared of him. We used to be, I, I used to run to the neighbours and hide behind their door because I was so scared of him.[25]

Another former student said that the Kuper Island, British Columbia, school

was better than being in the chaotic home life that we had. My parents went to residential school system, and they didn't know how to parent and suffered alcoholism. There was physical abuse at home, just the chaos of an alcoholic home.[26]

Forced departure
"I didn't want my dad to go to jail."

For many students, the trip to residential school began with the arrival of an official letter. When Josephine Eshkibok was eight years old, a priest came to her home in northern Ontario and presented her mother with a letter. "My mother opened the letter and I could see her face; I could see her face, it was kind of sad but mad too. She said to me, 'I have to let you go,' she told us. So we had to, go to, go to school at Spanish Residential School."[27]

Isaac Daniels recalled one dramatic evening in 1945, when the Indian agent came to his father's home on the James Smith Reserve in Saskatchewan.

> I didn't understand a word, 'cause I spoke Cree. Cree was the main language in our family. So, so my dad was kind of angry. I kept seeing him pointing to that Indian agent.
>
> So that night we were going to bed, it was just a one-room shack we all lived in, and I heard my dad talking to my mom there, and he was kind of crying, but he was talking in Cree now. He said that, "It's either residential school for my boys, or I go to jail." He said that in Cree. So, I overheard him. So I said the next morning, we all got up, and I said, "Well, I'm going to residential school," 'cause I didn't want my dad to go to jail.[28]

Donna Antoine was enrolled in a British Columbia residential school after a visit from a government official to her family.

> It must have been in the summer, the, the Indian agent came to, to see my father. I imagine it must have been the Indian agent because it looked pretty serious. He was talking to him for some time, and because we couldn't understand, we, we couldn't even eavesdrop what they were talking about. So after some time spent there, Father sat, sat us down, and told us that this Indian agent came to tell us, tell him that we had to go to school, to a boarding school, one that is not close to our home, but far away.

Donna Antoine.

The official had told her father that he would be sent to jail if he did not send Antoine to residential school. "We were sort of caught in, in wanting to stay home, and seeing our parents go to jail, and we thought, we must have thought who's gonna look after us if our parents go to jail?"[29]

In the late 1940s, Vitaline Elsie Jenner was living with her family in northern Alberta. "My, my mom and dad loved me, loved all of us a lot. They took care of us the best that they knew how, and I felt so comfortable being at home." This came to an end in the fall of 1951.

Vitaline Elsie Jenner.

> My parents were told that we had to go to the residential school. And prior to that, at times, my dad didn't make very much money, so sometimes he would go to the welfare to get, to get ration, or get some monies to support twelve of us. And my parents were told that if they didn't put us in the residential school that all that would be cut off. So, my parents felt forced to put us in the residential school, eight of us, eight out of, of twelve.[30]

Many parents sent their children to residential school for one reason: they had been told they would be sent to jail if they kept their children at home. Ken A. Littledeer's father told him that "if I didn't go to school, he'd go to jail, that's what he told me." As a result, he was enrolled in the Sioux Lookout, Ontario, school.[31]

Andrew Bull Calf was raised by his grandfather, Herbert Bull Calf. When he was enrolled in residential school in Cardston, Alberta, his grandfather was told "that if he didn't bring me, my grandfather would be … would go to jail and be charged."[32]

Andrew Bull Calf.

When Martha Minoose told her mother she did not wish to return to the Roman Catholic school in Cardston, her mother explained, "If you don't go to school, your dad is going to go to jail. We are going to get a letter written in red that's very serious."[33]

Maureen Gloria Johnson went to the Lower Post school in northern British Columbia in 1959.

> I went there with a bus. They load us all up on a bus, and took us. And I remember my, my mom had a really hard time letting us kids go, and she had, she had a really hard time. She begged the priest, and the priest said it was law that we had to go, and if we didn't go, then my parents would be in trouble.[34]

In the face of such coercion, parents often felt helpless and ashamed. Paul Dixon attended residential schools in Ontario and Québec. Once he spoke to his father about his experience at the schools. According to Dixon, "He got angry and said, 'I had no choice, you know.' It really, it really hit me hard. I wasn't accusing him of anything, you know, I just wanted some explanations. He said, 'I, I will, I will go, I would go in jail, I will go in jail if I didn't let you go.'"[35]

When she was four or five, Lynda Pahpasay McDonald was taken by plane from her parents' home on Sydney Lake, Ontario.

> I looked outside, my mom was, you know, flailing her arms, and, and I, and she must have been crying, and I see my dad grabbing her, and, I was wondering why, why my mom was, you know, she was struggling.
>
> She told me many years later what happened, and she explained to me why we had to be sent away to, to residential school. And, and I just couldn't get that memory out of my head, and I still remember to this day what, what happened that day. And she told me, like, she was so hurt, and, and I used to ask her, "Why did you let us go, like, why didn't you stop them, you know? Why didn't you, you know, come and get us?" And she told me, "We couldn't, because they told us if we tried to do anything, like, get you guys back, we'd be thrown into jail." So, they didn't want to end up in jail, 'cause they still had babies at, at the cabin.[36]

Dorothy Ross recalled how unhappy her father was about sending his children to residential school. "As we got older, I remember Dad, I knew Dad was already angry. He was angry at the school for taking us away, for taking myself and my siblings. He couldn't, couldn't do, he couldn't do anything to help us. Either, same thing with my mom, 'There's nothing I can do to help you.'"[37]

Dorothy Ross.

Albert Marshall hated his parents for sending him to the Shubenacadie, Nova Scotia, school. Many years later, he asked his brother what the family reaction had been to his being sent to school.

> He didn't answer me for a while, a long time. He says, "Nobody said anything for days," because my father was crying every day. Finally my father told the family, "I failed as a father. I couldn't protect my child, but I just couldn't because you know what the Mounties, the priest, the Indian agents told me? They told me, if I don't, if I resist too much then they would take the other younger, younger brother and younger, younger children." Then he says, "It was not a choice. I could not say, take them or take the three of them. But I couldn't say nothing and I know I have to live with that."[38]

Jaco Anaviapik's parents opposed his being sent to the Pond Inlet hostel in what is now Nunavut.

> When they started taking kids off the land to attend school the RCMP boat would pick us up. There is no doubt that our parents were intimidated by the police into letting us go. They were put in a position where they could not say no. Even though they

did not want us to go they were too afraid of the police, too afraid to stand up to the police. I am one of the lucky ones because my father did say no when they wanted to take me. He told them he would bring me himself once the ice had formed. I was brought here after the children who had been rounded up by boat had already started. That first year my parents came several times to take me home but they were refused by the area administrator. My sister told me that my parents were very sad at that time.

Rather than be separated from their children, his parents moved to Pond Inlet. "After two years had passed my family decided to move to Pond because they knew I had to go to school."[39]

In some cases, parents reluctantly sent their children because the residential school represented their only educational option. Ellen Smith's father attended the Anglican residential school at Hay River in the Northwest Territories. She believes that his experiences at the school led him to oppose her being sent to residential school. However, her grandfather believed it was necessary that she get an education.

> My dad reluctantly let me go to school because my grandpa said that "in the future she will help our people; she needs to go there." And that struggle occurred with my dad over the years. For eleven years, that I went to residential school. But my grandpa was the one that said, "They have to go. She has to go."[40]

She was sent to the Anglican school in Aklavik in 1953. She eventually attended three other residential schools.

Some parents wanted their children to gain the knowledge they believed was needed to protect their community and culture. When Shirley Williams's father took her to catch the bus to the Spanish, Ontario, girls' school, he bought her an ice cream and gave her four instructions: "One was remember who you are. Do not forget your language. Whatever they do to you in there, be strong. And the fourth one, learn about the *Indian Act*, and come back and teach me. So with those four things, he said that 'you don't know why I'm telling you this, but some day you will understand.'"[41]

One student, who attended the Gordon's, Saskatchewan, school, recalled the ways in which the churches competed against one another to recruit students.

> But when we look at the residential schools, you know, and the churches we recognize, you know, at least I've seen it, you know, that we've had these two competing religions, the Anglican and the Catholic churches both competing for our souls it seemed. You know, I remember growing up on the reserve here when they were looking for students. They were competing against each other. We were the prizes, you know, that they would gain if they won. I remember they, the Catholic priests coming out with, you know, used hockey equipment and telling us, you know, "Come and come to our school. Come and play hockey for us. Come and play in our band. We got all kinds of bands here; we got trombones and trumpets and drums," and all that kind of stuff. They use all this stuff to encourage us or entice us to come to the

Catholic school. And then on the other hand, the Anglicans, they would come out with what they called "bale clothes." They bring out bunch of clothes in a bale, like, a big bale. It was all used clothing and they'd give it to the women on the reserve here, and the women made blankets and stuff like that out of these old clothes. But that's the way they, they competed for us as people.[42]

Some children wanted to go to school, at least initially. Leon Wyallon, who attended the Roman Catholic residence in Fort Smith in the 1960s, said he looked forward to residential school "because I wanted to learn; learn to talk English and learn, so I can learn both languages at the same time." He hated his first year at the residence, particularly the restrictions on speaking his own language. But he said, "My mom and dad didn't listen to me; but they still sent me back."[43]

In other cases, missionaries convinced students of the benefits of going to school. Anthony Henry said that a priest named Father LaSalle convinced him to come to residential school at Kenora. According to Henry, his mother did not want him to go to residential school, but LaSalle, who spoke fluent Ojibway, convinced him it would be beneficial.[44]

A place of refuge
"They'd be in a good place."

Poverty and the inability to feed and clothe their children forced some parents to send their children to residential school. When Ivan George was enrolled in the Mission, British Columbia, school, his father was a single parent with six children under the age of fourteen. When the time came to return to the school after his first summer holiday, Ivan told his father he did not wish to return. "He says, 'You have to. I can't provide for you, or nothing to feed you, clothes on your back, education.' So, I went back, and I said, 'Oh, I better,' because you know where, what, what's going on, all that. So, I stayed the whole year without running away."[45]

Ivan George.

Cecilia Whitefield-Big George said her mother was not able to support her family when they lived in Big Grassy in northwestern Ontario.

> She would go and clean, work for people, eh, like
> do their laundry and clean their floors and clean the house for them and that's how she fed us. They'd give her food, eh. And then when the priest arrived he told her, you know they'd be in a good place if they went to school. And so that's how that happened. I, my little sister, she was only four years old. So that's how we first got picked up.[46]

One former student, whose grandparents had also attended residential school, placed his daughter in residential school when she was thirteen.

> I didn't have a wife at the time and I felt that was a good place for her, so I wasn't really fully aware of the, you know, the negative parts of, the parts, negative, negativity of residential school 'cause really, I guess, when I look at the residential school issue, you know, I saw, you know, physically, I guess, better than what I experienced at the reserve. On the reserve I had a very abusive dad, my dad was abusive, physically abusive, and we lived in a little log cabin and we didn't have regular meals.[47]

Ethel Johnson said she and her siblings were sent to the Shubenacadie school when her mother was diagnosed with tuberculosis.

> My father couldn't look after us. I was ten years old, there was another one, there was five of us, and the youngest was about nine months old, at the time. So the three of

us were old enough to go to residential school; I never even heard about it 'til then. 'Cause my father had to work and he had to maintain a house, fix our meals, he just couldn't do it. So I don't know where he found out or how this was possible, but we ended up going over there anyway. This was in '46.[48]

Dorothy Jane Beaulieu attended the Fort Resolution, Northwest Territories, school after the death of her father.

And they seemed to pick on orphans, you know. My father, I lost my father when I was, in 1949 we lost him. And I stayed here in a mission eleven and a half years, and I never went home for seven years. I had no, no, nowhere to go, you know. My sisters were living in Yellowknife, but they were all, you know, they were all married, and had children of their own. So you know I would, my sister Nora and I, we just stayed there, you know.[49]

Illness and family breakup meant that in some cases, children were raised by their grandparents. After Hazel Mary Anderson's parents separated in 1972, her grandmother took care of her and her two siblings. They lived on the Piapot Reserve in Saskatchewan until her grandmother was in her early seventies. At that time, the children were sent to residential school.[50] Prior to going to the Shubenacadie school, one student was being cared for by his grandparents. "I went there basically because I felt sorry for my grandparents who were trying to look after me and trying to keep, maintain, and they were struggling."[51]

One former Blue Quills, Alberta, student said:

We have, at that time, there was six of us who are older, who were living at the house, but there was three others, younger ones, who were from another father, but they lived with us. So, now in our family currently, we had twelve. But the oldest ones, the six of us, had to see and witness a lot of, a lot of violence, especially abuse with my mom and dad. We had two sisters, and four, or three brothers, and myself, that's six. I was the youngest of the siblings of that bunch.

But there was times when, you know, drinking would be to excess, so, so my moshum and my kokum would take us in to protect us from, from the fighting, and the pain and the struggles.

There was, as far as I can recall, one day there was some lady or social worker that just came to our house at my kokum's place, Jenny's, and they told us we were just going for a ride in a big, fancy car. And of course, you know, we were poor, we didn't have any of that stuff, so we thought it would be kind of nice, but nobody told us where we were going. So all I could remember was my auntie, my kokum, we are at the, the house, and waving goodbye, and all I remember was just peeking out the window in the back, and not understanding why, you know, Grandma crying. But we went, and they brought us to a big school, just out by the Saddle Lake Reserve. It was the Blue Quills school. And I was only five, so you know I was youngest of the six.[52]

In some cases, parents placed their children in the school to protect them from violence in the community. Both of Dorene Bernard's parents had attended the Shubenacadie school.

> My father spent eleven years in a residential school, from 1929 to 1940. My mom spent around seven years there during the 1940s. Whatever would have made them think that it had changed, that it was better in 1960s than it was when they were there? I don't know. But I could tell you that our lives outside the residential school was bad enough that she felt she was alone to make those decisions, that it was better for us to be there than with other family members, with our extended family. We were safer in her eyes to be there than at home.[53]

The journey

"The train of tears."

Frederick Ernest Koe recalled that one morning, there was a knock at his parents' door in Aklavik, Northwest Territories.

> Anglican Minister Donna Webster and RCMP officers at the door, and they're asking for me and telling me to pack up because I had to go. Well pack up, a few little things, no suitcases, my hunting bag is still kind of dirty, throw whatever stuff you had in it and off you go.
>
> And I didn't get to say goodbye to my dad or my brother Allan, didn't get to pet my dogs or nothing, you know, we're going. Marched over to Frankie's house which was just half a block away and picked him up and then we were marched to the plane, just like we're criminals, you know marching to this policeman to get on the plane.
>
> And that was my experience leaving Aklavik. And it was pretty monumental point in my life, very dramatic I guess. You don't realize this until after, because those times, you just did what the people in charge told you to do.[54]

Howard Stacy Jones said he was taken without his parents' knowledge from a public school in Port Renfrew, British Columbia, to the Kuper Island school.

> I was kidnapped from Port Renfrew's elementary school when I was around six years old, and this happened right in the elementary schoolyard. And my auntie witnessed this and another non-Native witnessed this, and they are still alive as I speak. These are two witnesses trying, saw me fighting, trying to get away with, from the two RCMP officers that threw me in the back seat of the car and drove off with me. And my mom didn't know where I was for three days, frantically stressed out and worried about where I was, and she finally found out that I was in Kuper Island residential school.[55]

Howard Stacy Jones.

For many residential school students, the school year started in a long ride in the back of a school-owned farm truck. Shirley Leon attended the Kamloops, British Columbia, school in the 1940s. She described her first memory of residential school as seeing the cattle trucks come onto the reserve, and scoop up the kids to go, and seeing my cousins cry, and then, and they were put on these trucks, and hauled off, and we didn't know where, and my grandmother and mother hiding us under the bed. And when the, the federal health nurse or the Indian agent would try to come into the house, my grandmother would club them with her cane.[56]

The day she left for the Lestock, Saskatchewan, school, Marlene Kayseas's parents drove her into the town of Wadena.

There was a big truck there. It had a back door and that truck was full of kids and there was no windows on that truck, it was dark in there.

And that's where we were put. There was a bunch of kids there from up north, Yellowquill, Kenaston, and my reserve. And all you hear was yelling and kids were fighting in there and some were crying. And we were falling down on the floor because there was no place to sit, we were standing up. And it seemed like such a long time to get there.[57]

Rick Gilbert's first experience with residential schooling came when his older siblings were sent away to school.

And I remember just directly outside of the house there was a cattle truck parked there and they were loading kids on the back of this cattle truck. And that's how they were taking my, well I am going to call them my brother and sister, they were taking my brother and sister away in this cattle truck to the mission. I didn't know then that that's what they were doing, but that's what happened.[58]

Alma Scott was taken to the Fort Alexander, Manitoba, school when she was five years old.

We got taken away by a big truck. I can still remember my mom and dad looking at us, and they were really, really sad looking. My dad's shoulders were just hunched, and he, to me, it looked like his spirit was broken. I didn't have the words at five for that, but I do now. I just remember feeling really sad, and I was in this truck full of other kids who were crying, and so I cried with them.[59]

Alma Scott.

Leona Bird was six when she was sent to the Prince Albert, Saskatchewan, school.

And then we seen this army covered wagon truck, army truck outside the place. And as we were walking towards it, kids were herded into there like cattle, into the army truck. Then in the far distance I seen my mother with my little sister. I went running to her, and she says, "Leona," she was crying, and I was so scared. I didn't know what was going on, I didn't know what was happening. My sister didn't cry because she didn't understand what we, we were, what's gonna happen to us. Anyway, it was time for me and her to go, and she, when we got in that truck, she just held me, pinched me, and held me on my skirt. "Momma, Momma, Momma." And then my mother couldn't do nothing, she just stood there, weeping. And then I took my little sister, and tried to make her calm down, I just told, "We're going bye-bye, we're going somewhere for a little while." Well, nobody told us how long we were gonna be gone. It's just, like, we were gonna go into this big truck, and that's how, that's how it started.[60]

Sam Ross recalled putting up a fight when the Indian agent came to his family's home in northern Manitoba to take him to residential school in Prince Albert, Saskatchewan.

I remember hiding under the bed there; they pulled us out from under the bed, me and my younger brother. We ran, you know, we cried a lot and but that didn't help better; they took us out. They took us out to the truck; all four of us. My other two brothers walked to the truck. But me and my late, younger brother, we fought all the way, right up, right to the station, train station, CNR station.[61]

As in Sam Ross's case, the truck ride was sometimes followed by a train ride. In the 1950s, Benjamin Joseph Lafford travelled by bus and train to the Shubenacadie school.

Sam Ross.

And I don't know who were there, anyway, there was a police officer and two people, told my father that "we're going to take your children to the better place." And my dad didn't understand because, my dad was getting sick, he had asthma. He didn't understand, then, and he agreed with them, anyway, he agreed with the people that would take us, all my brothers and my sisters to the place that I don't know.

So about a couple days later, a bus came in to our home, and told us, "Get on the bus," I don't know, could be an Indian agent, and the RCMP. Told us, "Go on the bus, go on the bus, we take you to a better place." So we had to agree with them because I didn't understand as a young boy. I had to listen to what they said because we listened to our dad, we listened to him because he knows what's best for us.

So we went on the bus, so they picked every child in our community, in my reserve. Picked every child, put them on the bus, send us to a train station at Grand Narrows, that morning, about, around 7:30, around there I think. And every child they put on, didn't say anything. They put them on the bus and through Grand Narrows, then we waited there. We didn't have no food, we didn't have no clothes to take with us. We just get on the bus and go.

So, that morning, we heard the, told my brothers we had to sit over here and wait for the train to come. So we heard a train, we heard a whistle and we said, and my brother said, "Oh, that's the train coming to pick us up, pick us up." I said, "Okay," you know. So when the train came, they put us on, Indian agents put us on, the RCMP put us on the train. Told us to sit over here. So it doesn't matter, so we left from Grand Narrows. Every station we stopped at, there was children, Native children, that had long hair when I looked out the window.

And I went, "Wow, there's more children going on the train, probably they're going the same way as I'm going." So at that time it didn't matter to me, so every station we stopped, there was Native children, girls and boys. And there was RCMP and an Indian agent lining them up, put them on the train, put them on the seats. No one's talking about anything, I didn't know them. Every station, and by the time we got to Truro, there was full of Native people, Native children on the train. Wow, there was a whole bunch of us. Had long hair, you know, had no clothes to take with them.

So we didn't know, we didn't understand. So we got to Truro, so we changed trains and then the conductor, he says, when we got to the point where we went, the conductor said, "Last stop for Shubenacadie. Last stop, get ready." So we were driving and we wouldn't take that long. So we got all the children, all the girls on one side and all the boys on one side. And we didn't understand nothing. And when the train came so far, I think it would be around 12:00, or between 12:00 or 12:30, we got to our destination and the conductor was saying, "Shubenacadie, Shubenacadie, next stop." So he was saying that, so we all stop and the Indian agent was sitting in the front there. He said, "Okay guys, get ready."[62]

Larry Beardy had a strong memory of the first train trip that took him from Churchill, Manitoba, to the Anglican residential school in Dauphin, Manitoba—a journey of 1,200 kilometres.

I think it was two days and one whole day of travel on the train to Dauphin. So, it was quite a, it was quite a ride. And when we boarded the train, I was very excited. It's like going on a journey, going for a, a travel. It's not my first time going on a train, but I was going alone. I was going with my sister and my other older siblings. And, and the train ride was okay for the first half hour or so, then I realized I was alone. My mother was not there. And like the rest of the children, there was a lot of crying on that train. At every stop if you understand the Canadian National Railway, families lived in sections every twenty, fifteen miles, and children will get on the train, and then there'd be more crying, and everybody started crying, all the way to Dauphin, that's how it was. So, there was a lot of tears. That train I want to call that train of tears, and a lot of anger, a lot of frustration. I did that for several years.[63]

Emily Kematch was sent from York Landing in northern Manitoba to the Gordon's school in Saskatchewan. When she was put on the train that was to take her there, she did not know she was being sent to school.

I didn't know I was going away to school. I thought I was just going for a train ride and I was just excited to go. My sisters and my brothers were on the train too and I felt like, I have family with me, but I didn't understand why my parents didn't come on with us. They were just on the side of the railway there and they were waving at us as the train was moving away. And I remember asking one of the kids from back home, "How come our parents aren't coming?" and then she said, that girl said, "They can't come 'cause we're going to school." And I was talking to her in Cree and I said, "Well, I don't want to go to school, I'd rather stay home and stay with my parents." And she said, she told me, "No, we can't, we have to go and get our education," and then at night as we were travelling along, I got really lonesome.

Because her siblings were going to the Anglican school in Dauphin, they got off there. Emily stayed on the train. "We were on the train, I'd say, like, three days to get to Saskatchewan and when we got there, three of my cousins were with me, those were the only ones I knew. Three boys, there's Billy, Gordon, and Nelson and I was the only girl from my hometown."[64]

Many students whose parents belonged to the United Church were sent from northern British Columbia to residential school in Edmonton because there was no United Church residential school closer to where they lived. Sphenia Jones's journey to residential school started from Haida Gwaii (also known as the Queen Charlotte Islands), off the coast of British Columbia.

Sphenia Jones.

And I went on a boat first from Haida Gwaii. There was really lots of Haidas that were going to Edmonton at that time, and some Skidegate, as well as Masset, and we got on a really big boat. They used to have a, they used to call it a steamer. It used to bring groceries and stuff like that maybe once a year, twice a year to Haida Gwaii, that's what they put us on, and then we got off the boat in Prince Rupert, and then they started hauling us on a train there.

The train station building is still there in Rupert, where we all had to wait. There was really lots of us. And I don't remember what month it was, or anything like that. But we used to have to do stops along the way, and pick up more Native children. And we were on the train, gee, for about four days, I think, something like that. And the more people they picked up, the more squished we all became in, inside the train, and we were packed in like a bunch of sardines. There was kids laying around on the floor, all along in, in where the walkway was supposed to be. And I could hear really lots of crying all the time, crying, crying, crying.

She recalled that at one stop, the train picked up an infant.

I could hear a baby crying about the second day, so I start looking, and I found this little one in the corner. There was a whole bunch of kids around. I don't know if they were alive or whatever, you know. I picked him up, anyway, and I remember packing him around. I lost the space that I was sitting at. So, I was walking around. I was lucky I had a coat. I took my coat off, I remember holding him, sitting, holding him, looking at his face. Nothing to eat, nothing to drink. I couldn't give him anything.[65]

Students from remote communities often were taken to residential school by small airplanes. At the end of the summer in 1957, a plane that was normally used to transport fish landed on the water at Co-op Point on Reindeer Lake, in northern Saskatchewan. John B. Custer recalled the roundup:

John B. Custer.

And all of a sudden I seen this priest coming, and this RCMP, and they told me let's go for a walk. So, I went, walked down the fish plane, and this is where they, they threw me in without the consent of my grandparents. And there was already a bunch of kids there. There was about at least twenty-five to thirty kids. And that's at the young age of seven years old, I remember this very well. This, the fish, the fish plane was, it had a very strong smell of fish, and he half-assed washed that plane, and it was, there was still slime fish in there, in that plane. And there was a whole bunch of kids there, and I was just wondering what am I doing in this plane? Most of the kids were crying, and I could see their parents on the shoreline, waving goodbye, and most of them were crying.[66]

Dorothy Hart grew up in northern Manitoba. She recalled how, when she was six years old, she and a friend were playing by a lake when a plane landed. "My friend took off first. I remember this 'cause it's, and this guy just grabbed me and put me on the plane. And there were other kids in the plane already. And this was how I ended up in Norway House. Not even saying, I didn't even see my grandparents."[67]

Florence Horassi was taken to the Fort Providence, Northwest Territories, school in a small airplane. On its way to the school, the plane stopped at a number of small communities to pick up students.

And then we got to, there's another place that we stop at, there's another, this one young boy got on the plane there. Had a lot, a lot of crying. There's ... a lot of kids in the plane. Some of them were sitting on the floor of the plane. It was just full. When the plane took off, there's about six or five older ones, didn't cry, but I saw tears come right out of their eyes. Everybody else was crying. There's a whole plane crying. I wanted to cry, too, 'cause my brother was crying, but I held my tears back and held him.

THE JOURNEY • 29

She and her brother were separated once they reached the school.

> When we got to Providence, my brother was scared. We got off the plane. There was
> nuns waiting for us on the shore, brothers, Father, priests. He, he was scared, so he
> grabbed hold of my hand, he was holding my hand. We don't have no luggage, or
> no, no clothes, just what we had on, just what we had on. And we walk up the hill, to
> the top of the hill, and my brother was so scared. He was just holding onto my hand
> so tight. And then top of the hill, the priest came, and he told me he's got to go this
> way, and, and then the Sister came over to me, told me you got to go this way. They're
> trying to break our hands apart, but he wouldn't let go of my hand, holding. And the
> priest was holding his hand, and the sister was holding my hand. They broke our
> hands apart like that.[68]

Joe Krimmerdjuar was taken to the Chesterfield Inlet school in the Northwest Territories
in 1957.

> And my mother was on the beach when I was boarding the plane. With few clothes
> I had, maybe one pair of pants, maybe a sock that my mother had put into her flour
> sack. And I know that she started walking home not even bothering to look at me.
> And today I think maybe she had tears in her eyes. Maybe she was crying.[69]

In the Northwest Territories, students often were taken to school by boat. Albert Elias
was sent to the Anglican school in Aklavik in 1952.

> So in 1952 we were sent away. In those days there's, you know, there's no airplanes
> like we have now. So the Anglican Mission schooner, a small boat, came down to Tuk
> and we were boarded, we were, you know, we got on the boat, and all excited and
> waving and, and we left Tuk. And then we travelled a ways along the, along the way
> to Aklavik was camps, hunting camps, fishing camps, and we stopped at those places
> and picked up students as we went along.

At one stop, all the children got off the boat. When it was time to get back on the boat,
the boy walking ahead of Albert decided to run away.

> Just before he stepped on the walk plank he dashed one side and he ran away. He ran
> away. And the Anglican missionary there, he ran after him and caught him and, and I
> saw for the first time how somebody could be so rough to a small child and carry that
> boy like a rag doll up to the boat. And I asked myself there, the fear, fear came to my
> being, you know, and I sensed fear, like, I never felt it before, and I said, "What have
> I got myself into?" you know. Before I even reached Aklavik I start seeing violence,
> you know, which I really never saw before. And that was, to me, it always, you know, it
> was always in my memory. So the first trauma, I guess.[70]

Sam Kautainuk was twelve years old when he was taken to the Pond Inlet school in what
is now Nunavut.

> The boat they used to bring us here is still there down by Ulayuk School. That's the
> boat that picked me up from our outpost camp. It was the RCMP, the Area Administra-

tor and two women. The special constable lifted me by my shoulders and put me in the boat so that I could go to school. They ignored my cries for my mother. I remember as the boat took us away I kept my eyes on my parents' tent until I couldn't see it anymore. That moment was the most painful thing I ever experienced in my life.[71]

Arrival
"I've always called it a monster."

Nellie Ningewance was raised in Hudson, Ontario, and went to the Sioux Lookout, Ontario, school in the 1950s and 1960s. Her parents enrolled her in the school at the government's insistence. She told her mother she did not want to go.

But the day came where we, we were all bussed out from Hudson. My mother told me to pack my stuff; a little bit of what I needed, what I wanted. I remember I had a little doll that my dad had given me for a Christmas present. And I had a little trunk where I made my own doll clothes. I started sewing when I was nine years old. My mom taught us all this though, sewing. So I used to make my own doll clothes; I packed those up, what I wanted.

Nellie Ningewance.

I guess I had mixed feelings. I was kind of excited to go away to go to school. My mom tried to make it feel comfortable for me and I know it was hard for her and hard for me. But when the time we were ready to leave, they had a bus; and there was lots of people with their kids waiting to leave. And I made sure I, I was the last one to board the bus, 'cause I didn't want to go.

I remember hugging my mom, begging her, getting on the bus; waving at them as they were going, pulling away. I don't remember how long the ride was from Hudson to Pelican at the time, but it seemed like a long ride....

When we arrived there, again I was, I made sure I was the last one to get off the bus. And when I arrived there, a guy standing at the bottom there helping all the students to get off the bus, reaching out his hand like this; I didn't even want to touch him. I didn't even want to get off. I'm hanging to the bar; I didn't want to get off. To me he looked so ugly. He was dark, short, and he was trying to coax me to come down the stairs and to help me get off the bus. I hang onto the bus and they had to force me and pull me down to get off the bus.

The next three days I guess was sort of, like it was like floating.... I remember crying then calming down for a while, then crying again.... When we arrived we had to register that we had arrived then they took us to cut our hair. The next thing was to get our clothes. They gave us two pairs of jeans, two pairs of tee-shirts, two church dresses, they were beautiful dresses; two pairs of shoes, two pairs of socks, two pairs of everything.

And we had a number; they gave us a number and that number was tied in our, in all our clothes; our garments, our jackets, everything was numbered. After that we were told to be in the, go in the shower; at least fifteen of us girls all in one shower. We were told to strip down and, with all the other girls; and that was not a comfortable feeling. And for me I guess it was violating my privacy. I didn't even want to look at anybody else. It was hard.

After that, they gave us our toothbrushes to brush our teeth. And they asked us to put our hands out and they put some white dry powder stuff on our hands. I didn't know what it was. I smelt it, but now today I know it was baking soda. I didn't realize what it was then.[72]

Campbell Papequash had been raised by his grandfather. When his grandfather died in 1946, Papequash "was apprehended by the missionaries and taken to residential school."

When I was taken to this residential school you know I experienced a foreign way of life that I really didn't understand. I was taken into this big building that would become the detention of my life and the fear of life. When I was taken to that residential school you know I see these ladies, you know so stoical looking, passionate-less and they wore these robes that I've never seen women wear before, they only showed their forehead and their eyes and the bottom of their face and their hands. Now to me that is very fearful because you know there wasn't any kind of passion and I could see, you know, I could see it in their eyes. When I was taken to this residential school I was taken into the infirmary but before I entered the infirmary, you know, I looked around this big, huge building, and I see all these crosses all over the walls. I look at those crosses and I see a man hanging on that cross and I didn't recognize who this man was. And this man seemed dead and passionate-less on that cross. I didn't know who this man was on that cross. And then I was taken to the infirmary and there, you know, I was stripped of my clothes, the clothes that I came to residential school with, you know, my moccasins, and I had nice beautiful long hair and they were neatly braided by mother before I went to residential school, before I was apprehended by the residential school missionaries.

And after I was taken there they took off my clothes and then they deloused me. I didn't know what was happening but I learned about it later, that they were delousing me; 'the dirty, no-good-for-nothing savages, lousy.' And then they cut off my beautiful hair. You know and my hair, my hair represents such a spiritual significance of my life and my spirit. And they did not know, you know, what they were doing to me. You know and I cried and I see them throw my hair into a garbage can, my long, beautiful braids. And then after they deloused me then I was thrown into the shower, you know, to go wash all that kerosene off my body and off my head. And I was shaved, bald-headed.

And then after I had the shower they gave me these clothes that didn't fit, and they gave me these shoes that didn't fit and they all had numbers on them. And after the shower then I was taken up to the dormitory. And when I went to, when I was taken up to this dormitory I seen many beds up there, all lined up so neatly and the beds made so neatly. And then they gave me a pillow, they gave me blankets, they gave me sheets to make up my bed. And lo and behold, you know, I did not know how to make that bed because I came from a place of buffalo robes and deer hides and rabbit skins to cover with, no such thing as a pillow.[73]

Marthe Basile-Coocoo recalled feeling a chill on first seeing the Pointe Bleue, Québec, school.

It was something like a grey day, it was a day without sunshine. It was, it was the impression that I had, that I was only six years old, then, well, the nuns separated us, my brothers, and then my uncles, then I no longer understood. Then that, that was a period there, of suffering, nights of crying, we all gathered in a corner, meaning that we came together, and there we cried. Our nights were like that.[74]

Pauline St-Onge was traumatized by just the sight of the Sept-Îles school. She fought back when her father tried to take her into the school. "I thought in my child's head I said: 'you would... you would make me go there, but I will learn nothing, nothing, nothing.'"[75]

Louise Large could not speak any English when her grandmother took her to the Blue Quills, Alberta, school in the early 1960s.

My grandma and I got into this black car, and I was kind of excited, and I was looking at the window and look. I'd never rode in a car before, or I might have, but this was a strange person. I went to, we drove into Blue Quills, and it was a big building, and I was in awe with the way it looked, and I was okay 'cause I had my grandma with me, and we got off, and we went up the stairs. And that was okay, I was hanging onto my grandma, I was going into this strange place. And, and we walked up the stairs into the building, and down the hallway, going to the left, and there was a room there, and two nuns came.

As was often the case, she was not used to seeing nuns dressed in religious habits. "I didn't know they were nuns. I don't know why they were dressed the way they were. They had long black skirts, dresses, and at that time they looked weird 'cause they had these little weird hats and a veil, kind of like a black bridesmaid or something, and they were all smiling at me."

She was shocked to discover she was going to be left at the school. The nuns had to hold Louise tight to stop her from trying to leave with her grandmother.

And I wasn't aware at that time that my grandma was gonna leave me there. I'm not ever sure how she told me but they started holding me and my grandma left and I started fighting them because I didn't want my grandma to leave me, and, and I started screaming, and crying and crying, and it must have been about, I don't know, when I look back, probably long enough to know that my grandma was long gone. They let me go, and they started yelling at me to shut up, or I don't know, they had a real mean tone of voice. It must have been about, when I think about it, it was in the morning, and I just screamed and screamed for hours. It seemed like for hours.[76]

Rachel Chakasim and her friends were excited about the prospect of going to residential school from their home community of Moosonee, Ontario. They all ran down to the water's edge to get on the float plane that would take them to school. On their arrival, they were taken to the school by the same truck that was used to haul garbage to the local refuse site. From that point on, the experience was much more sombre.

And I can still recall today the, the quiet, the quiet, and all the sadness, the atmosphere, as we entered that big stone building. The excitement in the morning was gone, and everybody was quiet because the ... senior students that had been there before knew the rules, and us newcomers were just beginning to see, and we were little, we were young.

I remember how they took our clothes, the clothes that we wore when we left, and they also cut our hair. We had short hair from there on. And they put a chemical on our hair, which was some kind of a white powder.[77]

Rachel Chakasim.

Linda Head was initially excited about the prospect of a plane trip that would take her to the Prince Albert, Saskatchewan, school. "My dad kissed me, and up I went, I didn't care [laughs] 'cause this was something new for me." The plane landed on the Saskatchewan River. "There was a, a car waiting for us, or the truck. But I got into the car, and the boys were in the truck, like an army, an army truck. They stood outside the, outside, you know, at the back, not inside." The students were driven to the school, which was located in a former military barracks.

And we all, there was a crowd when we got there, a crowd of, you know, other students, and we went to the registration table. They gave us, told us which dorm to go, and, and there was a person standing, but the kids were, you know, lining up, and this person took me to the line. And when the line was full, I guess when we were, they took us to the dorm.... We had our numbers, and a bed number. And she told us to settle down. Well, I wasn't understanding this 'cause it was English, but I followed, you know, watch, watch everybody, and ... she took my hand, and guided me to the bed, and the number showed me what number I was, number four, and we had to find number four. So that's how it was then.

My stuff, I had to set it down, then I, I was under, under the bed, not the higher up, I had the lower bed. So, I was just lying around there ... the music was loud, the radio.

Everybody was talking in Cree, some of them in Cree, some of them in English, well a little bit of English. And my cousins ... we were in together some of them, some of us at the same age, so they came over and talked to me. I said, "Well, here we are." Here I was missing home already.[78]

Gilles Petiquay, who attended the Pointe Bleue, Québec, school, was shocked by the numbering system at the school. "I remember that the first number that I had at the residential school was 95. I had that number—95—for a year. The second number was number 4. I had it for a longer period of time. The third number was 56. I also kept it for a long time. We walked with the numbers on us.[79]

Mary Courchene grew up on the Fort Alexander Reserve in Manitoba. Her parents' home was just a five-minute walk away from the Fort Alexander boarding school.

> One morning my mom woke us up and said we were going to school that day and then she takes out new clothes that she had bought us and I was just so happy, so over the moon. And, she was very, very quiet. And she was dressing us up and she didn't say too much. She didn't say, "Oh I'll see you," and all of that. She just said, she just dressed us up with, with no comment. And then we left; we left for the school.

When the family reached the school, they were greeted by a nun. Mary's brother became frightened. Mary told him to behave himself. She then turned around to say goodbye to her mother but she was gone. Her mother had gone to residential school as a child. "And she could not bear to talk to her children and prepare her children to go to residential school. It was just too, too much for her." Courchene said that on that day, her life changed. "It began ten years of the most miserable part of my life, here on, here, in the world."[80]

Roy Denny was perplexed and frightened by the clothing that the priests and sisters wore at the Shubenacadie school.

> And we were greeted by this man dressed in black with a long gown. That was the priest, come to find later. And the nuns with their black, black outfits with the white collar and a white, white collar and, like a breast plate of white. And their freaky looking hats that were, I don't, I couldn't, know what they remind me of. And I didn't see, first time I ever seen nuns and priests. And they, and they were speaking to me, and I couldn't understand them.[81]

He had not fully understood that his father was going to be leaving him at the school. "So when my father left I tried to stop him; I tried, I tried to go, you know, tried to go with him, but he said, 'No, you got to stay.' That was real hard."[82]

Calvin Myerion was sent to the Brandon, Manitoba, school. He recalled being overwhelmed by the size of the building.

Calvin Myerion.

The only building that I knew up to that time, that moment in my life was the one-storey house that we had. And when I got to the residential school, I seen this big monster of a building, and I've never seen any buildings that, that large, that high. And I was, I've always called it a monster, I still do today, because of not the size of it, but because of the things that happened there.[83]

Archie Hyacinthe said he was unprepared for life in the Catholic school in Kenora.

It was almost like we were, you know, captured, or taken to another form of home. Like I said, nobody really explained to us, as if we were just being taken away from our home, and our parents. We were detached I guess from our home and our parents, and it's scary when you, when you first think, think about it as a child, because you never had that separation in your lifetime before that.

So that was the, I think that's when the trauma started for me, being separated from my sister, from my parents, and from our, our home. We were no longer free. It was like being, you know, taken to a strange land, even though it was our, our, our land, as I understood later on.[84]

Dorene Bernard was only four and a half years old when she was enrolled in the Shubenacadie residential school. She had thought that the family was simply taking her older siblings back to the school after a holiday.

I remember that day. We went down there to take my sister and brother back. My father and mom went in to talk to the priest, but they were making plans to leave me behind. But I didn't know that, so I went on the girls' side with my sister and she told me after couple hours went by that they had already left. I would say it was pretty difficult to feel that abandoned at four and a half years old. But I had my sister, my older sister Karen, she took care of me the best way she could.[85]

When parents brought their children to the school themselves, the moment of departure was often heartbreaking. Ida Ralph Quisess could recall her father "crying in the chapel" when she and her siblings were sent to residential school.

He was crying, and that, one of the, these women in black dresses, I later learned they were sisters, they called them, nuns, the Oblate nuns, later, many years after I learned what their title was, and the one that spoke our language told him, "We'll keep your little girls, we'll raise them," and then my father started to cry.[86]

Vitaline Elsie Jenner resisted being sent to school.

And I didn't want to go to the residential school. I didn't realize what I was going to come up against upon being there. I resisted. I cried and I fought with my mom. My mom was the one that took us there and dragged, actually just about dragged me there, because of my resistance, not wanting, I hung onto everything that was in the way, resisting.

The separation at the Fort Chipewyan school in northern Alberta was traumatic.

And so when I went upon, when we went into the residential school, it was in the parlour, and there was a nun that was receiving the students that were going into the residential school, and I, you know, like I hung onto my mom as tight as I can. And what I remember was she had taken my hand, and what she did, what my mom did, I, I don't remember the rest of my siblings, it's just like I kind of blocked out, because that was traumatic already for me as it was, being taken there, you know, and this great big building looked so strange and foreign to me, and so she took my hand, and forcefully put my hand in the nun's hand, and the nun grabbed it, so I wouldn't run away. So, she grabbed it, and I was screaming and hollering. And in my language I said, "Mama, Mama, *kâya nakasin*" and in English it was, "Mom, Mom, don't leave me." 'Cause that's all I knew was to speak Cree. And so the nun took us, and Mom, I, I turned around, and Mom was walking away. And I didn't realize, I guess, that she was also crying.[87]

Lily Bruce's parents were in tears when they left her and her brother at the Alert Bay, British Columbia, school.

And our parents talked to the principal, and, and then Mom was in tears, and I remember the last time she was in tears was when my brother Jimmy was put in that school. And her and Dad went through those double doors in the front, and the principal and his wife were saying that they were gonna take good care of us, that they were gonna treat us like they were our new parents, and not to worry about us, and just bringing our hopes up, and so Mom and Dad left. And I grabbed my brother, and my brother held me, we just started crying. [audible crying] We were hurt because Mom and Dad left us there.[88]

Lily Bruce.

Margaret Simpson attended the Fort Chipewyan school in the 1950s. She was initially excited to be going to residential school because she would be going with her brother George.

I was happy I was going with him and my dad took us and there we're walking to the, to this big orange building. It was in, and we got there and I was so happy 'cause I was going to go in here with George and I was going to be with him but you know this was far as it was going to go once we made it in there.

He went one way and I was calling him and this other nun took me the other way, so we separated right there. Right from there I was wondering what is happening here? I was so lost, I was so lost. And they brought me downstairs and then I looked and all of a sudden I seen my dad passing on the other side of the fence, he was walking. I just went running I seen the door over there and I went running I was going to go see my dad over there. But they stopped me and I was crying and I was telling my dad to come and he didn't hear me and I was wondering what is happening, I don't even know.[89]

The rest of a new student's first day is often remembered as being invasive, humiliating, and dehumanizing. Her first day at the Catholic school in Kenora left Lynda Pahpasay McDonald frightened and distressed.

And I had, I must have had long hair, like long, long hair, like, and my brothers, even my brother had long hair, and he looked like a little girl. Then they took us into this, it was like a greeting area, we went in there, and they kind of counted us, me and my siblings. And I was hanging onto my sister, and she told me not to cry, so don't cry, you know, you just, you listen. She was trying to tell me, and I was crying, and of course me and my sister were crying, there's three of us, we're just a year apart. Me, Barbara, and Sandy were standing there, crying. She was telling us not to cry, and, and just do what we had to do.

And, and I remember having, watching my brother being, like, taken away, my older brother, Marcel. They took him, and he had long hair also.

And we were taken upstairs, and they gave us some clothing, and they put numbers on our clothes. I remember there's little tags in the back, they put numbers, and they told us that was your number. Well, I can't remember my number.

And, and we seen the nuns. They had these big black outfits, and they were scary looking, I remember. And of course they weren't really, they looked really, I don't know, mean, I guess.

And, and we, they took us upstairs, I remember that, and they gave us these clothes, different clothes, and they took us to another room, then they kind of, like, and they took our old clothes, they took that, and they made us take a bath or a shower. I think it was a bath at that time.

After we came out, and they washed our hair, and I don't know, they kind of put some kind of thing on our hair, like, you know, our heads, and they're checking our hair and stuff like that. And then they took us to this chair, and they put a white cloth over our shoulders, and they started cutting our hair. And you know they cut real straight bangs, and real short hair, like, it was real straight haircuts. I didn't like the fact that they cut off all our hair. And same with my brother, they had, they cut off all of, most of his hair. They had a, he had a brush cut, like.[90]

When Emily Kematch arrived at the Gordon's, Saskatchewan, school from York Landing in northern Manitoba, her hair was treated with a white powder and then cut. "And we had our clothes that we went there with even though we didn't have much. We had our own clothes but they took those away from us and we had to wear the clothes that they gave us, same sort of clothes that we had to wear."[91]

Verna Kirkness attended the Dauphin, Manitoba, residential school. On arrival at that school after a lengthy train trip, she said, she was stripped of all her clothing.

Verna Kirkness.

They didn't tell me that they were gonna do that. And they poured something on my head, I don't know what it was, but it didn't smell too good. To this day, I don't know what it is. But from my understanding, from people explaining it to me, it was coal oil, or some, some kind of oil, and they poured that on my head, and then they cut my hair really, really short. And then, and when we, we sat, I remember sitting, I don't know it's, it looked like a picnic table. It was in the corner, I think it was in the corner, and I sat there. I was looking around, and I was looking for my sister.

And then I, and then I think we were given a dough-nut, or some kind of pastry, and then we were sent to bed. And I remember my first bed. It was right by the door. And then as when you walk in, it was on your right-hand side, and I was on the top bunk, the first bunk bed, I was on the top bunk, and that's my first, my very first night there.[92]

At the Blue Quills school, Alice Quinney and the other recently arrived students were told they were to be given a bath.

I had never been naked in front of anybody ever before, except my mom, who would give us a bath in, in the bathtub at home, in a, in a round tub, you know the old round tubs that they had, the steel tubs, that's the kind of, you know. And so that was hard too, they told us before, when we went down to the bathroom, we all had to strip, and they put this nasty smelling stuff in our hair, for bugs, they said, if we had brought any bugs with us. So, they put all that stuff, and some kind of powder that smelled really bad. And then we were, we had to take off all our clothes, and, and go in, in the showers together.[93]

On her arrival at the Alberni, British Columbia, school, Lily Bruce was separated from her brother and taken to the girls' dormitory.

I had to take a bath, and it was late at night, and I kept crying, and she was calling me a crybaby, and just kept yelling at me, and said if I woke up anybody, I was in deep trouble. "And if your mother and dad really cared about you, they wouldn't have left you here." [audible crying]

And then she started pulling my long hair, checking for lice. [audible crying] After she checked my hair and shampooed my hair, I had to have vinegar put in there, and being yanked around in that tub, too, had to wash every part of my body or else they were gonna do it, and I didn't want, I didn't want them to touch me.[94]

Helen Harry's hair was cut on her arrival at the Williams Lake, British Columbia, school.

And I remember not wanting to cut my hair, because I remember my mom had really long hair, down to her waist. And she never ever cut it, and she never cut our hair either. All the girls had really long hair in our family. And I kept saying that I didn't want to cut my hair, but they just sat me on the chair and they just got scissors and they just grabbed my hair, and they just cut it. And they had this big bucket there, and they just threw everybody's hair in that bucket.

I remember going back to the dorm and there was other girls that were upset about their hair. They were mad and crying that they had to get their hair cut. And then when that was all done, we were made to wash our hair out with some kind of shampoo. And I just remember it smelling really awful. The smell was bad. And this is, I think it had something to do with delousing people, I'm not sure.[95]

In 1985, Ricky Kakekagumick was one of a group of children who were flown to the Poplar Hill, Ontario, school. On arrival, the boys and girls were separated and marched to their dormitories.

When we got there, there's staff people there, Mennonite men. They're holding towels. So, we just put our luggage down on the floor there, and they told us, "Wet your hair." I had long hair, like, I was an Aboriginal teenager, I grew long hair. So, they told us, "Wash your hair." Then they had this big bottle of chemical. I didn't know what it was. It looked like something you see in a science lab. So, they were pumping that thing into our hand, "And put it all over your head," they said. "So, it will, this will kill all of the bugs on your head." Just right away they assumed all of us had bugs, Aboriginal. I didn't like that. I was already a teenager. I was already taking care of myself. I knew I didn't have bugs. But right away they assumed I did because I'm Aboriginal.

So after we washed our hair, everybody went through that, then we went to the next room. Then that's where I see a bunch of hair all over the floor. I see a guy standing over there with those clippers, the little buzz, was buzzing students. I kept on moving back. There was a line there. I kept going back. I didn't want to go. But came down to the end, I had no choice, 'cause everybody was already going through it, couldn't go behind anybody no more. So, I made a big fuss about it, but couldn't stop them. It was a rule. So, they, they gave me a brush, and they gave us one comb, too, and told us this is your comb, you take care of it.[96]

As a child, Bernice Jacks had been proud of her long hair. "My mom used to braid it and French braid it and brush it. And my sister would look after my hair and do it." But, on her arrival at residential school in the Northwest Territories, a staff member sat her on a stool and cut her hair. "And I sat there, and I could hear, I

Bernice Jacks.

could see my hair falling. And I couldn't do nothing. And I was so afraid my mom ... I wasn't thinking about myself. I was thinking about Mom. I say, 'Mom's gonna be really mad. And June is gonna be angry. And it's gonna be my fault.'"[97]

Victoria Boucher-Grant was shocked by the treatment she received upon enrolment at the Fort William, Ontario, school.

> And they, they took my braids, and they chopped my, they didn't even cut it, they just, I mean style it or anything, they just took the braid like that, and just cut it straight across. And I remember just crying and crying because it was almost like being violated, you know, like when you're, when I think about it now it was a violation, like, your, your braids got cut, and it, I don't know how many years that you spent growing this long hair.[98]

Elaine Durocher found the first day at the Roman Catholic school in Kamsack, Saskatchewan, to be overwhelming.

> As soon we entered the residential school, the abuse started right away. We were stripped, taken up to a dormitory, stripped. Our hair was sprayed.... They put oxfords on our feet, 'cause I know my feet hurt. They put dresses on us. And were made, we were always praying, we were always on our knees. We were told we were little, stupid savages, and that they had to educate us.[99]

Brian Rae said he and the other boys at the Fort Frances, Ontario, school were given a physical inspection by female staff.

> You know, to get stripped like that by a female, you know, you don't even know, 'cause, you know, it was embarrassing, humiliating. And, and then she'd have this, you, you know, look or whatever it was in her eyes, eh, you know. And then she would comment about your private parts and stuff like that, eh, like, say, "Oh, what a cute peanut," and you know, just you know kind of rub you down there, and, and then, you know, just her eyes, the way she looked. So that kind of made me feel, feel all, you know, dirty and, you know, just, I don't know, just make me feel awful I guess because she was doing that. And then the others, you know, the other kids were there, you know, just laughing, eh, that was common. So, I think that was the first time I ever felt humiliated about my sexuality.[100]

Julianna Alexander found the treatment she received upon arrival at the Kamloops, British Columbia, school demeaning.

> But they made us strip down naked, and I felt embarrassed, you know. They didn't, you know I just thought it was inappropriate, you know, people standing there, watching us, scrubbing us and everything, and then powdering us down with whatever it was that they powdered us with, and, and our hairs were covered, you know, really scrubbed out, and then they poured, I guess what they call now coal oil, or whatever that was, like, some kind of turpentine, I'm not sure what it was, but anyway, it really stunk.[101]

On their arrival at residential school, students often were required to exchange the clothes they were wearing for school-supplied clothing. This could mean the loss of home-made clothing that was of particular value and meaning to the students. Murray Crowe said his clothes from home were taken and burned at the school that he attended in north-western Ontario.[102] When Wilbur Abrahams's mother sent him to the Alert Bay school, she outfitted him in brand-new clothes. When he arrived at the school, he and all the other students were lined up.

> They took us down the hall, and we were lined up again, and, and I couldn't figure out what we were lined up for, but I dare not say anything. And pretty soon it's my turn, they told me to take all of my clothes off, and, and they gave me clothes that looked like they were second-hand, or but they were clean, and told me to put those on, and that was the last time I saw my new clothes. Dare not ask questions.[103]

John B. Custer said that upon arrival at the Roman Catholic school near The Pas, Manitoba, all the students had their personal clothing taken away. "And we were dressed in, we were all dressed the same. Like, we had coveralls on. I remember when I went over there, I had these beaded moccasins. As soon as I got there, they took everything away."[104]

Elizabeth Tapiatic Chiskamish attended schools in Québec and northern Ontario. She recalled that when she arrived at school, her home clothing was taken from her.

> The clothes we wore were taken away from us too. That was the last time we saw our clothes. I never saw the candy that my parents packed into my suitcase again. I don't know what they did with it. It was probably thrown away or given to someone else or simply kept. When I was given back the luggage, none of things that my parents packed were still in there. Only the clothes I wore were still sometimes in the suit-case.[105]

Phyllis Webstad recalled that her mother bought her a new shirt to wear on her first day at school at Williams Lake. "I remember it was an orange shiny colour. But when I got to the Mission it was taken and I never wore it again. I didn't understand why. Nothing was ever explained why things were happening."[106] Much later, her experience became the basis for what has come to be known as "Orange Shirt Day." Organized by the Cariboo Regional District, it was first observed on September 30, 2013. On that day, individuals were encouraged to wear an orange shirt as a memorial of the damage done to children by the residential school system.[107]

When Larry Beardy left Churchill, Manitoba, for the Anglican school in Dauphin, he was wearing a "really nice beautiful beaded" jacket his mother had made. "I think it was a caribou, a jacket, and she, she made that for me because she knew I was going to school." Shortly after he arrived at school, "all, all our clothes were taken away. My jacket I had mentioned was gone. And everybody was given the same, the same kind of clothing, with the old black army boots, we used to call them, and slacks."[108]

Ilene Nepoose recalled that the belongings she took to the Blue Quills residential school were taken away from her upon arrival. "I even brought my own utensils [laughing] and I never saw those things again, I often wonder what happen to them. But I remember at the end of the first school, the first year—they take our personal clothes away and they give us these dresses that are made out of flour sacks."

When she was to return home at Christmastime, the staff could not find the clothes she had worn to come to school.

Ilene Nepoose.

> I saw them on this other girl and I told the nuns that she was wearing my dress and they didn't believe me. So, that girl ended up keeping my dress and I don't remember what I wore, it was probably a school dress. But, that really bothered me because it was my own, like my mom made that dress for me and I was very proud of it and I couldn't—I wasn't allowed to wear that again.[109]

Nick Sibbeston attended the Fort Providence school for six years. He was enrolled in the school after his mother was sent to the Charles Camsell Hospital in Edmonton for tuberculosis treatment. The only language he spoke was Slavey (Dene); the only language the teachers spoke was French.

> On arrival was you're given a bath and you're de-liced and you're given a haircut and all your clothes are taken away. I know I arrived with a little bag that my mother had filled with winter things, you know, your mitts ... but all of that was taken away and put up high in a cupboard and we didn't see it again 'til next June.[110]

When Carmen Petiquay went to the Amos, Québec, school, the staff "took away our things, our suitcases, my mother had put things that I loved in my suitcase. I had some toys. I had some clothing that my mother had made for me, and I never saw them again. I don't know what they did with those things."[111]

Martin Nicholas of Nelson House, Manitoba, went to the Pine Creek, Manitoba, school in the 1950s. "My mom had prepared me in a Native clothing. She had made me a buckskin jacket, beaded with fringes.... And my mom did beautiful work, and I was really proud of my clothes. And when I got to residential school, that first day I remember, they stripped us of our clothes."[112]

Frances Tait was sent to the Alberni, British Columbia, school in 1951 when she was five years old. For her, as for so many students, the moment of arrival was a moment of tremendous loss.

> And even right from day one, I remember they took everything I had. I went to that school with a silver teapot that my mother had left for me, and my family made sure

that I had it. As soon as I walked into that school, they took all my clothes, and they took the teapot. And I never saw it again. And I got a haircut; I was issued school clothing.[113]

When Dorothy Ross went to school at Sioux Lookout, her clothes were taken from her and thrown away. "I was hanging on to my jacket really tight. I didn't want to let go. So once I set my jacket somewhere, I lost it. 'Cause what if my mom comes, I was looking for my mom, I need my jacket. They took that away from me."[114]

On her arrival at the Presbyterian school in Kenora, Lorna Morgan was wearing "these nice little beaded moccasins that my grandma had made me to wear for school, and I was very proud of them." She said they were taken from her and thrown in the garbage.[115]

The schools could not always provide students with a full range of shoe sizes. Geraldine Bob said that at the Kamloops school, "you got the closest fit whether it was too big or too small; so your feet hurt constantly." In the same way, she felt the clothing was never warm enough in winter. "I just remember the numbing cold. And being outside in the playground and a lot of us would dig holes in the bank and get in and pull tumbleweeds in after us, to try to stay warm."[116]

Stella August.

Stella August said that at the Christie, British Columbia, school, "we all had to wear the same shoes, whether they fit or not, and, and if they didn't fit, if we were caught without our shoes, we'd get whacked in the ear with our shoe."[117]

Other students recalled the school-issued clothing as being uncomfortable, ill-fitting, and insufficient in the winters. William Herney said that at the Shubenacadie school, the students would often huddle together in an effort to keep warm.

> It was, it was just like a circle. The inner circle was the three-, the four-, five- year-olds and seven-year-olds in that circle, small ones, and the older you are, the outer circle you were, and the oldest ones wanted the outest, and the, the outer circle, the farthest out. We would huddle up in there, just huddle in close together to give that body heat. And the young ones were protected from the elements. And, well, we huddled up around there for maybe an hour, an hour and a half, and until suppertime, when, when the bell rang, you were all piled in there.[118]

Margaret Plamondon said the children at the Fort Chipewyan, Alberta, school were not dressed warmly enough for the winter recess periods.

> And then it doesn't matter how cold it is, at recess, and you can't wear pants, you have to wear a little skinny dress, and it doesn't matter how cold it is, you were out there, and they wouldn't let you come in, even if you're crying and you're cold. You

had to go play outside during recess, fifteen minutes, you can't get in, they lock the door on you, even if you try to go in, and same thing on weekends. There's no, it doesn't matter how cold it is in the wintertime, we have to ... sometimes we'd stand there by the door, freezing, freezing to death, a whole bunch of us, you know, just little kids, don't understand why we can't go in to warm up.[119]

The students' wardrobe at the schools was also limited in terms of quantity. Joanne Morrison Methot said that the students at the Shubenacadie school had a minimal supply of clothing.

> And we didn't have a lot of clothes. We only had maybe two pair of pants, two socks, like two bras, two panties, and maybe two nightgowns, that's all we had. Sundays, it was a dress-up dress, like, for Sundays. We only wore that to go to church, and patent leather shoes, and little white socks. After church, we had to go back upstairs and change our clothes.[120]

Students spoke of the time they spent caring for their clothing. Shirley Ida Moore recalled that as a child at the Norway House, Manitoba, school, she used to get into trouble because she could not keep her clothes as neat and clean as was expected.

Shirley Ida Moore.

> We had these uniforms, they were, they were, we had a white blouse and then these tunics and I think they had like, three, three of those big pleat, pleaty things all around it. And every Sunday we had to iron those things razor sharp; like the pleats had to be sharp. And, and your shoes had to be polished and they had to be like glass. And, that's what I, that's what I got into trouble; that's why, because like, I was only little and she expected me to be able to iron those things like that well, and I couldn't and nobody could help me; so I would get punished. Just punished, and punished and punished.[121]

Language and culture
"How am I going to express myself?"

Many of the students came to the school fluent in an Aboriginal language, with little or no understanding of French or English. At school, they encountered English- or French-speaking teachers and supervisors, who typically had no understanding of the children's languages, and were actively, and often aggressively, involved in trying to deny their use. For children who could neither understand these new authorities nor speak English or French, the first few months in the school were disorienting and frightening. Arthur Ron McKay arrived at the Sandy Bay, Manitoba, school in the early 1940s with no knowledge of English.

> I didn't know where to go, not even to the washroom sometimes. I just wet myself because I didn't know where to go and I couldn't speak to the teacher, and I know that the nuns was the teacher and I couldn't speak English. They told me not to speak my language and everything, so I always pretended to be asleep at my desk so they wouldn't ask me anything. The nun, first time she was nice but later on as she began to know me when I done that to lay my head on the desk pretending that I was sleeping not to be asked anything. She come and grab my hair, my ears and told me to listen and to sit up straight.[122]

When she first went to the Amos, Québec, school, Margo Wylde could not speak any French. "I said to myself, 'How am I going to express myself? How will I make people understand what I'm saying?' And I wanted to find my sisters to ask them to come and get me. You know it's sad to say, but I felt I was a captive."[123]

William Antoine grew up speaking Ojibway on the Sheshewaning Reserve in Ontario. When he was seven, he was taken to the Spanish, Ontario, boys' school.

> I was in Grade One, the work that was given to me I didn't know anything about and, and the teacher was speaking English to me and I didn't understand what he was saying. That's why it was so hard; I didn't understand English very much. I understand a little bit, at that time, but I did not understand what he told me. And he would get mad at me and angry at me because I couldn't do my work.

William Antoine.

I could not, I couldn't do it because I didn't understand what he was telling me, what to do. So it was hard.[124]

When he first went to the Fort Albany, Ontario, school, Peter Nakogee could speak no English.

Peter Nakogee.

That's where I had the most difficulty in school because I didn't understand English. My hand was hit because I wrote on my scribblers, the scribblers that were given on starting school, pencils, erasers, rulers and that, scribblers, and textbooks that were given. "Write your names," she said, so they don't get lost. But I wrote on my scribblers in Cree syllabics. And so I got the nun really mad that I was writing in Cree. And then I only knew my name was Ministik from the first time I heard my name, my name was Ministik. So I was whipped again because I didn't know my name was Peter Nakogee.[125]

For Marcel Guiboche at the Pine Creek school, the experience was frightening.

Marcel Guiboche.

A sister, a nun started talking to me in English and French, and yelling at me. I did not speak English, and didn't understand what she, what she was asking. She got very upset, and started hitting me all over my body, hands, legs and back. I began to cry, yell, and became very scared, and this infuriated her more. She got a black strap and hit me some more. My brother, Eddie, Edward, heard me screaming, and came to get me.[126]

Calvin Myerion recalled not being allowed to speak his language at the Brandon school.

And the time went on, and I was told not to speak my Native language, and I didn't know any other language other than my Native language. I didn't know a word of English, and my brother, who had been there before me, taught me in, said in my language not to talk the language. But the only way that I could communicate was through my language.[127]

The shock of her first night at the Alberni school left Lily Bruce in tears. Eventually, her auntie, who was a student at the school, was brought in to speak to her.

I was just getting dressed into pyjamas, and I never, I never spoke English. [crying] My auntie was told to tell me that I wasn't allowed to speak Kwak'wala anymore. I told her, "But Auntie, I don't know how to speak English." And she says, "Well you're gonna have to learn pretty quick." [crying] She said, "From now on, you have to speak English." I don't know how long it took me. I kept my mouth shut most of the time. I'd rather keep quiet than get in trouble.[128]

Andrew Bull Calf recalled that at the residential school in Cardston, Alberta, "I got strapped a lot of time because I didn't know English, you know, and the only language we spoke was Blackfoot in our community and so I got strapped a lot for that."[129] Percy Thompson recalled being slapped in the face for speaking Cree shortly after his arrival at the Hobbema school in Alberta. "How was I to learn English within three or four days the first week I was there? Was I supposed to learn the English words, so the nun would be happy about it? It's impossible."[130]

When two sisters attended the Anglican school at Aklavik, they could not speak English. But, according to one sister, the staff would "spank us when we tried to talk our language. So, we just keep away from one another."[131] Alfred Nolie attended the Alert Bay school, where, he said, "they strapped me right away, as soon as they heard me talking our language. I didn't know what they were saying to me."[132]

Martin Nicholas said that at the school he attended in Manitoba, the prohibition on speaking one's own language left him isolated. "I would be punished if I spoke my language, yet, that's the only language I knew. So, what am I supposed to do? So, I kept quiet." Because he did not speak English, he became alarmed if anyone spoke to him.[133]

Meeka Alivaktuk came to the Pangnirtung school in what is now Nunavut with no knowledge of English.

Alfred Nolie.

> For example, I knew how to knit. I learned before we came to school how to knit mittens but when we got to school and the teacher was speaking to us in English and he was saying "knit, purl, knit, purl," I had no idea what that meant so I put down my knitting and just sat there. The teacher came up to me and slapped my hands because they didn't know what to do and I couldn't understand what he was telling me. That's how my education began.[134]

After growing up speaking only Cree in northern Manitoba, Emily Kematch found that "learning how to speak English was a struggle." She said that "the only way I got by was my friend Sally taught me words, 'this is how you say, say words.' She taught me what to do so I wouldn't get into trouble and we weren't allowed to cry. If we cried, we got spanked."[135]

At the Qu'Appelle, Saskatchewan, school in the mid-1960s, Greg Rainville said, he was punished for speaking his own language and for failing to carry out instructions given him in a language he did not understand. "The nuns would get frustrated with you when they talked to you in French or English, and you're not knowing what they're talking about, and you're pulled around by the ear."[136]

When Robert Malcolm came to the Sandy Bay school, he did not speak a word of English.

> I had to learn the hard way to communicate in school what the, the nuns or the teachers wanted. And if you didn't, if you didn't understand that, it was you were being punished, sometimes physically, and then sometimes emotionally. Like you were made fun of sometimes by other people in your class, like if I said, or did something wrong everybody would laugh at you.[137]

Rules against the use of Aboriginal languages were intended to force students to learn English (or French) as quickly as possible. These rules and the anxiety they caused remain among the most commonly cited elements of residential school experiences. Jacqueline Barney said that one of her report cards from the Sault Ste. Marie, Ontario, school complained that "Jackie still insists on speaking Cree."[138] Dianne Bossum recalled being told not to speak her own language at the La Tuque, Québec, school she attended in the late 1960s and early 1970s.[139] Geraldine Shingoose recalled being punished for not speaking English at the Lestock, Saskatchewan, school. "I just remember, recalling the very first memories was just the beatings we'd get and the lickings, and just for speaking our language, and just for doing things that were against the rules."[140]

Geraldine Shingoose.

Dorothy Nolie recalled that at the Alert Bay school, she was caught speaking in her own language at the dinner table. "They put me in the middle of the floor, in front of everybody, and that was my punishment for speaking our language. I was hungry. I never ate nothing. Looked around, looked around, everybody eating. That's how mean they were to me, to all of us kids in there."[141]

At the Roman Catholic residence in Fort Smith in the 1960s, Leon Wyallon recalled, he was punished for speaking his own language.

> We can't even talk in our own language. The minute you talked your own language then you would get sent to the corner. The minute those Grey Nuns find out that you're talking in your own language, whispering, you'd, if you don't tell us now then you get strapped on the hand until you say, what did you say. They let you stand in the corner 'til suppertime.[142]

David Nevin recalled seeing a young girl "savagely" beaten by staff at the Shubenacadie school for refusing to stop speaking Mi'kmaq.

> This went on for—seemed like an eternity, and no matter what they did to her she spoke Mi'kmaq. You know, and to this day I, you know, that has been indelible in my

mind and I think that's one of the reasons why when I went to school there I always spoke English, that fear of being hit with that strap, that leather strap.[143]

Alan Knockwood recalled being strapped for speaking his own language at Shubenacadie.

Just for saying thank you to someone who gave me something in the school. I was caught by a brother or one of the workers, and I was strapped so severely that when we went to supper my cousin Ivan had to feed me because my hands were so swollen from the straps. And I remember sitting at the corner of the table and the guys got up and hid me, stood up and hid, so Ivan could feed me a few mouthfuls of food.[144]

Allen Kagak recalled being disciplined for speaking Inuktitut at the Coppermine tent hostel in the Northwest Territories (now Nunavut). "I couldn't speak English, they tell me to speak English, but I couldn't help it, I had to speak my Inuktitut language. When I speak my Inuktitut language, they, teachers, strapped, strapped, strapped me, pulled my ears, let me stand in a corner all morning."[145]

Richard Kaiyogan also attended the Coppermine tent hostel.

But over the years, if you talk in your own language you get strapped, and later on, I had to learn the hard way but myself, I think over the years I earned that, we earn it, take this education. One time I got strapped and I didn't want to get strapped anymore so I said to myself, I said, "What am I here for?" You know, education, I guess. Anyway, my culture is going to be—my language will be lost in the way. Okay, why not think like a white man? Talk like a white man? Eat like a white man, that's what, so I don't have to get strapped anymore. You know, I followed their own rules.[146]

On his first day of school in Pangnirtung, the teacher overheard Sam Kautainuk speaking to a friend in Inuktitut. "He took a ruler and grabbed my head like this and then smacked me in the mouth with the ruler four times. That was very painful, it hurts! It hurt so much. That happened just for speaking to my friend in my own language."[147]

There are also reports of students being forced to eat soap if they were caught speaking an Aboriginal language. Pierrette Benjamin said this happened at the school at La Tuque.

They put a big chunk, and they put it in my mouth, and the principal, she put it in my mouth, and she said, "Eat it, eat it," and she just showed me what to do. She told me to swallow it. And she put her hand in front of my mouth, so I was chewing and chewing, and I had to swallow it, so I swallowed it, and then I had to open my mouth to show that I had swallowed it. And at the end, I understood, and she told me, "That's a dirty language, that's the devil that speaks in your mouth, so we had to wash it because it's dirty." So, every day I spent at the residential school, I was treated badly. I was almost slaughtered.[148]

Alphonsine McNeely attended the Roman Catholic school at Aklavik in the 1940s. On one occasion, she and a friend were overheard by a nun teaching each other their respective languages.

She took me, I don't know why they always target me. So anyway, she took me to the sink, and she took this, they had this Sunlight soap, it's kind of a big bar, she took a brush, a floor brush, and she, she, I thought she was gonna tell me to scrub the floor or something. Instead of that she, she grabbed my hair, and she started rubbing my mouth with that.[149]

Ken A. Littledeer recalled seeing a fellow student at the Sioux Lookout school having his mouth washed out with soap for speaking an Aboriginal language. "I watched that incident, and, and I didn't like what I seen, bubbles coming out. It sounded like as if they were gonna kill him, or is he breathing, I would say, 'cause I see bubbles coming out of his nose and his mouth, and gagging."[150]

At the Shubenacadie school, a staff member once caught William Herney speaking Mi'kmaq with his brother.

And she says, "What are you two boys doing?" "Nothing, Sister." "Oh, yes, I heard you. You were talking that language, weren't you?" "Yes, Sister." "Come here," she said. I went over. She took a stick. She leaned me over to the bathtub, the bathtub, grabbed me by the neck, and I don't know how many whacks she gave me over my bum, and I was crying like I don't know what. Then, she took a piece of soap, and she washed my mouth in it. I can still even taste that lye soap. All my life I tasted that taste. And she said, "You don't talk that language here. That's a no, no, no, you don't, you understand?" Looks at me straight in the eye. She said, "Do you understand that?" And I said, "Yes, Sister, I understand."[151]

William Herney.

In Roman Catholic schools in the West and North, it was most common for many of the staff members to have come originally from Québec or Europe. The fact that these staff members were allowed to speak to one another in French (their first language) bothered many students. Mary Courchene once asked one of the staff of the Fort Alexander, Manitoba, school,

"How come you get to talk your own language and we don't?" It was just, you know wanting to know why they could speak French and we couldn't speak Ojibway inside the, inside the school. We spoke it outside, but we couldn't speak it inside, inside the house; inside the school. And she looked at me and she was very angry but she didn't say anything.

Mary Courchene.

Later that evening, she was told to apologize to the nun in the dining room. At first she objected, only to be told that

> "No one's going to eat until you say you're sorry." Of course I had to say I was sorry; I didn't want all the rest of the students to have to go without supper, and just because I wouldn't say I was sorry.

> So I said I was sorry and but it was, I was made to feel humiliated. And there were, there was always humiliations like that, that made you feel small. And of course it was meant for the other, all the other students to laugh at this person that was made to feel ashamed. So it was always you know, that kind of, that kind of thing. So we weren't, we weren't encouraged to be ourselves. We weren't encouraged to, to do what was best for us. It was always what those ... anyway.[152]

Students also objected to the fact that if they were taught an additional language, it was French. Lydia Ross attended the Cross Lake, Manitoba, school. "And in my Grade Eleven essay, I wrote out a French essay of 500 words, with all the verbs and adjectives, I had 90% in there. That's how, that's how much French that they taught me, and not my language. I couldn't speak our language."[153]

Despite the usual instruction to conduct school life in English (or in French in some of the Québec schools), many students continued to speak their own language when they could. Monique Papatie said that at the Amos, Québec, school, students "went to a corner to speak our language, even if we weren't allowed to do that. We kept our language, the Anishinabemowin language, and I speak it very well today, and this is what I want to teach the children, my mother's grandchildren and great-grandchildren."[154] Arthur Ron McKay said he was able to hang on to his language at the Sandy Bay school.

> Or else you'd get your ears pulled, your hair or get hit with a ruler. Well anyway, I just kept going and I couldn't speak my language but then I was speaking to boys in the, 'cause they came from the reserve and they speak my language. We use to speak lots, like behind, behind our supervisors or whatever you call it. That's why I didn't lose my language; we always sneak away when I was smaller.[155]

Ronalee Lavallee said that at the Grayson, Saskatchewan, school in the 1970s, there were a number of students from northern Saskatchewan who spoke fluent Cree. At night, they would teach the language to the other students. "We wanted to learn this language, and how we used to take turns watching for the nuns so that we wouldn't get into trouble. And I think, just think, that was 1970 or '71, that's not so long ago, and they were still doing that to us?"[156]

From the student perspective, the overall message was to speak English (or French). There were some exceptions. Mary Stoney said that at the school she attended in Alberta, at least one priest made an effort to preserve Aboriginal languages. "We were lucky to have Father Mullen, who helped preserve our Cree language by translating the Bible and hymns. If not, the language would be in worse shape. In school we often spoke Cree to each other, but some Sisters were strict with the rules and some were not."[157] Both Catholic and Protestant missionaries had a long history of learning and encouraging the use of Aboriginal languages in religious settings. At the Beauval, Saskatchewan, school, Albert Fiddler recalled, Aboriginal languages were restricted to use in religious classes.

> But that's the only thing they allow is learning how to pray in Cree. They won't allow us to talk to each other, and they make sure that we don't, we don't talk to each other in Cree either. We only, they only teach us how to pray in Cree in catechisms in the classroom, but not to talk to each other because it's un-polite for somebody that doesn't understand Cree.[158]

Alex Alikashuak said that at the school at Churchill, Manitoba, which operated in the 1960s, there were no restrictions on the use of Aboriginal languages.

> We, we almost never spoke English. The only time we spoke English was when we ran across, like, see the thing is in our school, some of our dormitory staff were Inuit people too, so we, we couldn't speak to them in English, anyway. The only time, real time we spoke English was when we were in the classroom, or we're talking to one of the administration staff, and or somebody from town that's not Inuit, but otherwise we, everybody spoke our language.[159]

The rule in the Aklavik residence, according to Ellen Smith, was "English please, English please." But, she said, "when we went on the playground in Aklavik we spoke our language; run around. There they even took us out on the land; in the springtime. We went muskrat trapping."[160]

Despite the encouragement that was offered in some schools, and the students' efforts to keep their language alive, the overall impact was language loss. Russell Bone felt he lost the ability to speak his language at the Pine Creek school.

> I realized that nobody was, never used to talk their language. Some would, some would speak their language as long as the nuns weren't around, eh. And then, I started losing it. Forgetting how, what to say, about the words; what they meant; and when somebody, let's say, there'd be two people talking, eh, two young guys talking their language, and I wouldn't understand. I'd lost it.[161]

Of her experiences at the Baptist school in Whitehorse and the Anglican school in Carcross, Rose Dorothy Charlie said,

> They took my language. They took it right out of my mouth. I never spoke it again. My mother asked me why, why you could hear me, she's, like, "I could teach you." I said, "No." And she said, "Why?" I said, "I'm tired of getting hit in the mouth, tired of it. I'm just tired of it, that's all." Then I tried it, I went to Yukon College, I tried it, and then my own auntie laugh at me because I didn't say the, the words right, she laughed at me, so I quit. "No more," I said. Then people bothered me, and say, "How come you don't speak your language?" And I said, "You wouldn't want to know why." So, I never speak, speak it again.[162]

Robert Joseph went to residential school at the age of six as a fluent speaker of Kwak'wala. "By the time I left that school, eleven years later, of course nobody in the school spoke that language. There are only 100 of us now in the entire Kwakiutl Nation who speak the language."[163]

Prior to the expansion of the residential school system in Québec in the 1960s, some Aboriginal students from that province were sent to schools in Ontario. Paul Dixon was one of these students. His younger brother, however, was educated at a residential school in Québec. "So, I couldn't talk to my brother in French 'cause I didn't know French, and he couldn't talk to me in English." His mother had insisted that they learn their Aboriginal language, which meant that they did have a language in common.[164]

When John Kistabish left the Amos school, he could no longer speak Algonquin, while his parents could not speak French, the language that he had been taught in the school. As a result, he found it almost impossible to communicate with them about the abuse he experienced at the school. "I had tried to talk with my parents, and, no, it didn't work. It's that we lived with them like if it was... We were well anyway because I knew that they were my parents, when I left the residential school, but the communication wasn't there."[165]

In some cases, the residential school experience led parents to decide not to teach their children anything but English. Both of Joline Huskey's parents attended residential school in the Northwest Territories. As a result of their experience in the schools, they raised their daughter to speak English.[166] When Bruce R. Dumont was sent to residential school in Onion Lake, Saskatchewan, his mother warned him not to speak Cree. She told him that "you got to learn the English language and, you know, so we, you know, we were instructed at home, and spoke freely, spoke Cree at home, but at school we, we weren't allowed to speak, speak our language."[167]

Bruce R. Dumont.

Andrew Bull Calf recalled that at the residential school in Cardston, students were not only punished for speaking their own languages, but they also were discouraged from participating in traditional cultural activities.[168]

Evelyn Kelman attended the Brocket, Alberta, school. She recalled that the principal warned the students that if they attended a Sun Dance that was to be held during the summer, they would be strapped on their return to school. "Today I still know one or two people who didn't go because they were afraid of that."[169]

Marilyn Buffalo recalled being told by Hobbema school staff that the Sun Dance was devil worship. "We were told by untrained, unprofessional teachers who took great joy in beating the heck out of the boys and the girls, that we were never going to amount to anything. And called savage."[170]

Sarah McLeod attended the Kamloops school. When she went home for the summer, her grandmother would teach her about traditional ways of healing.

> My grandmother would saddle a horse for me, telling me, "Go get this medicine for me up on the hill." She'd name the medicine, and I was, like, eight years old, I'd get on a horse, and I'd go all by myself, and I'd get the medicines. I know which medicines she's talking about. I'd get off my horse, and I'd put some in the sack, and I'd have to go look around for a big rock, so I can get back on my horse again.

One year, she returned to school with a miniature totem pole that a family member had given her for her birthday. When she proudly showed it to one of the nuns, it was taken from her and thrown out.

> I looked at her. I said, "But that's my birthday present." "No, that's no good. That's all devil you see in that totem pole. It's all devil, can't you see all the devil in there? You throw it away right now." And she made me throw it in the garbage, and it was, I didn't know, I said to myself, "Oh, my gosh. All this time I was, I was hugging this devil?" You know I didn't know that.[171]

At Akaitcho Hall, the residence in Yellowknife, Northwest Territories, Mary Olibuk Tatty roomed with students from a variety of backgrounds.

> Three years of my life, I lost my Inuit values, even though I, I'm very strong. My mom was very strong at throat singing, and drum dancing, or whatever. But being a female Inuk, very proud Inuk I am, doesn't matter if my grandpa's a Newfie, what hit me was I couldn't say the Lord's Prayer in my room unless I whispered it, because I grew up so Anglican, because my roommate was Dogrib [Dene], or *Kabluunak* [a white person], 'cause they would ask me why are you, why are you saying this?

The common language of the residence and school was English. "The thing is I notice I spoke a lot of English to them, because back in my head, we had no choice but to speak English, 'cause our supervisors were all *Kabluunak*, nothing against *Kabluunak*, my grandpa's white, but I wish we had more support at residential schools with our Inuit values."[172]

Even when it did not directly disparage Aboriginal culture, the curriculum undermined Aboriginal identity. Thaddee Andre, who attended the Sept-Îles, Québec, school in the 1950s, recalled how as a student he wanted "to resemble the white man, then in the meantime, they are trying by all means to strip you of who you are as an Innu. When you are young, you are not aware of what you are losing as a human being."[173]

One former student said that her time at the Catholic school in The Pas, Manitoba, left her feeling ashamed to be Aboriginal.

> Even our own language was considered ugly; we weren't allowed to speak Cree language. I wasn't allowed to be myself as a Cree woman. Everything was filthy, even our monthlies and that's how I learned it at home and what I learned from the residential school, everything was ugly. And that's where I learned a lot of ugliness also, I became a compulsive liar, learned to live in the world of denial. When I was younger, I

learned how to hate, I hated my own mother, I blamed her for allowing us to be taken away even though at that time I didn't realize she didn't have a choice. It wasn't until 1990 that she told us that "I didn't have a choice. It was either that, or me going to jail. I had to let you kids go to school," 'cause that's when I disclosed to them both my mom and dad what I went through in residential school in 1990, August of 1990.[174]

Gordon James Pemmican recalled how at the Sioux Lookout school, the students used to watch western movies. "The ones they made us watch, Indians never won. I don't recall any show where Indians ever won. When we went out to play cowboys and Indians, none of us wanted to be the Indian."[175]

On occasion, some of the staff at the Blue Quills school had the students put on what one former student called "little powwows."

Gordon James Pemmican.

> "Okay, everyone, want to see you guys dance like Indians," like, you know, like you pagans, or you people, you know, to go in the circle, and then she says, "Here's your drum, and here is your stick," and of course he sang though. I remember he's still a good singer, but they would laugh when he would bang that dust, that tin, steel dustpan, eh.

> But they had laughed at some of this, you know, make us do some of the things that was culturally done, eh, but to turn it around and make it look like it was more of a joke than anything else. It was pretty quiet when we would do those little dances. There was no pride. It's just like we were all ashamed, and we were to dance like little puppets.[176]

It was during a confirmation class at the Sept-Îles, Québec, school that Jeanette Basile Laloche rebelled against the suppression of Aboriginal language and culture.

> They gave us a lesson on the Pentecost, and then the principal Father came with the inspector. You had to be good in you person, and you had to have good posture. Then, they explained to us the Pentecost. Then he said: "The Apostles had tongues of fire on the top of the head, then they started speaking all languages." Then there I said: "No, no, they didn't speak my language." Then there, he insisted, he said: "Yes, Jeanette, they spoke your language." I said: "No, it is impossible that they could have spoken my language." Because, I began to be a rebel then: the God that my grand-mother taught me about, my grandparents taught me, he was nothing like theirs. Then there, I said: "No, they didn't speak my language." I shouldn't have, we didn't have a word to say, and I remember what he said: "Put your hand on the desk." You couldn't contradict them, I placed my hand on the desk, and with the ruler, I had to repeat, repeat that the apostles spoke my language. Me, it took time before I said it, but you know that's it, I was marked: I was hit with the ruler, with ... there was a

blade on the end of the ruler. I wrote a poem about it, my writing, and it was: "I was a little flower that was uprooted and transplanted into another world." My values were disrespected, my beliefs humiliated, I suffered infanticide. After all those horrors, my body, my mind had to adhere.[177]

Bedwetting
"Shame on you."

The trauma of being taken from their parents and placed in an alien, highly disciplined, and at times violent institution contributed to the development of involuntary bedwetting among many students. For the most part, in response, the schools employed punitive, shaming strategies. These measures were largely self-defeating, since they only intensified the feelings of anxiety and insecurity that underlay the problem.[178]

On his first night at the Beauval, Saskatchewan, school, Albert Fiddler, who had never lived in a building with indoor plumbing before, wet his bed. As he recalled, in the morning, a priest

> threw me in over my knees in front of the kids there, screamed, "you wet your bed" or something. I understand a little bit here and there what they were saying, anyway, because I had heard a little English before here and there. He grabbed my little underwear open, which I had to wear I guess. Slapped my buttocks like crazy there so that I'd never do that again. No explanation, not even asking who I am, and who I, what the hell, and then he gave me in front of the whole, the kids to see me there being bare ass, and I don't forget that.[179]

Russell Bone had a similar experience at the Pine Creek school. He too began wetting his bed once he came to residential school. He told the Truth and Reconciliation Commission of Canada that in the morning, a staff member "grabbed me from behind of the head, behind the hair, like the hair and she pushed my face into it. And she rubbed my face in it. 'Don't you ever do that again!'"[180]

The Commission also heard about cases where bedwetting began after specific acts of abuse. Shortly after he was sexually abused by a staff member at the Blue Quills school, one student began wetting his bed at night.[181]

Helen Kakekayash recalled being sent to the basement of the school in McIntosh, Ontario, for wetting her bed. "I don't know how long I would stay there, and they would bring my food there, and they would tell me to wash my blanket."[182]

Alfred Nolie wet his bed on his first night at the Alert Bay school.

> And then next morning, went for breakfast, went for a shower, and then they came and grabbed us after supper, and made us wash our sheets and blanket by hand. After that, they made us scrub the stairs on the school. This is all the way from the bottom to the top, this large stairs, and there's steel plates on there, and I didn't know that. One of the staff saved me, and my pants were soaked with blood, both sides, 'cause I was kneeling down. I didn't know what to say, but he seen my pants was just

covered with blood, both sides, because of the two days I was scrubbing the stairs and no school.[183]

The humiliation was often deliberate. At the Blue Quills school, all the students were lined up each morning. Then, according to Louise Large, those students who had wet their beds were taken out of line. "And I remember the nuns making fun of them, and, you know, they were made to be laughed at."[184]

Patrick James Hall recalled the treatment that children who wet their beds received at the Brandon school.

> A lot of children are wetting their beds, and then, you'd get up in the morning and you'll, the ones who wet their beds won't get up right away. They'll just lay there. And then we went to the shower, so everyone will go. And there'll be, like, eight, nine kids in there that are, don't wanna get up, eh. So he'll go there and whip the sheet off, and get up and yell, just whip them on the ass real hard, and they'll go stand in the corner. And then the next one "pshhh." Then, he'll make them stand there. He'll do that to them, and then make them stand there for a while. Then, all in all, the other boys will, will be done showering. He'll bring them back, then he'll make those boys tease them, eh, about their, about pissing their pants. And then, he'll make them take all their dirty laundry, then they'll just take it down and drop it somewhere there by down the stairs, then, where the shower is. But he'll make you have a cold shower first, so you don't have, just to make you remember.[185]

At the girls' school in Spanish, Ontario, Josephine Eshkibok had trouble with bedwetting. "First time I wet the bed I had to stand in front of 125 girls; they'd be all going like this to me, 'Shame on you.'"[186]

At the Qu'Appelle, Saskatchewan, school, Wesley Keewatin recalled, the staff would tip over a bed with the child still in it if they thought the child had wet the bed during the night. "If they were still sleeping they'd just grab their, their beds and flip them right over. You know they'd go flying."[187] Wendy Lafond said that at the Prince Albert, Saskatchewan, school, "if we wet our beds, we were made to stand in the corner in our pissy clothes, not allowed to change."[188]

Don Willie recalled that students who wet their beds were publicly humiliated at the Alert Bay school. "And they used to, they used to line up the wet bed, bedwetters, and line them up in the morning, and parade them through, parade them through breakfast, the breakfast area, pretty much to shame them."[189]

Frank Tomkins said that at the school at Grouard, Alberta, the staff once made a boy who could not control his bowels eat some of his own excrement. When he complained about this incident to his father, word

Wendy Lafond.

got back to the staff member, who beat Frank. At this point, his father withdrew him from the school.[190]

William Francis Paul said that at Shubenacadie, students who had been designated as bedwetters were compelled to wear a type of hospital gown that they referred to as "Johnny shirts." "Nobody tied your Johnny shirt. You were, your butt was exposed. Every time I opened my eyes, I'd see everybody's butt."[191] Joseph Ward spent one year in what was referred to as the "wet dorm" at the Shubenacadie school.

> Everybody wet the bed in that dorm you know and, and I heard horror stories about that dorm, but I don't know, I can't remember. Other than, taking our pyjamas and whatever we had and our sheets, to one pile, in the morning; and going for a shower. You know, just was like that for a whole year. I wet the bed, every day, like clock-work.[192]

Mary Rose Julian said she used to feel very sorry for the boys at Shubenacadie who wet their beds.

> I used to feel bad for the boys, you know, that wet their beds. You know they would have to carry their sheets on top of their heads, and parade through the refectory to the laundry room. And I had my head down, I didn't want to look at them, I was so, I know they were embarrassed. But I was afraid for my brother. But luckily, I never saw him go through, you know, the lineup.[193]

Benjamin Joseph Lafford recalled being humiliated at the Shubenacadie school for wetting his bed.

> I wet the bed and this Brother Sampson came in the morning, came to wake us up, "Everybody get up and wash up" and everything and he'd look at the beds and he said, "Oh somebody pissed the bed. Oh we've got a pitty potter here," a pissy potter or whatever they called it and you know and I was one of them that pissed the bed because I wanted to piss so bad at nighttime and then we got punished for that. I got punished for that. Every time I wet the bed I had to carry my blanket over my head, take it downstairs, go through the cafeteria where all the girls are and the boys are and everybody was looking at me carrying my pissy blankets over my head to go take it to where they would clean, do the laundry or something and I had to go sit down.[194]

In an effort to prevent bedwetting, some schools used to limit access to water at night. Aside from being punitive, the method is both counterproductive—since students do not learn how to control a full bladder—and unhealthy.[195] Benjamin Joseph Lafford recalled that at the Shubenacadie school, the washrooms were locked up at night.[196] Another Shubenacadie student, Joanne Morrison Methot, also recalled being denied water at night. "But we were so thirsty at times, so we used to go in the bathroom, open that tank, and drink the water from there. And I said, 'Well if I die, well, it can't be anybody's fault but mine, because I'm thirsty and I want some water.'"[197]

Ron Windsor said that at the Alert Bay school, students who were recovering from an illness were also denied access to water at night.

> We had no place to drink water, and we had a little ... bathroom there. And I was one of them that drank water from the toilet bowl, because I was caught by the matron, and after that they just locked it. We had no place to go when we got better, then we have to go downstairs to use the washroom. But there was still a lot of other guys there that couldn't move yet, and I still could see them crying, and I was crying with them.[198]

Ron Windsor.

Nora Abou-Tibbett said that students at the Lower Post, British Columbia, school were not allowed to drink water at night.

> And you know many of us, we were energetic, and you come in from outside and everything, and then you have to go and all wash up, and wash your feet, whatever, and then you go right to bed, no water. And so, I used to get to the sink, and I have this facecloth, and I just pretend I'm wash, well, I'm washing my face, and then I just run cold water on, you know, just fill it with cold water, and pretend I'm wring, wringing it out, but I just put it to my face, and I drink the water out of there, you know. So that's how we drank water.[199]

Daily life
"We were programmed."

Daily life in a residential school was highly regimented. John B. Custer said the students at the Roman Catholic school near The Pas "were treated like, I don't know, a herd of cattle, I guess. We had to line up for everything. Line up to go to the toilet, line up to go wash, line up to go take a shower, line up to go to play, line up to go to school, eat."[200]

Life in the Shubenacadie school was strictly controlled in the early 1940s when Noel Knockwood attended the school.

> We used to wake up in the morning, even before we had time to go to the bathroom, we would kneel down and we would say our prayers. 'Course it was orchestrated by the nuns and they told us what prayers to say.

> Then after prayers we were able to use the washroom and get dressed, then we would go downstairs in a single file. And then we would find our place in, in, in a, in a kitchen where, where we sat and we stood by our plates and waited for the nun to go give the command to sit down and she would clap her hands and by that sound we would all sit down. Then we would say grace, 'course they were Catholic prayers, Catholic grace that we said. We were forbidden to speak our own language.[201]

Lydia Ross said that the students at the Cross Lake, Manitoba, school were organized "just like an army.... And we used to go, oh, then the other one is you always file, file it by your number, always for everything. Go, go to cafeteria, you go by your number. Go to classroom, you go by number all in one row, up the stairs, up to the classroom. And everything was routinely done."[202]

Mel H. Buffalo spoke of how beds were to be made in precise, military style.

Mel H. Buffalo.

> There's a main sheet from above and the second sheet goes partway and you pull it under. And then the other sheet that covers—there's three—there's two sheets that cover and then the main blanket, that one, that covers as well. And then your pillowcase. There are two pillowcases, one that goes one way and the other goes the other way. And your dirty one comes to changing room, you have to take everything off and throw them in the centre of the common room and that goes to the laundry room. There's a laundry crew that picks that up, in a little cage, and takes that down to the laundry room and

brings it back the next day. So, after you've made your bed and the supervisor has inspected it to make sure there's no wrinkles or crinkles—if there is, he'll just rip off the whole thing again and you have to do it over 'til you get it right. First few times I was there, I couldn't get it right every morning. I used to have to do it at least twice and maybe if—if I'm—or if he's in a pretty bad mood, I could probably—he'd probably make me do it about three times.[203]

At the Sturgeon Landing school in Saskatchewan, one former student said, the students had to stand like soldiers: "We had to hold our head straight and not look anywhere else. We couldn't at all look at anybody. Especially not the boys where they were. No, we weren't allowed to look anywhere. We had to line up when we walked in school."[204]

Daniel Andre had a detailed memory of the routine at Grollier Hall, the Roman Catholic residence in Inuvik, Northwest Territories.

> Our day consisted of just getting up the morning at, I don't know when, 6:30, 7:00, and we'd get up and say our prayers, and then go, and get dressed, and go for breakfast. And then after breakfast, we were all assigned a chore, so we did the chore, and then from there we just did whatever we did until school, and then we'd get dressed and go to school. And then come home at lunch, and have lunch, and then go back to school, and then come home, and, and or go to Grollier home. And then from 3:30 to 5:00, we would just, we'd play outside, or play in the gym, or whatever was, maybe something was assigned, like, go for a walk or whatever, and we'd do that until supper, and then have supper. And then in the evening after supper, about a half an hour later, we were assigned to gym time, which was in the evening from six to eight, something like that. It was 'til 8:00 o'clock, anyway. And then after we were done in the gym we'd just go back upstairs, and then everybody had to have a shower. So, we showered and put on our pyjamas, and then the boys would be, they'd be sent to bed by groups, like the first group, second group, third group, depending on your age. And so we went to bed, and then we'd just get up the next day, and it happened all over again.
>
> And then on Saturday and Sunday, we have a late breakfast. Sister Tremblay would bring our cereal and whatever, toast and whatnot, up to the, the boys' end, and, and we'd have breakfast, cereal and toast. And then, yeah, and sometimes we went down to the cafeteria, but depending how many students were upstairs, she would bring the stuff up, and then we'd eat, and then have lunch after that, after, and then we'd go for a walk in the afternoon. In the winter, or summer, spring, whenever it was, we always went to our walk to get out of the building, by a supervisor, a student supervisor from downstairs, the seniors, and sometimes they hired adults from the community or whatever. And, and yeah, so that was our life.[205]

Many students spoke of life that was regulated by the ringing of a bell. At the schools that Percy Tuesday attended in northwestern Ontario, everything was done with a whistle, a buzzer or a bell. We were programmed, and we couldn't go or nothing. When the bell rang that's when you got up and when, you know, every-thing. When the whistle blew, you were playing outside, you had to come running in, and everything told you what to do. Every, you knew what everything meant to a buzzer or whistle; you know what you had to do. Even when we lined up to go and eat, we lined up at our benches, we'd stand there 'til the nun, I think, rang a bell or something for us to sit down, and then to start eating, you know.[206]

Stella Bone, who attended the Sandy Bay school in the 1960s, recalled

those bells that they used to use ring, ring, ring, okay, "Time to get up." Ring, ring, ring, like, you know, bells throughout the day. Ring, ring, ring, recess bell, eh. Well, mind you, there was recess bells in other schools, too, but this drilling, conditioning was automatic, eh. And if you didn't do it, then of course, there was a consequence to that, really tough consequence.[207]

Bernadette Nadjiwan said that at the Spanish, Ontario, girls' school, "I became acquainted with a regime of rules, which at first feel rigid and regimental." She too remem-bered the bells. "It rang in the morning when we'd wake up, to wake us up, to get ready for school, the bell rang again, and to get ready for bed, even to go to classes. We were so well trained, and everyone was likened to a soldier."[208] David Charleson said that at the Christie, British Columbia, school, "the bell would ring, and it would ring again to wash up, and it would ring again to line up at the dining room area, and I know we had to totally be quiet. We couldn't even talk to each other in the dining room while we're eating. Couldn't even ask for salt and pepper in language, English language."[209]

The schools afforded the children little in the way of privacy or dignity. Louise Large recalled "those little bathrooms" at the Blue Quills school.

There was maybe six in a row, and six sinks. And the nun stands there, and give us two little pieces of toilet paper, and they were almost see-through, and that's what we had to use to wipe ourselves after we used the bathroom. And later in the evening, we would get our panties checked and to see if there was, if they were soiled.[210]

Ilene Nepoose recalled that students were not allowed to close the bathroom doors in the Blue Quills dormitory. "It had to be opened and we were given three squares of toilet tissue, that's all we could use, that's all, three squares."[211]

Larry Roger Listener recalled how, when he attended residential school, female staff would supervise the boys when they were taking showers. "One had a ruler, would tell us, 'clean there, clean there, and wash there.'"[212]

Lydia Ross recalled that at the Cross Lake, Manitoba, school,

When you were small in a dormitory, we were in rows, two rows this way, two rows that way, and there was a, a little hole in there where the nun used to peek out of there with her white, she just wore white. You know those nuns, you only saw their face and their hands, that's it, you didn't see any, any of them dressed as an ordinary street person. They always wore, wore those, those black clothes.[213]

Vitaline Elsie Jenner recalled her first sight of the junior dormitory at the Fort Chipewyan, Alberta, school.

And I looked up there, and, you know, and little rows of beds, you know, really not very close, 'cause they had a little space in between, so they can walk through. They walked through every night, you know, make sure that, make sure that your hands are not playing with yourself, 'cause that's all they ever thought of was gross things in their minds, you know. It was just awful.[214]

When checking students for health problems, the staff in some schools paid little attention to the children's dignity. Shirley Waskewitch felt humiliated by her experiences at the Catholic school in Onion Lake, Saskatchewan.

I had scabs, I had developed scabs all over my body, and they were all over my body, and they weren't looked after. This one time in the high dormitory with the, where the big girls slept, we're all standing in line, washing in our basins. The girls were standing in line with their basins just washing up, and, and this nun come and got me, and stood me up in front of all the girls, and kind of turned me around, and I was kind of bent over, and she must have took a ruler, I think it was a ruler, and she pulled my bloomers down, and lifted my nightgown to expose me in front of everybody, to expose the scabs I had on my bum.[215]

For administrative reasons, Indian Affairs and the school administrators assigned each residential school student a specific number. In many schools, these numbers were used on a daily basis instead of names. Many students found the experience degrading and dehumanizing. At Cross Lake, Lydia Ross said,

My name was Lydia, but in the school I was, I didn't have a name, I had numbers. I had number 51, number 44, number 32, number 16, number 11, and then finally number one when I was just about coming to high school. So, I wasn't, I didn't have a name, I had numbers. You were called 32, that's me, and all our clothes were, had 32 on them. All our clothes and footwear, they all had number 32, number 16, whatever number they gave me.[216]

Marlene Kayseas never forgot the number she was given at the Lestock, Saskatchewan, school. "I remember when I first went, my number was 86. I was a little small girl and I was in a small girls' dorm. And you had to remember your number because if they called you, they wouldn't call you by your name, they'd call you by your number."[217]

Lydia Ross.

Martha Minoose recalled how the students were numbered at the Roman Catholic school in Cardston, Alberta. "They didn't call us by our name, they just called numbers. So my number was 33 in the small girls. When I went to the senior girls, my number was 15. So our clothes were marked and they just call out numbers."[218]

Martha Minoose.

At the Sandy Bay school, Stella Bone was number 66. "And everything that I had was marked with that number, eh. It may not affect others as much as it affected me, but being a number."[219] Bernice Jacks felt that the practice at the Kamloops school denied her any personal identity. "I was called, 'Hey, 39. Where's 39? Yes, 39, come over here. Sit over here, 39.' That was the way it was. And that's ... I say it just the way they said it. I was 39."[220]

Wilbur Abrahams recalled how, on the first day of school at Alert Bay, British Columbia, the students were all given numbers.

> They told us to remember our number, instead of calling my name, they'd call my number, and if you don't remember your number, you, you know you get yelled at. And I, I think we did extra chores, so you had to really keep memorizing your number. Mine was 989. And it was, so that's how they got my attention, you know, when they wanted you for something that, you know, could be for anything, could be for job placements or something, I don't know, you, 989, you had to pay attention, and just be there, I guess, or just be aware.[221]

Antonette White, who went to the Kuper Island school, said that "even though you have family, you still feel separated, you still, you don't have a name, you don't have an identity, you just have a number, and mine was 56."[222]

Kiatch Nahanni, who went to several residential schools and residences in the Northwest Territories, including those at Fort Providence and Fort Smith, recalled how strange and frightening she found the school at first. Not only was the language different, but she also lost her name and became simply a number. "Because I was given a number and whenever your number was called you, you, you had to be on the defensive because I think you were in trouble."[223]

At the Sioux Lookout school, students also were called by their numbers. According to Ken A. Littledeer, "They called me number 16, because that's the number that I was given when I walked in through those doors. So, 16, I was called. Whenever I heard that 16, I'm supposed to pay attention."[224] Lorna Morgan recalled that at the Presbyterian school in Kenora, "they just gave me a number, which I'll never forget, you know. This is your number. When we call this number, you know, that's you, you know. And it was number 16, and I'll never forget that number."[225]

Strange food
"We were very lonely without those berries."

In their home communities, many students had been raised on food that their parents had hunted, fished, or harvested. Strange and unfamiliar meals at the schools added to their sense of disorientation. Daisy Diamond found the food at residential school to be unfamiliar and unpalatable. "When I was going to Shingwauk, the food didn't taste very good, because we didn't have our traditional food there, our moose meat, our bannock, and our berries. Those were the things that we had back home, and we were very lonely without those berries."[226]

Florence Horassi had a strong memory of her first meal at the school at Fort Providence, Northwest Territories.

> And when we ate, it was a hung fish. I recognize some fish, 'cause we have, have hung fish for our dog food. When I was small, I see that. It was covered so much in pepper. It was just black. Not cooked good, there's blood on it, and it was rotten. And I wanted to throw up. I threw up. And the nun came to me, she stood at the back, she dig in her pocket, and took a clothespin out, put it on my nose, and told me to eat.

She was not used to the milk that was served at the school: "And the milk, they had cows. I believe it came from the cows, 'cause it was really, at least for me, it was so thick I couldn't drink it. And she pulled my head back, and told me to take the, she put my head up, like over my hand, and she pour it down, just dripping."[227]

Some schools did make allowances for traditional foods. Simon Awashish recalled being allowed to trap for food while attending the Amos, Québec, school.

> One thing that we were allowed to do, to do, put out some snares. These were one of the activities we liked to do. We were a group of young children. We were about aged thirteen or fourteen, and we would go out and set snares. And when we brought in hares, we were asked if ... there was some members of our nation that came to work in the kitchen, and we asked them to cook the hare for us in the traditional Atikameg way, in order to keep some sort of contact with our traditional food that we had before, before we were separated from our community.[228]

Dora Fraser, from the eastern Arctic, found it difficult to adjust to the food served in the hostels. "We were eating canned food, beans, peas, red beans. The food was terrible, but this, this family was eating well, like, country food comes in and they eat, and we were fed sometimes leftovers. Sometimes we didn't eat it all."[229]

Even when traditional foods were prepared, the school cooks made them in ways that were, to the students, strange and unappetizing. Ellen Okimaw, who attended the Fort Albany, Ontario, school, had vivid memories of poorly cooked fish being served at the schools. She said that when a First Nations man had provided the school with fish, the school cook had simply "dumped the whole thing, and boiled them like that, just like that without cleaning them."[230]

Ellen Okimaw.

School meals
"You didn't get enough."

Again and again, former students spoke of how hungry they were at residential schools. Students who spoke of hunger also spoke of their efforts to improve their diet secretly. Woodie Elias recalled being hungry all the time at the Anglican school in Aklavik in the Northwest Territories. "You didn't get enough; hungry. So once in a while we go raid the cellar and you can't call that stealing; that was our food. I got somebody, go in the kitchen and get the bread."[231]

Dorothy Nolie said she was hungry all the time in the Alert Bay school. She thought it a lucky day when she was told to cut bread in the kitchen.

> We'd eat it while we're cutting it, so that was good
> for a while. We were cutting bread for a long time,
> and kids would come to me and ask me for bread,
> and I'd sneak it to them, 'cause I know they were
> hungry, too.[232]

Of the food at the Fort Alexander school, Faron Fontaine said that all he could recall was

Dorothy Nolie.

> kids starving. Kids going in the kitchen to steal
> food. Lucky thing I knew some people that worked
> in there with my grandfather, they used to steal me,
> sneak me some food all the time, send me an apple
> or sandwich or something. It's pretty good to have
> connections in there I guess. As for those other
> kids, I don't know how they survived. Maybe their stomach shrunk enough that what-
> ever they ate was filling them up, I don't know.[233]

Andrew Paul said that every night at the Roman Catholic school in Aklavik,

> we cried to have something good to eat before we sleep. A lot of the times the food we
> had was rancid, full of maggots, stink. Sometimes we would sneak away from school
> to go visit our aunts or uncles just to have a piece of bannock. They stayed in tents not
> far from the school. And when it's raining outside we could smell them frying dough-
> nuts, homemade doughnuts, and those were the days when we ate good.[234]

Nellie Trapper recalled that whenever she would go through the kitchen to the laundry room at the Moose Factory, Ontario, school, we used to steal food, peanut butter, whatever's cooking in a pot. There were big pots in there. I remember taking figs from that pot. I just happened to walk by, you had to walk through the kitchen to the, to go to the laundromat, drop off the laundry there. You'd always take something from the kitchen when we're walking by there.[235]

While girls took food from the kitchens, boys might raid the school gardens. Rick Gilbert worked in the gardens at the Williams Lake, British Columbia, school.

Kids would try and sneak to eat some of the carrots and potatoes and whatever else. If you get caught if we call it stealing, if you get caught stealing any of the vegetables to eat the punishment for that was that they would paint your hands red. And so you had to suffer the humiliation for days and a week until the paint wore off your hands. To let everybody know that you were a thief I guess.[236]

Doris Young said that hunger was a constant presence at the Anglican schools she attended in Saskatchewan and Manitoba. "I was always hungry. And we stole food. I remember stealing bread. And they, the pies that, that I remember stealing were lined up on a counter, and, and they weren't for us to eat, they were for the, for the staff."[237]

At the Sioux Lookout school in the 1960s, the boys would slip into the kitchen at night to take extra food. Ken A. Littledeer's job in the raids was to stand by the doorway and listen to the steps, listen to the stairs, and echo, to hear if somebody was coming.[238]

Don Willie was one of the boys who used to make midnight raids on the kitchen at the Alert Bay school. "I guess, and steal pretty much, like, just chocolate, chocolate milk and stuff like that. They'd have it, they'd just, just have it with hot water in the bathrooms, and when they were caught there, they'd end up being strapped. But also we used to get strapped for being caught out of bed."[239]

Ray Silver recalled that a small grocery store used to dump spoiled fruits and vegetables by a creek near the Alberni, British Columbia, school.

And us kids, we used to sneak from the school, we must have had to walk about a mile, sneak away from the school, sneak over the bridge, and go to that dump, and pick up apples, they were half rotten or something, and they threw out, they were no more good to sell, but us kids that were starving, we'd go there and pick that stuff up, fill up our shirts, and run back across the bridge, and go back to the school.[240]

Mary Beatrice Talley.

Many students spoke of the lack of variety in the school menu. At the Assumption, Alberta, school, Mary Beatrice Talley recalled, there was "porridge every morning. Evening, eggs and potatoes. That's all we have. Milk and coffee, I think the bigger girls, they take coffee. They have milk and tea there too. But food is—every day, same, same, same."[241] Many students recalled being served porridge every morning.

At the boys' school in Spanish, Ontario, William Antoine remembered:

> In the morning they would give you porridge; every morning, every morning. They call it "mush" back then. It was like lumpy, you know, very lumpy. It didn't taste very good ... but you had to eat it in order to, to have some food in you. You know you had to eat it so that's, and you had to get used to it. You had to get used to, you know. We got bread with no butter, just dry bread. Got a little milk, you know.[242]

Gerald McLeod said that at the Carcross school in Yukon Territory, "you would never see eggs, you know, for a couple of months. It was always mush. A lot of people didn't like eating liver. They had liver there that people couldn't eat, and they forced us to eat it."[243]

Louise Large said that at the Blue Quills school, the

> porridge would be burnt, black toast, and some lucky kids would get, no not, not burnt. But the food was horrible. I remember that I had to eat, because I was the youngest, every meal I had to eat everybody's leftover, and then I became real fat and chubby in school, 'cause we weren't allowed to throw away food, and because I was the smallest, I guess I was bullied into eating everybody's garbage.[244]

Shirley Ida Moore, who attended the Norway House, Manitoba, residential school in the 1960s, echoed the sentiments of other former students.

> And, I hated, I hated, I hated breakfast. I didn't mind very much eating over there, but I hated breakfast because, I think what I didn't like was we always had to eat porridge; and this porridge was, like it, I was, I eat porridge at home before but it was good. You know when the porridge they gave us was, like when they put it into your bowl, it was this big lump; big ball, lump.[245]

Chris Frenchman recalled being forced to eat at the Hobbema, Alberta, school. "You either ate it or we, we would go hungry to bed. So we had no choice but to eat it."[246]

Mel H. Buffalo recalled being punished because he refused to eat his breakfast at the Edmonton, Alberta, school.

> I was the last one to be let out of the cafeteria because I wouldn't eat my porridge. And they said, well you'll have this porridge again at lunch, and sure enough, again at lunch, and then again at supper, and the next day they got me a fresh bowl of porridge, but they said the same thing. And I still refused to eat that porridge, and I was taken to the principal's office, and I got five straps on each hand, and sent to my, to a room by myself, with no contact with the other students.[247]

Darlene Thomas said students were forced to

> eat that, whatever it was in our bowl, or our plate, we'd have to eat every bit of it. And if we got sick, we got strapped. And I start, put that food in my mouth and I wouldn't swallow it and keep putting food until I got a big piece and then I wrap it in the tissue

and put it back in my sleeve and when I get caught I find another place, put it in my sock or pull up my, pull up my tunic and tie a knot in my bloomers, 'cause we had those big long bloomers we had to use. So I tie a knot with that tissue and all that ugly food so I wouldn't get sick.[248]

Darlene Thomas.

Connie McNab found it difficult to eat the food served at the Lapointe Hall residence in Fort Simpson, Northwest Territories.

> And we sat down to eat, and the pork chops were just dry and I was so thirsty; my mouth was dry and I couldn't swallow. I couldn't eat them and they kept saying, "You have to eat. They're going to check." And I couldn't, I tried the wax beans, wax green beans; I ate some of those and it went on like that. And they wouldn't let them take food to me.[249]

The conflict over food turned to abuse when students could not keep their food down. Bernard Catcheway recalled that in the 1960s at the Pine Creek, Manitoba, school, "we had to eat all our food even though we didn't like it. There was a lot of times there I seen other students that threw up and they were forced to eat their own, their own vomit."[250]

Connie McNab.

Diane Bossum said that at the La Tuque, Québec, school, "We were obliged to eat everything we had on our plates. At a given time, I had, I got a soup, but in the soup there was an insect. Then I showed the soup to my educator. After that, she asked 'do you want another soup?' 'No.' But she brought another soup. I didn't want to eat, but my soup was there. I had to eat anyway."[251]

Bernard Sutherland recalled students at the Fort Albany, Ontario, school being forced to eat food that they had vomited up. "I saw in person how the children eat their vomit. When they happened to be sick. And they threw up while eating. And that when he threw up his food. The food is not thrown away. The one whose vomit he eats it."[252]

Ethel Johnson had vivid memories of watching her younger sister struggling to eat food that she was not used to eating at the Shubenacadie school.

> She didn't like it. And the nun was behind her saying, "Eat it." They used to call her pussy when she was in school; blue eyes I guess. And she couldn't eat it, and she started crying. And then she tried to make her eat it; and she couldn't. And then she threw up, and then she put her face in there. And she couldn't; when you're crying you can't eat anyway.[253]

Mary Beatrice Talley recalled one conflict between a staff member and a student over food at the Assumption, Alberta, school.

> And then our supervisors, they were sisters, and then she comes to this girl and then she told her that you have to eat the fat and everything. And this girl doesn't like it. So she just shoved it in her mouth like this. Just put everything in her mouth and asked her to swallow it. And we're watching that too, me and my friend, we're having supper. And then this girl was just crying and she told her to swallow it. And I—we're seeing—we're saying that she might choke on it. And we told Sister, we told Sister not to do that. And she told us, you two, you shut up. It's none of your business. I'm the one that's looking after you girls. And then that girl was just crying and she was just throwing up and she went to the washroom. I see that too.[254]

Victoria McIntosh said she was harshly disciplined for refusing to eat porridge with worms in it at the Fort Alexander school.

> I really, really dislike porridge. And there was an incident where I wouldn't eat porridge, and, the first time, and I looked down, and there was a bowl in front of me, and I noticed there was worms in it, and I wouldn't eat it, and the nun come behind me, and she told me, "Eat it," and I wouldn't eat it, just nope, and she, she slammed my face in, in the bowl, and picked me up by my arm, and she, she threw me up against the wall, and she started strapping me. And I don't remember going up the stairs, but I remember her, she had my arm, had me up by one arm. And I don't remember that, that time gap in between, but after that I remember something broke inside of me that I wasn't stubborn, but I had to listen or else. And everybody was really terrified of this nun.[255]

At the Sandy Bay school, Stella Bone recalled, "we were made to eat our food regardless what type or shape or in what condition it was. And if we didn't eat, if we didn't eat it, or if it made us sick, you're guaranteed to eat your sick and your food at the same time. Even if you're gagging, you're just, used to be just, you had to eat it." She thought that nutrition was better in her home community. "At least, at home, I would have rabbit, fish, bannock, potatoes, you know. I thought about those things when I'd be starving in there."[256]

Many of the schools used to provide the students with a vitamin-enriched biscuit that had been developed by Indian Affairs in the 1940s.[257] Alfred Nolie said that at the Alert Bay school, these biscuits were issued daily. "They gave us one biscuit in the afternoon, maybe two or three o'clock in the afternoon. We all line up. They gave us one biscuit for snack in the afternoon."[258] Shirley M. Villeneuve, who attended the Fort Simpson, Northwest Territories, residence, recalled that the students used to refer to them as "doggie biscuits."

> I wouldn't eat it, I would give it to somebody else. And the, the nun, the nun she saw me doing that and she didn't like that.
>
> She didn't like that I gave it away and she says, "Why you gave it away?" I says, "Because I don't, I'm not hungry; I don't want it." And she says, "Well, it's good for you,

it's good for you," she kept telling me. And I said, "No, I don't want it. I don't want it," and so I was, I was scared.[259]

Stella Bone also reported her difficulty in eating the nutritional biscuit when she attended the Sandy Bay school. "They used to be really hard, eh, so you'd have to suck on it really long to make it soft, you know, just to appease your, your hunger, I guess."[260]

Mel H. Buffalo recalled with distaste the vitamin pills and biscuits that students were given.

> They would ask you to swallow one of these every day. If you had bit into it—oh man, it was horrible, the taste was in your mouth for days. So you'd try not to bite it because—we would dare some of the new kids to bite the pills but they'd only do it once and that was it. And we used to—when we ran out of pucks, we'd use those cookies for pucks because they were hard. And we didn't have any of the regular pucks so, we saved up a bunch of those and used those.[261]

Complaints about the limited, poorly prepared, monotonous diet were intensified by the fact that at many schools, the students knew the staff members were being served much better fare. When she helped in the kitchen to prepare staff meals at the Sechelt, British Columbia, school, Daisy Hill could not help noticing "how well they ate compared to the food that was given to us, students."[262]

Daisy Hill.

At the Kamloops school, Julianna Alexander was shocked by the difference between the student and staff dining room.

> On their table they had beautiful food, and our table, we had slop. I call it slop because we were made to eat burnt whatever it was, you know, and compared to what they had in their dining room. You know they had all these silver plates, and beautiful glass stuff, and all these beautiful food and fruits and everything on there, and we didn't even have that. And so I, I became a thief, if you want. You know I figured a way to get that food to those hungry kids in intermediates, even the high school girls, the older ones were being punished as well.[263]

At the school she attended in Saskatchewan, Inez Dieter said, "the staff used to eat like kings, kings and queens." Like many students, she said she used the opportunity of working in the staff dining room to help herself to leftovers. "I'd steal that and I'd eat, and I'd feel real good."[264]

When Frances Tait was given a position in the staff dining room, she said, she thought she had "died and gone to heaven 'cause even eating their leftovers were better than what we got. And anybody who got a job in there, their responsibility was to try and steal food and get it out to the other people."[265]

Hazel Bitternose, who attended schools in Lestock and Qu'Appelle, Saskatchewan, said she enjoyed working in the priests' dining room. "They had some good food there and I used to sneak some food and able to feed myself good there. So that's why I liked to work there."[266]

Gladys Prince recalled how at the Sandy Bay, Manitoba, school, the "priests ate the apples, we ate the peelings. That is what they fed us. We never ate bread. They were stingy them, their own, their own baking."[267]

Doris Judy McKay said that at the Brandon, Manitoba, school, cleaning up the staff dining room was a prized chore. "There'd be about three or four of us working, we'd race for the supervisors' dining area because, why we raced was because they left a, like platter of their meal there. Like say if they had steak, chicken or, pork chops, and we'd race for that eh, 'cause what we got wasn't very much."[268]

Betty Smith-Titus said that her father paid extra to the Baptist-run school in Whitehorse, Yukon Territory, to ensure that she was given the same food as the staff. "I didn't get that. I ate like the rest of the kids. I ate the runny rolled oats in the morning, with a glass of milk. And my father paid for, I don't know how, how many years, and finally I told him I ate like the other kids, they didn't give me what the staff ate, so my dad didn't pay him anymore."[269]

Some students, however, spoke favourably of residential school food. One student, who attended the Gordon's, Saskatchewan, school in the 1950s, said, "You know, I've heard a lot of people say that, you know, their experience in residential school, their meals were terrible. That wasn't so in Gordon's. Gordon's provided really good meals, a lot of times they were hot, good meals."[270]

Some students also reported improvements in the food, over time. Mary Rose Julian thought the food at the Shubenacadie school in the 1950s was not "too bad."

> I did like the porridge that we got every morning, 'cause I was, I was brought up on porridge. So, the porridge was pretty good, because they put sugar in it while they were, they mixed it with sugar, and they never put sugar on the table, they mixed it, mixed the porridge with the sugar, and that was really good. Sometimes it was lumpy, you just bust the lumps in your mouth, you know, no big deal.

But there were limits to her praise. She recalled that fish was served on Wednesday and Friday.

> It wasn't, it wasn't like my, the way my father and mother prepared it. It was horrible. And then they put this sauce over it. It was white sauce, well, it was white, anyway, you know, and it was horrible. So, anyways, you had to eat that, and some kids didn't like it so much, you know, they got sick on it, but I didn't get sick on it. I managed to swallow it and everything. I forced myself to eat it. So, I start getting used to it after a while. So, the, the food and everything was fine.[271]

Chores

"We were like slaves."

Based on the chores that she and other students did at the Blue Quills school, Ilene Nepoose said, "We kind of run the school based on our own labour. We washed, we cleaned, they hired ladies to cook. There was no janitors, we were the janitors."[272] Reflecting on the work he did at the Roman Catholic school in Kamsack, Saskatchewan, Campbell Papequash also noted that the students provided much of the labour needed to keep the school in operation.

> I think there was a lot of slave labour in there because we had all the children, they all had to do, we all had our own jobs to do. You know all the residential school children maintained that whole building by cleaning it up and looking after the building. You know some guys worked in the boiler room and the furnace room, in the laundry room and with the dryers and the vegetables and working in the root cellar looking after the vegetables.[273]

Ula Hotonami recalled that at the school in Round Lake, Saskatchewan, she spent half the day in classes and half the day working.

> We had to learn how to cook, how to do laundry, how to iron, how to do all those things, wash dishes, whatever, and clean out the, the both dormitories, and sweep the steps, and all those thing we had to do, we had to learn and that. And so it was, it was something that I never really expected, like, when I went to school.[274]

Andrew Speck said that at the Alert Bay school, "early in the morning you're up, like 5:30, 6:00 o'clock in the morning 'cause you had to do your chores before you had your breakfast. If you weren't up there, you were, you were literally ripped out of bed and thrown in a cold shower."[275] Ellen Smith attended three different Anglican schools and residences in the Northwest Territories. In her memory, when students were not in class, they spent much of their time performing chores. "From the morning you get up seven o'clock in the morning, you were cleaning, cleaning, cleaning 'til you went to school. They kept us busy around the clock; right 'til we went to bed."[276]

One former student said that at the Shubenacadie school, chores took priority over classroom work. "I'm

Andrew Speck.

only in Grade Seven; I didn't even do Grade Seven! I spent most of the time working in a barn and duty. I got in there a little bit, you know, little bit of education or whatever they were commissioned to give to me, I didn't get."[277]

At the girls' school in Spanish, Ontario, Josephine Eshkibok said, she spent much of her time doing chores.

> We used to work ... one week in the dairy and one week in the chicken coop. And the housework, sewing room, laundry; so we had to do all that work. There was one day there I was doing, a lot of stairs because the school is so high; I did the stairs and I guess I didn't do them right. I must have left some dust or something there in the corner. The teacher came there, said, "You didn't do that right. Go back up there; start over again." So I did.[278]

Darlene Wilson felt that the students at the Alberni school had little time to themselves.

> Our time that we had was only time for us to do our job in the school. Some of us did the stairwells, some of us did the floors, stripping and waxing, laundry work, kitchen work, and some of us did dishes, pots and pans, helping with the cook, setting out the kitchen, the kitchen food. Our tables were set about four times a day for breakfast, lunch and supper, depending on the weekends. Each of us had our own jobs.[279]

Darlene Wilson.

There was a gendered division of labour, with the girls doing much of the cleaning and cooking. Geraldine Bob recalled that at the Kamloops school, the students did much of the cleaning. "We were just little kids, not even ten years old, eleven years old and we had to, if you can imagine the little kids in this school, cleaning the entire school and being forced to do things that are beyond them really. You know like cleaning the bathrooms, cleaning the tubs, shining the floors."[280]

Rose Marie Prosper's first chore at the Shubenacadie school was to sweep down the steps. "I had to sweep the steps down, make sure there was not a grain of sand or nothing in between those little runs. They checked everything we did. It had to be perfect. If not then we were made to do it over again, along with a strapping. I got strapped so many times down there because I had to learn about rules, regulations."[281]

Of the chores that she had to perform at the Sandy Bay school, Isabelle Whitford said, "We used to clean up in the, in the rectory. There was a long hallway. And then, they had hallways on the side for each rooms. We used to get on our hands and knees to wash the floors and wax them. We were like slaves."[282]

Emily Kematch said one of the things she learned at the Gordon's, Saskatchewan, school was "how to clean." As a result, she said,

> I'm good at making a bed. We were taught how to make a bed perfectly. How to fold it, like each corner had to be folded just right and tucked in under the mattress, like the bottom sheet and then we put another sheet on top and our blanket. They were called fire blankets back then and our pillow and they had to be just right, or we'd get punished, if our beds weren't fixed just right.[283]

Shirley Ida Moore recalled that at the Norway House school in Manitoba, the students were supposed to make their beds in such a way that the sheets would be taut enough for an inspector to be able to bounce a nickel. She could never do this.

> So my, my sister again would rescue me; she'd, she'd do her bed 'cause she could do it, 'cause she was bigger and then she'd come over and do mine so that, I didn't have to get punished so much all the time. And that's, that's what every morning was like, every morning waking up scared, afraid you are going to get punished.[284]

At the Fort Providence school in the Northwest Territories, Florence Horassi was assigned to clean toilets.

> This one time, they give me a chore to do the lavatory, that bathroom area, the sink, the toilets. I cleaned the whole thing. And Sister came in the room, and I was standing a little bit aways, like from the middle, and I told her, "I'm finished." So she had to inspect, and she told me, "You missed a spot there." And, like, what spot? I couldn't see no spot. "You missed a spot there. Look again." And I know I'm not supposed to talk back, you speak only when you're spoken to, and when you're not spoken to, you don't speak, and you never talk back. And when I said, "I didn't miss it, I washed it there." "I'll make you clean that," she said, and she went out. When she came back, she came back with a toothbrush.[285]

The boys usually worked outdoors. Thomas Keesick said that at the McIntosh, Ontario, school,

> we cut firewood, four-foot-long logs because the school at that time was being heated by two furnaces and we took turns. Half of the boys would go to morning classes, they call it, and they'd finish then go in the woods and cut wood or go in the barns to pick, clean the stables, pick up eggs. And there was an underground thing where they kept potatoes, carrots, cabbage, we worked there. We had gardens and stuff like that, that's what I remember.[286]

Rick Gilbert recalled that in the winter, the students at the Williams Lake school had to help put in the school's supply of firewood.

> We had to cut big logs and have them chopped up and then packed in. We had to pack them into each building because we had wood furnaces. And I remember having to pack some of that wood and in the wintertime when now you're freezing

'cause even though sometimes we did have gloves and it wasn't thick gloves. And sometimes we lost gloves 'cause kids are kids, you lose your gloves you put them somewhere and couldn't find them again. And then of course you'd get a strapping before they give you another set. And I remember that crying, packing this you know, a six-years-old packing blocks of wood inside.[287]

Roger Cromarty started at the Sioux Lookout school at the age of eight in 1945. He began by working in the barn. "First year and second year I was there, boys were expected to milk cows, and clean the school barn, and feed the farm animals, horses, cows and pig. Those assignments were designated for the bigger boys." The school was heated by a coal-burning furnace. "And that coal came off the railroad track, which was a mile away, and then we started hauling coal, and that part I did too, shovelling all the coal for the school, and shovelling it into the bin." Cromarty also recalled being expected to help clean the school. "On

Saturdays was, was the big day for cleaning. This, this is when we got on, on knee, hands and knees, and with just a scrub brush, we were expected to scrub the assigned chores we were given. And incidentally this, most of the floors were made of cement, so it was very difficult for, on our knees to, to do that." By 1952, his last year at the school, he was in charge of slaughtering animals for the kitchen. "I was a butcher for the whole school, cutting meat every day. That was my, my chore."[288]

Work at the schools could be dangerous. Joanne Morrison Methot said she was injured in the Shubenacadie laundry.

Joanne Morrison Methot.

> One time I was in there, and the thing was spinning, I don't know, to rinse the clothes, and I stuck my hand in there, and my hand twisted. It didn't break, though but it was just sore. But that wasn't her fault, that was my fault. I wanted to see what it was like. It was going so fast. And of course when you're young, you're curious, so I stuck my hand, and a good thing I didn't break my arm. Yeah, but I think there was one girl that did though, but I didn't, I just hurted it, but I didn't break it, thank God.[289]

Lizette Olson said the students had to clean all the windows at the Prince Albert, Saskatchewan, school. "This was a big school and we had to clean it all, the windows, everything. Now, all the windows—one, two, three, four, five—the sanatorium windows, we used to

Lizette Olson.

lift the window like this. Some sat out the window to clean it. If there was an accident, one would have fell to his death."[290]

In some cases, students were paid small amounts of money for the work they did. For her work in the school kitchen at Fort Resolution, Northwest Territories, Violet Beaulieu could remember being paid a dollar by the priest.

> This is my first dollar I ever earned. So, Sister said, "All line up now, we're gonna go." Wherever we went we always line up in two, and walking.

> We went to the store. She stood at the door there. She never told us anything before we went there. So, we all bought sweet stuff.

When the children got back to the school, their supervisor asked to see their purchases.

> When she look at mine, she says, "You bought only sweet stuff?" I said, "Yeah." "You should have bought something more useful." I didn't say nothing. I had nothing to say. I couldn't say nothing, you know.

> She just told me that. She said, "I'll let it go for now, but next month it's not gonna be, you're not gonna do that," she says. "You're not gonna buy candy."[291]

At the Roman Catholic school in Kamsack, Saskatchewan, Campbell Papequash had the opportunity to work with mechanized farm equipment.

> I came from a family, you know, from a family that knew how to raise, how to look after horses and raise horses, and look after cattle and they put me out there. But there is a few good things that I learned in residential school because when I look back at the farming industry you know they had modern equipment there, modern machinery in the residential school, you know, they had these tractors and they had these combines and they had these swathers.[292]

Bernadette Fox was one of a number of students who spoke with pride of the skills she developed at a young age in residential school. While at the Roman Catholic school in Cardston, Alberta, she said, she "learned to be a good housekeeper. I learned how to clean myself personally and I was taught how to do housekeeping, make our beds, clean the floors and keep everything tidy. And so I continued that on in my life with my children, which is a positive thing for me."[293]

Religious training
"I was so terrified of hell."

Religious observation and religious training were central to residential school life. Noel Starblanket recalled that prayer was a dominant aspect at the Qu'Appelle school.

> And then we'd finish, and we'd go to our, back to our playrooms, they called them, and we'd sit there until it was ready for class, then we'd go up for class, and when we sat down in class, they made us pray again. We have to pray. So, then we'd, we'd, we'd have our classes, and then, and then the noon bell rang, and we could hear the church bells. They have a big church there. Those bells would ring, and we'd have to pray again before we left the classroom. I think they called it the Angelus, or something like that. So, we'd pray again, and then we'd go to lunch, and, and before, when we sat down, they'd make us pray again. So, we prayed, and then we went back to our class, got ready for our playroom, went back, got ready for our class, class again in the afternoon. We went to class, they'd make us pray again, and then we'd go through our instructions, and then after school we'd come back, and they had, we had free time 'til about five or so, and then, then the nun would blow the whistle, and we'd have to come running in.[294]

Antonette White resented the amount of time that was given to religious observances at the Kuper Island residential school. "I think the worst thing, is the praying. It's, it's like you pray, pray, pray, and yet there's still no peace in that prayer of what they made you do."[295]

Geraldine Archie said that at the residential school she attended,

> they made us pray from morning until night, and we used to pray when we got up in the morning, and pray before we ate breakfast, and then pray again before we went and started class, and pray again when we went home, went downstairs for lunch, and prayed again to go to afternoon class, and then prayed again before supper, prayed again before bedtime. I was always kneeling down and I developed calluses on my knees. The schools were all the same there.[296]

Antonette White.

Roger Cromarty had similar memories of the daily routine at the Sioux Lookout school.

Daily, we had the morning services in the chapel, grace at every meal, prayers at every class, evening services in the chapel, and the prayers at bedtime. On Sundays this was different. Again, we had morning, morning church services at the chapel, afternoon church services, Sunday school, and evening services.[297]

Louise Large joked that there was so much prayer at the Blue Quills school that she was left with "boarding school knees."

It's always, you know, I'll make a comment, like, I don't need to pray anymore 'cause I prayed so much. I prayed first thing in the morning. When they opened the lights, you just shot out of bed, then we had to go on your knees, and close your eyes, and clamp your hands together, and, and pray, Our Father, Hail Mary. And then when we were done, we had to make our beds.[298]

Ronalee Lavallee was another former student who said that arthritis in her knees was the result of all the praying she had to do in residential school.[299]

According to Geraldine Bob, each day at the Kamloops school started with prayer.

Then we got dressed and we got, brushed our teeth, washed our face, combed our hair and we went to breakfast. And we prayed again and after breakfast we prayed to thank the Lord for what we had received. We went to school and we prayed before school; we had catechism. And before we went for lunch we prayed again; after lunch we prayed again, after school we went to more catechism lessons. And then prayed again before dinner, after dinner and then in the evening.[300]

Students also were introduced to the round of religious holy days. Rita Carpenter recalled how, when she lived at a hostel in Inuvik,

we went, we'd, we'd, we'd practise every Saints Day, every like, St. Thomas, St. Michael, St. Francis of Assisi, St. Christopher, St. Mary, St. Bernadette, St. everything; everything. And we had on all our clothes for this special mass that we're going to have; our little tam, our little dress, our little fur coat, our little brown tights, our bloomers. And we'd all march two by two over to the Igloo Church; pray to a different Saint.[301]

Victoria Boucher-Grant recalled that at the Fort William, Ontario, school, "I learned a lot about the Catholic church. I learned how to pray. I learned how to, this became a way of life, kneeling on my knees, and praying to, to some, some God that made me feel guilty because I was, I was not a very clean person." She also said that when they bathed, the students were told not to look at themselves. "So, we had this big guilt thing about our own bodies."[302]

Fred Brass recalled a copy of Father Lacombe's instructional ladder that hung at the end of the play-room of the Roman Catholic school in Kamsack, Saskatchewan. "There was a picture of stairs and at the

Victoria Boucher-Grant.

bottom of those stairs was Indian people and there was fire. And above the stairs there was Jesus and the angels, and that's what we were told, if we didn't change our ways that's how we were going to end up. That's a picture that will always stay in my mind."[303]

Joseph Martin Larocque found religious education at the Qu'Appelle school frightening.

> They scared us. From the time I was small 'til the time the, the priest, the nuns, the whole thing, they scared everybody with dead people, and, you know, talking about the devil. And, and they had this little chart, catechism, where here's you're going up this road, and the, the roads are winding like this, and the, the devil's with a pitchfork. I was scared for a long time.[304]

Fred Kistabish attended the Amos, Québec, school. There, he encountered Father Lacombe's Ladder.

Joseph Martin Larocque.

> I don't understand the religious teachings of the priests and the nuns. There was a big blackboard that says if you're good boy you'll go to heaven. On the other side of the drawing, there's if you commit mortal sins, this is where you're gonna go, and then you have Lucifer and hell, and it said always, always forever, forever. That's traumatizing for a twelve-year-old, or a fifteen-year-old, or a fourteen-year-old. Anyways, when I left the residential school, I knew that if I died, for sure I was going straight to hell because I was disobedient, because there are things lacking in my childhood.[305]

Martha Minoose encountered the poster at the Roman Catholic school in Cardston.

> At the front they had a poster. It was really long and there was a black ugly road going down and there were people in the fire at the bottom and their hands were raised and they were suffering and they were stuck there and the priest ... oh priest, he taught religion. He said if you want to go down this road, you are going to be in there. You are going to go to hell and then the other road was so beautiful, they had a picture, it was going to heaven. There was angels and the lord and talk and it was so beautiful and you didn't want to go with that other one, I was so terrified of hell.[306]

In religious studies, student discipline might be linked to the lessons that were being taught. Once, in the religious studies class at the Fort Chipewyan, Alberta, school, Vitaline Elsie Jenner was caught speaking to a friend during a lesson. She was called to the front of the class.

> I thought, oh boy, I'm in trouble now. So, I walked up to the front of the class, and he, and he made me turn around to face my peers, and how embarrassing that was. I was kind of, I was a shy, a shy gal, a shy girl, and I turn around, and I knew I was in

trouble, and he said, "I was teaching you. What did I tell you, anyway?" he said. And I said, "Something about forty days, forty nights Jesus fasted, right." He said, "Oh, see, you weren't listening," he said. "So, for your punishment," he said, "this is what you're gonna do. You're gonna," he took headpins out of his, on his desk, there was a little container full of headpins, he took it out of his desk, and he said, "Spread your hand out." So, I spread my hand out like this, both hands, and he started jabbing me in front of the students, jabbing me in the hand, and he said, "You're, you're gonna feel what Jesus felt on the cross. You're, you're gonna feel the same pain." So, he was just jabbing me and jabbing me and jabbing me, and my tears were just streaming down my eyes, and looking at all the, the students that were all looking at me, right. They were shocked, like. And then after that, he stopped, finally he stopped, anyway, and so he stuck me underneath his, underneath, they used to have a great big desk, he stuck me underneath his desk. He said, "This is where you're gonna stay now 'til the lesson is over. You're gonna hear it from where you are now." So, oh, my goodness, so I sat there, and I was just crying, but I cried quietly.[307]

Students were confused by the requirement that they regularly confess their sins. At the Grouard, Alberta, school, Frank Tomkins said, he never

really learned anything except to pray and catechism and confessions. And I used to lie like hell and go to confession. The priest would ask you all kinds of questions that had nothing to do with religion. They just wanna know all about you—what your thoughts and everything else. And I'd lie like hell because they used to say that God knew everything anyway! You know, God knew everything.[308]

Fred Brass said that at the Roman Catholic school in Kamsack, Saskatchewan, he was taught to lie. "I had to lie to keep from being beat and it is not a very nice feeling. When we went to confession, what they called confession, we had to lie, make up lies just to get through our confession."[309]

Frank Tomkins.

Although much of the initial religious training was done by rote, students internalized the lessons they were taught. In his later years at the Sandy Bay school, Arthur Ron McKay decided, in his words, "to try their way." He said he took to reading the Bible and became an altar boy.

That's how I lost all my ... beliefs, traditional things that I knew from my grandfather, the songs that he tried to show me because I knew some songs before I left for school and I forgot all about those songs, traditional songs, Sun Dance songs, even when I was younger, that young I knew and I knew how to do all the little things that the medicines, he used to pick. By this time then I was going back on the last years, I forgot all about those.[310]

Not all teachers attempted to frighten students out of their traditional beliefs. Ula Hotonami recalled telling a sympathetic teacher at the United Church school that she attended in Round Lake that her family did not attend church.

> I said, "We, I like to go to Sun Dances." I said, "It's getting summer time now, I want to go to Sun Dance, 'cause I always go to Sun Dance with my grandma and them, and we always take part in there. We fast, and we don't, she doesn't make us fast all day," I said, "because we're still young and, and that," I told her. "Then, but as we got older, our, our, every summer," I said, "was a little bit more hours we had to fast," I said, "but she made sure that we, she got us up before sunrise. We had to, we could eat before sunrise. And then she'd talk to the Elders after. She'd tell them how long we were gonna fast, and we would fast that long. We wouldn't eat nor drink, but she made us sit in a lodge, and listen to them talking and that."

According to Hotonami, the teacher told her,

> "Keep faith, 'cause you won't be here very long, then you could go back to that again," she'd tell, tell me that. And I told her, "But that's not right." I said, "Like, we have to go to church every Sunday, and I don't like going to church," I told her, and she said, "Well, we can't, we can't stop it," she said. "So just try hard, and just go to church, and just sit there."[311]

Many students were confused by the contradictory combination of religious teaching and harsh discipline. Julianna Alexander, a former Kamloops school student, said,

> You know they were trying to tell me that's this church, or this place we're in, you know, I had to do, I had to be this perfect, perfect person or whatever. And yet at the same time, that's not what I saw. Because I thought to myself, well, if you're a priest and nun, how come you're doing this to this child, or you're doing this to me, and I would say it out loud, and I'd get more lickings.[312]

Julianna Alexander.

For other students, a religious education was one of the key benefits of residential schooling. Mary Stoney was proud of both the religious training she received at residential school and the skills she took away from her education. "I learned a lot of good things at the residential school over the years, my church beliefs and culture has brought happiness and healing to my family."[313]

Elizabeth Papatie said she learned important skills at the Amos, Québec, school. "I learned to look after myself, to dress properly, and to, to brush my hair, and to be nice and tidy, because the woman I had stayed with, she had told me how to look after myself and be nice and tidy, and to my, my manners and to speak well."

She also valued her religious education. "I learned religion at a very early age. I learned about Christianity and I loved it. I love beautiful things, I love beauty."[314]

Separating siblings
"I think at that particular moment, my spirit left."

Inez Dieter said the only time she got to spend with her brother was when she was in class. "I used to turn around and smile at him and if I got caught, of course I'd go to the front again to be punished." Sometimes, she said, they would communicate with each other in sign language.[315]

Daniel Nanooch recalled how he and his sister were separated at the Wabasca, Alberta, school.

Daniel Nanooch.

> So even though I was there with my sister and I only seen her about four times in that year and we're in the same building in the same mission. They had a fence in the playground. Nobody was allowed near the fence. The boys played on this side, the girls played on the other side. Nobody was allowed to go to that fence there and talk to the girls through the fence or whatever, you can't. When I look at these old army movies, I see these jails, these prisoners standing there with rifles and there was a fence. It felt the same way, "Don't approach that fence" when I think back.[316]

Madeleine Dion Stout, who attended the Blue Quills school, thought the school deliberately discouraged the development of family connections.

> There was a sense of separation and the sense of, of not connecting to your own, you know, the people who would mean the most to you, your family members, and your community members, a complete separation. And if it wasn't that we were taught by my mother to always love one another no matter how big the transgressions we committed against each other, that we would always, always love one another, and I think that's, that's what we carry today, not what residential school taught us, but there's still a deep conflict there, you know, that separation, but be together, separate but be together. So, there's this, there's this, these conflicting messages I think that I still carry.[317]

Wilbur Abrahams had a strong memory of being separated from his sisters on their arrival at the Alert Bay school.

My sisters were kind of in front of me. My two sisters, and we got up the stairs, got up. Somebody guided us through the door, and going down the hallway, and I didn't realize it, but they were separating us, girls on this side, and boys on this side, and I was following my sisters. And all of a sudden this, I felt this little pain in my, my left ear, and this, I looked up, and I saw this guy with a collar, and he pulling me back with, by my ear, and telling me I was going the wrong way. You're going this way. Pull, still pulling my ear. I have always believed that, I think at that particular moment, my spirit left.[318]

The only reason Bernice Jacks had wanted to go to residential school in the Northwest Territories was to be with her older sister. But once she was there, she discovered they were to sleep in separate dormitories. "They wouldn't allow us to be with our sisters. The juniors had to be with the juniors. Intermediates have to be with the intermediates." On the occasions when she slipped into the older girls' dormitory and crawled into her sister's bed, her sister scolded her and sent her away. "My sister never talked to me like that before."[319]

Sheila Gunderson was in residential schools in the Northwest Territories from 1958 to 1971, living in both the Fort Providence school and Lapointe Hall (Fort Simpson). She was enrolled when her mother was institutionalized; she never met her mother again until she was sixteen years old.

And, I didn't know I had an older sister until I was I think probably thirteen years old and somebody came and introduced us and said that we were sisters. And anyway, then my older brother was also raised by my grandmother and so I got to know him and over the years he had left Simpson and I never really got to know him until the last few years and it's like, we're strangers 'cause we, we were, I was raised in residential school and he was raised by my grandmother.

But anyway, living in residential school, I don't know, it just seemed, you were alone. There was always so many people there and you were always [audible crying] you were always alone and you didn't know who to talk to because you weren't allowed to become friends or, or mingle with your brothers or sisters.[320]

Helen Kakekayash's older sister tried to comfort her when she first arrived at the McIntosh, Ontario, school. She recalled that "she would try to talk to me, and she would get spanked."[321]

When Peter Ross was enrolled at the Immaculate Conception school in Aklavik, Northwest Territories, it was the first time he had ever been parted from his sisters.

In all that time I was there I never had a chance to talk to my sisters. You know, we're segregated even in church. The girls had one side, the boys one side. You went to school, same thing. You never had a chance to, only at Christmas and Easter feasts I think is the only time that, we sat in the same dining room to eat together. And that's the only time, you know, my sisters and I had a chance to talk together.[322]

Older brothers and sisters were both a source of comfort and protection. It was not always an easy role to play. Margaret Simpson had to look out for her younger sister at the Fort Chipewyan, Alberta, school.

> I needed to protect my sister and boy, that was hard. Especially when she's going to get a strapping or something, maybe she wet the bed or something and is going to get a, be put in the water there, in the tub and I couldn't just go in there, and I tried once and I got a good licking for that. I was happy that she didn't just pee every night in bed. Some of the girls did every night and every morning they got up and they had to be in that tub. Never mind how cold it was, getting washed in there, there was no privacy, no nothing like that.[323]

At Lapointe Hall in Fort Simpson, Connie McNab found herself separated from her older sister. "I remember telling her like, 'Don't leave me.' She would come and sit with me and at night one of her dorm mates would come and get me and bring me there so I could just see her at night; after everything was dark, 'cause I had nobody and I was seven, six."[324]

Bernard Catcheway said that even though he and his sister were both attending the Pine Creek, Manitoba, school, they could not communicate with each other. "I couldn't talk to her, I couldn't wave at her. If you did you'd get, you know a push in the head by a nun; you know because you were not loved."[325]

Bernard Catcheway.

The rules regarding the separation of siblings could be violently enforced. Dorene Bernard said that one day at the Shubenacadie school, she saw her brother

> walking down a hallway to go to church. We met right at the same, we met right across from each other turning the corner to go down to the chapel. And when I waved to him, 'cause we weren't allowed to speak, so I kind of waved to him, and he kind of waved back, and one of the boys, the men, that were watching the boys, they weren't a priest, they weren't a brother, they were just civilians, men. [A staff member] grabbed Robert out of the line and threw him against the radiator right outside the priest's office, and he smashed his head on a radiator and he was rolling around on the floor holding his head, and then Morris was kicking him, telling him to "Get up! Get up!" And I turned around and seen that and I ran out, ran back to help him. And I ran back and I jumped on his back and I started pulling his hair, telling him to "Leave him alone, he didn't do anything." And I was ten years old at that time and I bit him, I scratched him. I knew I was going to get it and I knew Robert was going to get it; he was going to get beaten bad.

> So we were fighting, and of course, yeah, I did, I got, you know, I got locked in the dormitory and I wasn't allowed out. And I was, I don't remember if they brought me

food or not, but it didn't really matter, my punishment was that I would never be able to speak to him, my brother.[326]

On her second day at the Kamloops school, Julianna Alexander went to speak to her brother.

> Did I ever get a good pounding and licking, get over there, you can't go over there, you can't talk to him, you know. I said, "Yeah, but he's my brother." You know it's not any, anybody different, you know, you can't talk to him, you can't go over there, can't sit with him, you know, so this was the beginning of our, our daily routine, I guess, you know, can't talk, can't see them, can't anything. I knew he was there, I just, you know, and he knew I was there, too.[327]

In strange surroundings, contact with siblings was especially important. Of her time at the Alberni school, Elizabeth Good recalled that "the only thing that was familiar to, to me were my siblings, and my home was a world away. And so whenever I did get to see them, it was, that was all that existed within the world was my siblings, I could see them, and I ached for them."[328]

In some cases, family members were not told if their siblings were sick, even when they were all enrolled in the same school. Joanne Morrison Methot recalled:

> I remember one time my brother, he had an abscess or something here, and it busted. They took him to the hospital. They didn't even tell us that my brother almost died. They didn't tell us nothing. Then we find out after, we just found out he was gone. I think it was to a hospital they brought him, and they didn't tell us my brother almost died. They didn't tell us anything, you know, like, if something happened.[329]

Beverley Anne Machelle said the separation from her siblings increased her sense of loneliness at the Lytton, British Columbia, school.

> I wasn't even allowed to talk to my brothers, and I had three brothers there. Two of those brothers committed suicide. Yeah, it really hurt not to be able to, and I couldn't even talk to my sister, and she was on the same side as me, but she was a, she was a junior girl. And maybe if she was, you know, in intermediate, I would have had more access to her. But it was, it was really lonely not having my mom, and not having my brothers or my sister.[330]

Gender relations
"You're boy crazy."

The policy of separating brothers and sisters was part of a larger policy of separating boys from girls. Lena McKay stayed at Breynat Hall, one of the two Roman Catholic-run residences in Fort Smith, Northwest Territories. She recalled the expectations for girls and boys there:

> And we're not allowed to talk to the boys. We, you know, we go for meals and that, 'cause they used to meet us in the stairway, like, you know, we'd turn our heads, she'd tell us we're pants crazy. Can't even leave our shirt, like this open, you know, button shirts. Boy, she, one time she came to me, she just about choked me, 'cause, you know, my shirt was, one button was open. Here she was just fiddling around, trying to, you know, she just about choked me buttoning my shirt, because she said, "You want to show yourself to, to the men?" you know. "You're boy crazy. You're pants crazy," things like that.[331]

Andy Norwegian said he found the separation of the sexes to be unnatural at Lapointe Hall, the Roman Catholic hostel in Fort Simpson.

> When I was still living at home we had the freedom to move around the community and interact with our female cousins. In just the first two months that I arrived here there were three boys that went to talk to some girls on the girls' side and what happened as a result of that was that evening we were called into the gymnasium like this, and the three boys were sent to the mechanical room and they were stripped down to their undershorts. They were forced to come out, one at a time, and lay down, face down on a table in the middle of the gymnasium. The boys that came out laid down on a table like this, face down, and the supervisor pulled down their undershorts and strapped them with a leather strap, about three inches wide and a half-inch thick. It had a wooden handle and he put both hands on it and strapped them across the buttocks and you could hear the impact throughout the whole gymnasium and also the boys that were on the table, every time they were hit, they would cringe and put their arms around the table very hard, and you could hear that too.[332]

Students often circumvented these restrictions. At the Blue Quills school, Ilene Nepoose said, boys and girls would meet in the boiler room. "I would be her lookout. I had to look out for anybody in authority. I don't know what the heck she did in there but she was in there with boys. She would say they would be necking. She made it sound like such a romantic moment."[333]

When she was fourteen years old, Isabelle Whitford, a student at a Manitoba school, became pregnant. "I just wanted to get out of school. And sure enough, they kicked me out of school."[334] John Edwards met his future wife when they were both living in Grollier Hall in Inuvik, Northwest Territories.

John Edwards.

> I told all the buddies there, you know, "Don't touch her, she's my girlfriend; going to be my girlfriend," and then I told her that. Got into a lot of trouble over her and, went into the girls' end and went upstairs to see her and told her that, you know, "I'm not going to do anything, nothing bad, just come to hold you and tell you that, you know I love you, I want you to be my girlfriend."
>
> And I was going to jump out the second storey window in the middle of the winter so I don't get caught. But the supervisor making her rounds and caught me and I just walked down the girls' end. Walked right down to the boys' end and I got, I had to wait in the hall. And they had their discussion and they came out and I had to go see the boys' supervisors.
>
> And, they told me, told me, what I did was very serious and shouldn't be done and it's not tolerable. So I'll probably get a suspension or grounded for sure. So they told me, "You want anything done? 'Cause we're going to have to call your parents." And I said, "Sure, call them," and they told them basically that I had been caught in the girls' end, in a girl's room and, "You have anything to say?" Said, "No; just got to deal with it" and, so I'm trying to phone and I just told them, "Mom, I met this girl and I think she's the one; I'm going to love her."[335]

Such romances were not uncommon. Donald Copenace's parents met at the Presbyterian school in northwestern Ontario.[336]

In addition to students' efforts to seek each other out, the schools themselves also arranged marriages. Violet Beaulieu was enrolled in the Fort Resolution school when she was four years old in 1936. An orphan, she was still in the school at age twenty-one in 1953. By then, she had rejected a number of men the school officials had tried to get her to marry.

> They had to get rid of me, I guess. Where are they gonna send me? They, 'cause they had to set up a marriage for me, somebody I didn't know. So, she sent me to bring a book to a priest. I brought a book to a priest, and he said, "Sit down, I want to talk to you." So, I sat down, and he says, "You're getting old." So, I thought I was old. And he says that you should be getting married, and so many guys came to see you, and you refused. So next time somebody comes, you go out there, and you're gonna marry that guy.

She said that on January 6, 1953, she was told there was someone at the school to see her.

> And then the parlour bell rang, and Sister said, "Somebody came to see you." So, I went to the door there, and he says, "I came to see Father to ask to marry you." It's, like, yeah, I said, "Okay," and I walk away. Then that was January 6, and I guess I didn't know the wedding was set for January 12th, six days later.

She was upset by the prospect of having the wedding announced in advance.

> I was gonna get married that Monday morning. And the custom then was Sunday church, they used to announce wedding, like, Monday morning. In those days, the church used to be just full of people. Every Sunday people would just, all the time. And that Sunday morning I got up, I was so sick. I was just throwing up. I was just sick just thinking that they're gonna announce my wedding, like, I'm gonna get married. I was so sick I couldn't go to church. They, you know, usually if you're sick they don't let you, I was sick. When the church was over, the girls came back, oh, they're just teasing, "Oh, Violet, you're getting married." And oh, I, I didn't like that, but I just, I had to do it.

She could recall little of the marriage ceremony itself.

> Next morning, 6:00 o'clock in the morning, my sister-in-law come, a wedding gown, veil, everything, and she was, oh, the whole set of clothes, helped me dress up now. And she must have knew by my expression that, I didn't say nothing to her, but she must have known I didn't want to. She kept saying, "Don't say no, don't say no," she kept saying to me. I didn't say nothing.

> And you know 'til to this day, I don't remember going in church. I blocked everything. I don't remember going in there. I know the church was full. I don't remember nothing. Only one time I came to when the priest asked me, "Will you take Jonas for your husband?" I woke up, and just like I woke up, not a sound, and they're waiting for my answer, and then, like, in the back of my head I could hear my sister-in-law saying, "Don't say no, don't say no." I said, "Yes." And from there, I don't know, just the day went. Like, that's how I got married, without, I didn't want to, and I still got married.[337]

For most of the period during which residential schools operated, no school system in Canada offered much in the way of sex education. It usually fell to parents to ensure that children received some information about puberty and sex, though there was no guarantee that would happen. Among First Nations people, puberty-recognition or passage ceremonies were generally held, during which women spoke to young girls and older men counselled young boys. Residential school students could not, however, turn to their parents or families for such knowledge, and tribal ceremonies were banned. Muriel Morrisseau said that she and the other girls at the Fort Alexander school did not know about the physical changes they would undergo at puberty.

I didn't know what was going on because they never told us. All they did was mark the calendar and give you a piece of rag that was already stained, dirty looking, ugh. We had to use that but I didn't even know what was happening with me. Even a brassiere, they gave us something to make us more flat, skin-tight homemade bras and you grow up very sad and I'm still, still lost. I figured out everything on my own, it's very hard, nobody to ask. I didn't want to ask the other girls when you start having puberty, I didn't even know the words. After I grew up I became pregnant because I didn't know the facts of life.[338]

Vitaline Elsie Jenner said students were left with a feeling of shame.

And you know they never explain anything, like you're developing into a woman, and all that good stuff, you know, which is not nothing shameful about it, it's, it's natural, you know. But to me I, I came out of it, out of there, just being shamed about everything. Everything was a shame, shame-based. And finally I got used to, you know, the every month and that, so I took care of myself that way.[339]

Her first menstrual period caught Alphonsine McNeely by complete surprise. At the time, she was attending the Roman Catholic school in Aklavik.

I told one of the older girls, "Sister is gonna really spank me now." I said, "I don't know, I must have cut myself down there because I'm bleeding now." My pyjamas is full of blood, and my, and my sheets, and I was so scared. I thought this time they're gonna kill me. And then she laugh at me, and she told me, "Go tell Sister. She's not gonna tell you nothing." I was scared. Told her, "Come with me." She came with me. And then I told her what happened. I showed her my pyjamas. She started laughing, and I start crying more, because why, why are they laughing? And I was already fourteen years old. And, and she said, that nun told me, "Even I go like that," she said. I used to think they never go

Alphonsine McNeely.

pee, they never go poop, or nothing, eh, so I was thinking how come they go like that then?[340]

One student, who attended school in northern Ontario, in the 1960s, was fifteen when she got married. "I didn't know anything. I was sixteen when I had my first child. No one ever told me what to expect. I didn't feel connected to my parents or anybody. I wasn't told anything, I wasn't told anything about how to raise, raise my children."[341]

Contact with parents
"I would hug her and I would kiss her."

Students keenly anticipated visits from their parents. Gerald McLeod recalled that when his parents visited him at the Carcross, Yukon Territory, school, they brought him candy and treats. When they left, the staff made him share it with other children. "They'd put it away, and they said, 'No, you can't have it. You got to share it,' and stuff like that. And it was just, you know, they had so much control over us."[342]

Because Nellie Ningewance's parents lived close to the school, they were able to visit her regularly. 'They'd come in by cab; stay over for the weekend Friday night and Saturday night and away they go again. They give me fruit, they buy me candy, bring me new clothes I couldn't even wear." They would also bring baked bannock. "We'd smuggle that under our pillows and have bannock, after the lights go out."[343]

Even though her parents lived only a five-minute walk from the Fort Alexander school, Mary Courchene saw them for only one hour a week.

> The parents were allowed to come into, to visit their children using the back door where the, where the boys' playroom was and the basement and that's where they would, they would wait. And then our names would be called in the, in our playroom across the way, in across the long corridor. And my, when my name would be called I'd be so happy. We'd line up and then we'd, we'd go walk, we had to walk, couldn't run. Walk to the, to the playroom and there was my mom and dad. They always sat on that side of that, on the left. And I would go rushing to, to my, to my mom. I would jump on her knee and I would hug her and I would kiss her.[344]

At some schools, the visits were closely monitored. Ben Sylliboy recalled that a nun was always present when his parents came to visit him and his siblings at the Shubenacadie school. "The nun told us to speak English so 'I can understand you.' So we couldn't tell them what was really going on in our world in that residential school."[345]

Loretta Mainville went to school at Fort Frances, Ontario, which was located near the reserve on which her parents lived. From the school, she could see her parents' house. On occasion, she caught sight of her parents.

> And I remember one time we were, we were always in lineups all the time, and, and one time we were going by a hall, and I saw him. He had work boots

Loretta Mainville.

and his work clothes, and he was talking to a nun, and apparently later on I found out that the nuns refused him a visit, but he tried to visit us all the time, but they wouldn't allow him.[346]

Madeleine Dion Stout had a vivid memory of her parents visiting her at the Blue Quills school.

> I remember looking out the window, look, thinking they were going to appear anytime, and so they did drive up, and I remember my father tying the horses to the posts at the school, and my mother getting out of the wagon. And I really, I looked harder at my mother for some reason. I saw her getting out of the wagon. She had, I can't remember what she had on, but I remember her red tam, and I remember how she wore it. Today, I'd probably describe it as very coquettishly, you know, sort of slanted. And, and [audible crying] I started crying then because I was missing them already. I knew they couldn't stay.[347]

Students were often encouraged to write home, but incoming and outgoing letters were read. One of Tina Duguay's letters to her parents was blocked because she had mentioned another student in the letter, and a second letter was blocked because she described school activities. "So, I used to wonder, 'what in the heck am I supposed to talk about?' You know I want to write letters to Mom and Dad, 'what am I supposed to say?' So, letter writing started to dwindle, and they didn't hear from me that often."[348]

Leon Wyallon felt terribly isolated from his parents when he lived in residence in Fort Smith. He also thought he could not describe what he felt in letters home. "Every time you write a letter they read it, and then they, I don't know what they do with it."[349]

Doris Young said that when she attended Anglican schools in Manitoba and Saskatchewan, she never received letters and parcels that her parents had sent her.

> My mother would, would write us letters, and my dad, and we never received them, or they'd send parcels, and they were opened, and we, we just don't know what happened to them, but I know that my mother when I, when I would, we'd come home, and said she would write to us. Her English was limited, but she still wrote, and my dad send, would send us money, but we never received it either.[350]

Because the staff read all outgoing letters, Josephine Eshkibok attempted to have a school employee smuggle a letter out for her.

> And one day I wrote a letter to my mother and it was that lady, an Indian lady that worked in laundry. I went to the laundry and I gave her that letter. I said, "Can you post this for me?" you know. I didn't want to tell anybody, just her. So she took that letter; I was so happy she's gonna post it. 'Cause I was writing to my mom, told her to come and get me; they're too mean over here, at the school; strap all the time.

The next day, she was called into the office. "There and on the table there was my letter. Then she opened it up you know, 'Is this your letter?' and I, I had my head down. And she read it, eh." The principal tore up the letter. According to Eshkibok, "I got a strap, as usual. I got the strap for sending that letter out."[351]

Given these restrictions, parents and children lost contact with each other. The problem was exacerbated if parents were not informed that their children were going to be transferred from one school to another. This happened to Doris Judy McKay in Manitoba in the 1950s. "I found out that I was transferred to Birtle without them letting my parents know or anything they just transferred us. Then my mother didn't find out 'til later on that we were in Birtle, when we wrote her a letter from there. She was pretty upset about it."[352]

Holidays provided some families with an opportunity to reconnect. However, Geraldine Shingoose's home in northern Saskatchewan was too distant from the Lestock school for her to return at Christmas and Easter. She stayed in the school for ten months out of the year.

> We didn't go home for Christmas, spring break, like all the other kids did, 'cause we lived so far. We lived up north in Saskatchewan. And, and then when I'd see my parents, it was such a, a beautiful feeling, just going back home to them for those two months. And, and then when September would come, I would, I would dread it.[353]

At the end of every summer, Ula Hotonami would try to talk her mother out of sending her back to school.

> And every summer when they'd go home for holidays for a couple of months, then I didn't really want to go back, you know, I'd want to stay out, but then, then my mother asked me why, and I told her, "'Cause I don't like getting lickings all the time," I told her. And I was getting lickings for no reason. Well, well I still, I used to get lickings for nothing. I don't know.[354]

Some children stayed at the schools year-round. Frances Tait recalled that every June, the school supervisor at the Alberni school would come with the list of students who were going home for the summer.

> And I remember hoping, crossing my fingers, crossing my toes that my name would be on that list, but it never was. And finally, one, one summer, I guess when I was about ten years old, I guess, in a way, I bet that I was thinking that maybe if I had a suitcase I would go home. So I went into the cloakroom, and I stole a suitcase and didn't put my name in it but put my brother's name in it and waited. And still, my name was not on that list. But because I stole the suitcase and because I had gone into the cloakroom without permission, I got punished. And it was to scrub the stairs from top to bottom with a toothbrush.[355]

Frances Tait.

Don Willie recalled how hard it was on students at the Alert Bay school as they waited at the end of the school year to see if their parents would come to take them home. "Kids would take turns sitting by the window, waiting for somebody to pick them up, pressing their faces against the window, and they were all happy if somebody came to pick them up, but pretty sad when nobody came."[356]

For students whose families had fallen apart, life at the school was particularly lonely. One former student recalled that at the Chapleau, Ontario, school, he never got letters from home.

> Other kids on holidays, going home, everybody's supposed to be good. I knew I wasn't going home; and my mom was drunk . 'Cause one brother said, "Your, your mother's drunk right now drinking." They phoned the store that's in Mobert, "She's incapable of accepting," taking his call or something. There was no phone to the house, but I mean there was phone that goes down to the store. And, he said, I guess the brother said, "No, your mother's not in the condition right now." I knew right away what was happening, I'm not going home man.[357]

Wilbur Abrahams and his sisters were not sent home from the Alert Bay school for the summer holiday.

> I remember the first year that, summertime, just before the summer holidays they had, they had a list of names, and the students that were going home for the summer. My name never came up. Must have been hard on my sisters, too, because they, they had the same list up on that side. I don't know, maybe there was about a handful of us that never went home. And it, it was a little, a little more freedom.[358]

Wilbur Abrahams.

Victoria Boucher-Grant attended the Fort William, Ontario, school. She was one of the children who did not get to go home in the summer.

> But in those times that I, when my uncle wasn't there, there was three of us that our, our families never came to get us in the, in the summer. One, the other was a boy, and two girls. And everybody used to think we were orphans, but we weren't orphans. It's just that our big family never came to get us.[359]

Ben Sylliboy, a student at the Shubenacadie school, was not able to go home for the summer holidays. "Some people were lucky, they went home in June; June 30th was known as Freedom Day for all the boys that were fortunate enough to go home a couple of months of the summer. But there was quite a few of us that didn't go home. We stayed at the residential school all summer. It was hard."[360]

Julianna Alexander recalled that at the Kamloops school, the "girls that were allowed to go home, or the boys that were allowed to go home were only allowed because their parents could afford to take them home, and the majority got left there for the holidays. And that was kind of like hell, because the load of having to do all the dirty work there."[361]

William Francis Paul said he enjoyed staying at the Shubenacadie school in the summer. "There was no school. We were outside all day. It seemed like that was the only time we had a lot of fresh air. We got to be outside most of the day, and we got to mingle with other kids, instead of your teacher, where I was outside."[362]

Darryl Siah said that some of the summer activities that were organized at the Mission, British Columbia, school were the best part of his residential school years. "But the best part was, we weren't, we couldn't go to our homes for the summer, we got to stay here for a while and go on camping trips, and we were canoe pulling and stuff, hiking up the cross up here in the mountain was good."[363]

Darryl Siah.

Mary Teya said the summers with her parents were the best memories of her life.

> For two months our parents would take us right out, back out to our fish camp and that would be one of the best memories in my life. Where we would be able to speak our language and live our way of life. For two months we stayed out there. We never came into town. And that's how come I think today I still have my language and I still have my way of, my way, my culture and my tradition and all the wonderful values of being a Gwich'in person, I still hold that. And I thank God for that.[364]

For some students, visits home had their own unique stresses. When Kiatch Nahanni and her sisters returned home from residential school in the Northwest Territories, they found that they were estranged from their father.

> He would talk to us in Slavey, and we would answer him back in English; because we understand what he said. And so when I was in Grade Three I, I came home and he, he talked to me in Slavey and I opened my mouth, nothing came out. I was, and I answered back in English and so that summer my cousin talked to me and slowly I got the language back. But it was like that every summer for the longest time.[365]

Residential schooling left Rosie Kagak completely unprepared for a return to her home community, and forgetful of traditional ways and foods.

> Finally, we're on our way home and I'm looking at everybody in the plane wondering where we're going. We land in Kugluktuk, originally Coppermine, and my parents travelled to Coppermine from their outpost camp to pick us up. One of my older

brothers came with a dog team to where the plane had landed on the ice. He took me and my brothers to the tent and this lady looks at me and tells me to sit beside her. I'm looking at her, and beside her was a man. She said something to me I could not understand. So I looked at my older sister, and I asked her, "What is she saying?" And she picked up a piece of frozen char and had her hand out with the char for me to have. I looked at her, I looked at her, I looked at my older sister, and I asked her, "Why does she want me to eat raw fish?"[366]

After years of separation, many family connections were broken. When Dorothy Hart returned to her home in northern Manitoba after six years in residential school, she discovered that her mother had remarried.

We were so happy to knock on their door; but this man appeared. And I called my mom, and she saw us, but she couldn't do anything. That guy said, "They're not staying here." He shut the door. So I took my sisters to my granny's, that's in Hart's Point. And we just got home after all these years. [audible crying][367]

Going away to residential school in the Northwest Territories brought Frederick Ernest Koe's home life to an end.

I said that year had a monumental effect on my life and my relationship with my family because I came, spent a year here, went back, everything that I thought I owned was gone and a month or so later my family moved over here because my dad moved with the armed forces, and you know, we lived here. And from that day on, the day we moved here, I never, ever went hunting with my dad again.[368]

Mollie Roy said that her years at the Spanish, Ontario, girls' school left her struggling with a sense of abandonment.

I think the thing about the school more than anything else is the feeling of abandonment. Why was, why was I there, and why didn't you come to see me? Because all of us, with the exception of few, were just, parents were, like, ten miles down the road, ten miles, and the people wouldn't even come. You know it's not that my parents didn't have a car. My dad worked at Denison, and made good money, and, like, there was no, you know, you'd wait and wait, and nobody showed up, and I think that's the thing more than anything else that bothered me. It's not the school, it's the fact that I wasn't wanted.[369]

Florence Horassi said that at the residential school she attended in the Northwest Territories, she was made to feel ashamed of being Aboriginal.

When I was in residential school, then they told me I'm a dirty Indian, I'm a lousy Indian, I'm a starving Indian, and my mom and dad were drunkards, that I'm to pray for them, so when they died, they can go to heaven. They don't even know my mom had died while I was in there, or do they know that she died when I was in there? I never saw my mom drink. I never saw my mom drunk. But they tell me that, to pray for them, so they don't go to hell.[370]

Agnes Moses said that her time in residential schools in northern Canada left her wanting "to be white so bad."

> The worst thing I ever did was I was ashamed of my mother, that honourable woman, because she couldn't speak English, she never went to school, and we used to go home to her on Saturdays, and they told us that we couldn't talk Gwich'in to her and, and she couldn't, like couldn't communicate. And my sister was the one that had the nerve to tell her. "We can't talk Loucheux [Gwich'in] to you, they told us not to."[371]

Cecilia Whitefield-Big George said that at the Catholic school in Kenora, she was "taught that my parents were drunks. Not being taught but being told, my parents were drunks. And to this day I wondered, how did they know a drunk if they were so holy?"[372]

By belittling Aboriginal culture, the schools drove a wedge between children and their parents. Mary Courchene recalled that in the 1940s at the Fort Alexander school in Manitoba, she was taught that

> my people were no good. This is what we were told every day: "You savage. Your ancestors are no good. What did they do when they, your, your, your people, your ancestors you know what they used to do? They used to go and they, they would worship trees and they would, they would worship the animals."

She became so ashamed of being Aboriginal that when she went home one summer, she

> looked at my dad, I looked at my mom, I looked at my dad again. You know what? I hated them. I just absolutely hated my own parents. Not because I thought they abandon me; I hated their brown faces. I hated them because they were Indians; they were Indian. And here I was, you know coming from. So I, I looked at my dad and I challenged him and he, and I said, "From now on we speak only English in this house," I said to my dad. And you know when we, when, in a traditional home where I was raised, the first thing that we all were always taught was to respect your elders and never to, you know, to challenge them. And here I was eleven years old, and I challenged.

Her father's eyes filled with tears. Then he looked at her mother and said, in Ojibway, "I guess we'll never speak to this little girl again. Don't know her."[373]

Feelings of shame complicated many parental visits. At the Amos, Québec, school, Carmen Petiquay felt ashamed of her parents also.

> And I was ashamed of my parents because I was told Indians smell bad and they don't talk, and I said to myself, "As long as they don't come," 'cause I was ashamed I hoped they wouldn't come because I, I hoped that they would come sometime. At, at one point my parents came and I was happy. I was pleased to see them, and I hoped that they would leave soon. Because it hurt so much to be taken away from one's parents like that, and it hurts to say things about one's parents and to be ashamed of them. I had believed because I was told that Indians smell bad and that they don't

wash. And my mother brought me an orange, and I kept the orange for the long time, I never even ate it, I kept it because it came from my mother. This is something that I now regret having thought that of my parents, that they smelled bad.[374]

After six years at the Mohawk Institute in Brantford, Ontario, Jennie Blackbird came to see the English language as being superior to her family's language.

> When I returned home, I heard my grandparents and my family around me, only speaking our language. I was a very angry person when I heard them speak the Anishinaabe, our language. I remember telling my grandparents, don't you dare talk to me in that language, and feeling superior to them, as they did not know how to make the English sounds. This, I now regret having said that to my loved ones.[375]

Jennie Blackbird.

When Vitaline Elsie Jenner went home for the summer holidays from the Fort Chipewyan school in Alberta, she was ashamed of her ancestry. "In the summers, when I went home from the residential school, I did not want to know my parents anymore. I was so programmed that at one time I looked down at my mom and dad, my family life, my culture, I looked down on it, ashamed, and that's how I felt." [audible crying]

She tried to deny who she was.

> I didn't want to be an Aboriginal person. No way did I want to be an Aboriginal person. I did everything. Dyed my hair and whatever else, you know, just so I wouldn't look like an Aboriginal person, denied my heritage, my culture, I denied it. I drank. I worked as well. I worked and partied hard. When I had that opportunity on my days off, I would party.[376]

When he returned home after spending three years at the Anglican school in Aklavik, Albert Elias no longer fit in with his family.

> I was a different person, you know. I had, I kind of knew everything after being in residential school. I couldn't, I couldn't, you know, get along and cope with life in Tuktoyaktuk 'cause I was rebelling against my parents and didn't listen to them and I was changed. I, and I had lost my language, but, you know, I'm very lucky, in those days everybody in Tuktoyaktuk still spoke Inuvialuktun, so it didn't take me long to learn my language back, so, and I know lots of people that are, don't have that experience.[377]

When Betsy Olson went home after three years at the Prince Albert school, she had difficulty adjusting to reserve life.

And, the food we had the first day was a rabbit, a rabbit, and I couldn't eat it. I told my sister, "I can't eat this. This is Peter Rabbit. I can't eat Peter Rabbit," I told her, 'cause Peter Rabbit was our favourite story in our books there, and I couldn't eat Peter Rabbit. All the wildlife we had for about a month, Mom had to buy white man's food to feed me 'cause I couldn't eat our, our way of eating back home. I couldn't eat soup. I couldn't eat fish. I couldn't eat bannock. Couldn't eat nothing. I had to, so Mom had to get extra money to try and buy extra food just for me.[378]

Ellen Smith, who was born in Fort McPherson, Northwest Territories, found that residential schooling made it impossible for her to fit back into her home community. "I can't sew; I can't cut up caribou meat; I can't cut up moose meat; work with fish and speak my language. So I was starting to become alienated from my parents and my grandparents; everything."[379]

Raphael Victor Paul spent ten years at the Beauval, Saskatchewan, school.

Raphael Victor Paul.

I thought for a long time that I was better than my parents. That's the thought that they gave you, because my parents didn't talk English, but I did. My parents were very Catholic, and I was very Catholic, but I knew both languages, the catechism and all that. So, you get, I got the feeling that maybe I know more than my parents.

His father believed that the residential school education had prevented his son and his friends from learning the skills they need to survive.

He said, "You know you guys that went to residential school are useless, because you don't know how to survive like they did." 'Cause they never taught us that, you know, how to. At that time, there was no welfare, there was, there was no running waters or lights, so we had to do all those things by ourselves, but we didn't know how. So, the people that went back had to relearn how to survive. And at that time, survival was fishing, hunting, and trapping. To this day, I don't know how to hunt. I can trap, I can fish, but I don't know how to hunt, 'cause I, I was never taught that.[380]

Some people never adjusted. Although she had not enjoyed her time at the Alberni, British Columbia, school, Frances Tait discovered she could not find a place for herself in her home community when she returned. "I couldn't survive in the village. I was different. I was an outcast. And my brothers weren't there." As a result, she asked to be sent back to Alberni, where she boarded with a Euro-Canadian family.[381]

Fear, loneliness, and emotional neglect
"Homesickness was your constant companion."

A majority of the former students who spoke to the Commission emphasized a general atmosphere of fear that permeated their school lives. Despite being surrounded by dozens of children, they were lonely and deprived of affection and approval.

Raymond Cutknife recalled that when he attended the Hobbema school, he "lived with fear." As he grew older, this turned into anger and bitterness.

> The abuse that I went through and then I grew with anger, as I grow a little older, and that stayed with me for a long, long time. Anger into bitterness as I grew a little older again and you know at the, and it's about the mid-grades or going into Grade Nine, and then the last part of my experience with my life, that reflected on hatred, with such intense hatred that I never thought what it meant but when I think about that, you know it, as I grow older even today when I think about it you know, I didn't realize how close I came to destroying my own life spiritually speaking, that is.[382]

Of his years in two different Manitoba schools, Timothy Henderson said:

> Every day was, you were in constant fear that, your hope was that it wasn't you today that were going to, that was going to be the target, the victim. You know, you weren't going to have to suffer any form of humiliation, 'cause they were good at that. You know and they always had nasty, nasty remarks all day long. There was never, you never heard a kind word; I never heard a kind word.[383]

William Herney, who attended the Shubenacadie school, recalled the first few days in the school as frightening and bewildering.

Timothy Henderson.

> And you had to understand, you had to learn. Within those few days, you had to learn, because otherwise you're gonna get your head knocked off. Anyway, you learned everything. You learned to obey. And one of the rules that you didn't break, you obey, and you were scared, you were very scared. You, you don't know what to come up with next. I was scared. I was, like, always afraid, always looking over my shoulder.[384]

Shirley Waskewitch said that in Kindergarten at the Catholic school in Onion Lake, Saskatchewan, "I learned the fear, how to be so fearful at six years old. It was instilled in me. I was scared and fearful all the time, and that stayed with me throughout my life."[385]

At the Fort Alexander, Manitoba, school, Patrick Bruyere used to cry himself to sleep. "There was, you know, a few nights I remember that I just, you know, cried myself to sleep, I guess, because of, you know, wanting to see my mom and dad. I could never figure out why we had to be in there, you know."[386]

Ernest Barkman, who attended the Pine Creek school, recalled, "I was really lonely and I cried a lot, my brother who was with me said I cried a lot."[387]

Paul Dixon, who attended schools in Québec and Ontario, described life at residential school as one of unbearable loneliness.

Patrick Bruyere.

> You hear children crying at bedtime, you know. But all that time, you know, you know we had to weep silently. You were not allowed to cry, and we were in fear that we, as nobody to hear us, you know.
>
> If one child was caught crying, eh, oh, everybody was in trouble. You'd get up, and you'd get up at the real fastest way. Now, they hit you between your legs, or pull you out of bed by the hair, even if it was a top bunk, you know. Homesickness was your constant companion besides hunger, loneliness, and fear.[388]

Rick Gilbert said that in the junior dormitory at the Williams Lake school, children cried themselves to sleep at the beginning of each school year.

> That one kid would be lonesome and starting to cry and then pretty soon the next bed another kid heard that and started crying and that's how it really spread next bed and next bed. And pretty soon almost the whole dorm was filled with kids crying because they are, you know and then, just knowing that they're not going to be, their mom and dad's not going to be coming to tell you goodnight and that things are okay. Nobody who has, that was one thing about this school was that when you got hurt or got beat up or something, and you started crying, nobody comforted you. You just sat in the corner and cried and cried till you got tired of crying then you got up and carried on with life.[389]

Bob Baxter said it was hard to come up with good memories of his time at the Sioux Lookout school. One of his strongest recollections was "the loneliness of being alone and being away from your parents." At night, he said, the dormitories were full of lonely children. "I remember when the lights used to go out everybody used to cry when I first got there, I guess being lonesome, I guess. All the kids are, he's crying, and I guess I was crying, too."[390]

Betsy Annahatak grew up in Kangirsuk, in northern Québec, which was then known as Payne Bay. When her parents were on the land, she lived in a small hostel in the community. Like many students, she has strong memories of the loneliness she experienced at the school.

> I remember the, the time the first few nights we were in the residential school, when one person would start crying, all the, all the little girls would start crying; all of us. We were different ages. And we would cry like little puppies or dogs, right into the night, until we go to sleep; longing for our families. That's the memory I have.[391]

Betsy Annahatak.

Noel Knockwood recalled boys crying themselves to sleep at the Shubenacadie school in the 1940s.

> At nighttime I could hear some boys trying to smother their, their crying by putting a pillow over their mouth. And they would, not be heard too much, but we could hear them because they were in the same room with us. And, and we slept in a large dormitory which had perhaps about twenty-five or thirty beds and we were side by side. So we could hear some kids crying at night and they would say, you know, "I'm lonesome, I want my mother, I want my father."[392]

For the first three days that Nellie Ningewance was at the Sioux Lookout school, all she did was cry.

> There was lots of us; other girls didn't seem to, seem to be doing the same thing, the younger ones. So my, my hiding place was in the washroom. I'd sneak to the washroom and sit in the washroom and they would look for me; I wouldn't answer. I hid in the washroom. I sat on the toilet tank with my feet on the toilet seat; and nobody didn't see me where I was. I wouldn't open the door. Somebody had to crawl under to get me out.[393]

On her first night at the Spanish, Ontario, girls' school, Shirley Williams recalled, "no sooner did we have the, the lights off, and in our, our beds, I could hear people sniffling, and I knew they were crying. I think the loneliness swept in and for me, too, and but I slept at least, you know, but I think I woke up every hour and that, but I did, but I did go to sleep finally."[394]

Daniel Andre was frightened and lonely when he went to Grollier Hall, the Roman Catholic residence in Inuvik, Northwest Territories. "And the hardest part that I had to deal with was when I would go to sleep at night, and I'd cry myself to sleep every night, wondering what I did wrong to, to be away from my mom and dad, and not to have them with me, or beside me, or protecting me."[395]

Students commented on how they felt lonely even in a crowded school. Alan Knockwood said about his time at Shubenacadie, "Biggest thing I remember from the school was that I was lonely. I was surrounded by people all the time, but I was alone. And it took a long time for me to finally acknowledge that I do live in a loving community."[396]

Despite the fact that there were over 100 students at the Mission, British Columbia, school, Jeanne Paul felt alone and isolated.

> But again it was the loneliness of, of crying under my sheets at night, you know, just covering my head, underneath my blankets and sniffling, you know, very quietly, so nobody could hear me. And I imagine there were a lot of other ones in the room, I didn't know, might be having the same problem as well.[397]

Jeanne Paul.

Josiah Fiddler went to school at McIntosh, Ontario.

> My first few weeks in school, I cried every day. Either it was on the beating of the seniors, the beatings, the pulling of the ears by the nuns, and my first introduction to the principal was a slap across the head and told me to get downstairs and join the other 100 boys there. After those first few weeks I finally said, I'm not going to give them that satisfaction any more, I stopped crying. And to this day, I haven't cried. I really can't. And I feel so good for people that have the ability to be able to cry because as I said, I don't know how to cry.[398]

Nick Sibbeston, who was placed in the Fort Providence school in the Northwest Territories at the age of five, recalled it as a place where children hid their emotions. "In residential school you quickly learn that you should not cry. If you cry you're teased, you're shamed out, you're even punished. So you brace yourself and learn not to cry, you have to be a big boy, you have to toughen up." There was one nun at the school who would give students an empty sardine can in which to collect their tears. "And I've always thought, you know, what's so hard about just putting your hand on a child and saying, 'Don't cry, don't be sad,' you know, but there was never anything of that."[399]

Jack Anawak recalled of his time at Chesterfield Inlet in the 1950s that "there was no love, there was no feelings, it was just supervisory. For the nuns that were in there it was just, they supervised us, they told us what to do, they told us when to do it, they told us how to do it, and we didn't even have to think, we didn't even have to feel."[400]

Murray Crowe was very homesick at the school he attended in northwestern Ontario.

> At nights I was crying. And, I was crying and there was other students that were crying. We had double bunks; we were all crying in the dorm. And then the workers

there, they kept taking other kids out because they were disturbing the other kids from sleeping and....

When I couldn't stop crying they came and got me. And they came and got me; they took me out, out to the dark room we called it. And they pulled my trousers down and they spanked me. But I didn't stop crying; I was screaming and crying. They checked me up. They checked me, they locked me there, in the dark room. And they checked me and I wouldn't stop crying and I was hurting, because they, they, they hit me too hard; and I was so, I was hurt so much.[401]

Murray Crowe.

Of her years at Shubenacadie, Joanne Morrison Methot said, "We never, nobody ever told us they loved us. We couldn't hug each other, you know, like, you know, [the sister] said, 'You can't do that.' You know you can't say you love somebody, or hug somebody, you can't kiss boys, and stuff, and of course I was too young for that, but she said we couldn't do that."[402]

Even though Lydia Ross's parents lived in the same community in which the school was located, she rarely saw them when she was enrolled at the Cross Lake, Manitoba, school. "If you cried, if you got hurt and cried, there was no, nobody to, nobody to comfort, comfort you, nobody to put their arms. I missed my mom and dad, and my brothers and sisters."

On one occasion, she looked out the school window and saw her father.

I knocked on the window, and he looked and I said, I waved at him. I wanted to go outside, but you're not supposed to. If you see your parents out on a Sunday, you're not supposed to go to them. You can't go and hug your little brother and sister, and go and talk to your mom and dad. You can only see them from a distance.[403]

Robert Malcolm said that when he was placed in the Sandy Bay school in Manitoba, he was "taken from a loving environment and put into a, a place where there was no love, and that we had to fend for ourselves pretty much. It was very traumatizing that we, we had to go through something like that."[404]

Clara Quisess was six when she was sent to the Fort William, Ontario, school. She found the experience traumatic. She became fearful of the nun who had responsibility for her at the school.

I had to learn the language that she was teaching me to speak. I was not allowed to talk in my language that whenever she asked me something, whenever she tried to tell me to pronounce this, I have to talk in English, no Native language. And she would yell at me if I was saying, I'm trying to tell her I don't understand and I'm confused and I don't know what to say and how to say it, I was very scared of her. She was always raising her voice at me and she always had this angry look on her face and it felt really intimidating. And I was homesick. I was, like, crying and she yelled at me and told me to stop crying and she called me a crybaby in front of the students and it made me not want to cry anymore. I didn't like her. Deep inside I hated her for being so mean to me and when she told me not to cry and she told me not to speak my language, I felt like I had to keep everything inside me and it made me lonely, that there's nothing out here that could make me happy and feel like it was home.[405]

For Florence Horassi, loneliness was a constant feature of life at the schools she attended in the Northwest Territories.

Like, the nuns in there, they're cold. There was nobody there to give any hugs. There was nobody there to say goodnight. There was nobody there to even wipe your tears, or we will hide our tears. We're not to cry, so we have to hide and cry. But at night, you could hear a lot of muffling crying, muffling, sometime all night. Late at night you can hear somebody crying. I don't know what time it is. There's no time or nothing that I know, but I know it's very late at night. There's nobody to tell us. Everything we do in there is wrong, wrong, wrong, wrong, is what I hear. Couldn't do anything right.[406]

This lack of compassion affected the way students treated one another. Stephen Kakfwi attended Grandin College in Fort Smith, Northwest Territories, when he was twelve years old. "And one day, a week after I got to Fort Smith, I had a meltdown 'cause I realized I wasn't going to go home for ten months and I was homesick, and my older brother didn't know what to do with me." When another student came into the room and asked what was wrong, Kakfwi's brother said, "He's homesick."

"He'll get over it," [the other student] said, turned around and walked back out. And I think that's how we were, you know, every kid that came after that, that's what we all said, "He'll get over it." No hugs, nothing, no comfort. Everything that, I think, happened in the residential schools, we picked it up: we didn't get any hugs; you ain't going to get one out of me I'll tell you that.[407]

Victoria McIntosh said that life at the Fort Alexander, Manitoba, school taught her not to trust anyone. "You learn not to cry anymore. You just get harder. And yeah, you learn to shut down. And you know those feelings are there, and but they're, they're so deep down inside, you know, and they come out as some pretty, some pretty wicked nightmares at times, and then some days are good."[408]

Victoria McIntosh.

Megan Molaluk lived at both the Anglican and Catholic hostels in Inuvik. As was the case with many students, her loneliness led her to engage in behaviour intended to get her kicked out of school.

> I missed camping, I missed having country food. There are so many things I wanted to say, all right, but I really wanted to go home. It was bugging home, and bugging, bugging, bugging. I guess they got tired of me bugging them, so they moved me to Grollier Hall. I didn't know nobody over there. So I start behaving, I asked Mr. Holman if I could move back. I'm tired of being with strangers everywhere.

> So I started doing bad things in Inuvik, drinking, sneaking out. I hated doing those things, but I really wanted to go home.[409]

Despair

"The first time in my life that I attempted suicide."

Childhood loneliness often drove students to take desperate and destructive measures. Elizabeth Joyce Brass attempted to take her own life at the Dauphin, Manitoba, school in the 1960s.

Elizabeth Joyce Brass.

> And I remember one time going downtown with, and this was probably when I was, like they had junior dorm, intermediate dorm, senior dorm, I was in the senior dorm at that time. I must have been about eleven, twelve years old, and I remember, and I don't even know where this thought came from, but I remember I wanted to go downtown, and I had a plan, I was gonna go steal some Aspirins, which I did. I can't remember what store it was, and, you know, later on that night I, I took a whole bunch of them, and I remember, you know, going to sleep, and then I remember the next morning, you know, someone waking me up, but I couldn't hear them, because there was that really loud buzzing in my ears, so I guess that, you know that was, that must have been the way the Aspirin had affected me. And I couldn't get up, and I could remember the supervisor, you know, telling me, you know, "You're just not wanting to go to school today," you know, "You're just pretending to be sick." And she sent me off to see the nurse. And on my way I, you know, threw up, and it was all brown, and so I went and seen the nurse on the top floor, and same thing, too, she says, "You need to get to school. There's nothing wrong with you." So that was, you know, the first time in my life that I attempted suicide, and, you know, just at a young age.[410]

Antonette White has her own disturbing memories related to suicide. The students at her Kuper Island school were forced to look at a suicide victim.

> I remember the one young fellow that hung himself in the gym, and they brought us in there, and showed, showed us, as kids, and they just left him hanging there, and, like, what was that supposed to teach us? You know I'm fifty-five years old, and I still remember that, and that's one thing out of that school that I remember.[411]

Helen Harry recalled how at the Williams Lake, British Columbia, school, girls played a gruesome game of defying death. They wrapped towels around their necks and pulled on them, taking themselves to the edge of unconsciousness.

I remember this one time one girl would stand there and one girl would stand there, then they'd just pull the towel really hard 'til we blacked out. I remember one time, it felt like I almost died because they couldn't get me to come back. So they went and got some water and they splashed it on my face because they got really scared, because most times you would lay on the floor for a while but then you'd just come out of it. You'd come out of the ... I don't know what. You'd black out for like a minute or two but you always came out of it. And I, that one time they couldn't get me to come out of it. And they caught us doing that, they caught us because we would sneak and do that.[412]

Hiding the truth

"A guilty conscience and a bad attitude."

Some lessons the schools taught too well: many students commented that one of the legacies of their time at residential schools was the ability to hide their feelings and give the responses that were needed to 'get by.' Margaret Simpson, who attended the Fort Chipewyan, Alberta, school, described it as a survival technique.

> I learned how to lie, to lie so that I will get away with whatever Sister wanted me to do and that whatever she wanted to hear, that's what I told her even if it was a lie. So it got easier and I got pretty good at lying and I had a real time to get out of that lying as I got older in life to be able to tell the truth and to know the difference of what was happening because of that lie that it became such a habit for me. I had a real hard time even after I left the residential school.[413]

Ken A. Littledeer said that at the Sioux Lookout school, he was taught "how to lie, I learned how to steal, to be mischievous."[414]

Noel Knockwood said that at the Shubenacadie school, he learned to fake submission. "We learned how to play the game and acknowledged and bowed our heads in agreement and whatever they said we agreed with them, because they were too powerful to fight and they were too strong to, to, for us to change their, their habits and their ways of living."[415]

John B. Custer learned to rebel at residential school. The only things he took away from his years at the Roman Catholic school near The Pas, Manitoba, were

Noel Knockwood.

> a guilty conscience and a bad attitude. So instead of learning anything in that residential school, we, we learned just the opposite from good. We learned how to steal, we learned how to fight, we learned how to cheat, we learned how to lie. And to tell the truth, I thought I was gonna go to hell, so I didn't give a shit. I was sort of a rebel in the residential school. I didn't listen, so I was always being punished.[416]

Hazel Ewanchuk attended two residential schools in southern Manitoba, where she learned that love was a lie.

You know we were ordered around like, we were already big girls, you know. We had to take the orders no matter what. You couldn't say, you know, I can't do that, you did it, or else you got a strapping, and we had Bible study every night. I didn't mind that. I thought, what are they preaching here about love? Where is that love? You know. There was no love for us. They made a liar out of Bibles and liars of themselves too.[417]

Elaine Durocher felt that she received no meaningful education at the Roman Catholic school at Kamsack, Saskatchewan. Rather, she learned the tools for a life on the fringes of society in the sex trade.

They were there to discipline you, teach you, beat you, rape you, molest you, but I never got an education. I knew how to run. I knew how to manipulate. Once I knew that I could get money for touching, and this may sound bad, but once I knew that I could touch a man's penis for candy, that set the pace for when I was a teenager, and I could pull tricks as a prostitute. That, that's what the residential school taught me. It taught me how to lie, how to manipulate, how to exchange sexual favours for cash, meals, whatever, whatever the case may be.[418]

Classroom experience

"They used to make an example of me all the time."

For many students, classroom life was foreign and traumatic. David Charleson said he found the regimentation at the Christie, British Columbia, school so disturbing that he

> never wanted to learn, so I jumped into my shell. I took Kindergarten twice because of what happened to me. I didn't want to learn. I never went home with any A's, or B's, or C's, and it was all under, under the bad, my baddest part of the book of knowledge. That's the way they graded me. That's what they put in my mind, I'm dumb, stupid, and they used to make an example of me all the time, 'cause I was one of the bigger kids in the school.[419]

At the Birtle, Manitoba, school, Isabelle Whitford said, she had a hard time adjusting to the new language and the classroom discipline. "I wasn't very good in math. I was poor. And, every time I couldn't get an answer, like, you know, she would pull my ears and shake my head. And I couldn't help it 'cause I couldn't understand, like, you know, the work."[420]

Betsy Olson described class work at the Prince Albert, Saskatchewan, school as a torment, in which her "spelling was always 30, 40, it was way down. And when we did spelling, sometimes I freeze, I couldn't move, I just scribbled because I couldn't move my hand. I can't remember to spell B, or E, or C. My mind was a blank. I could not bring any letters out. I just freeze."[421]

Noel Knockwood recalled that he was often frozen with fear in class:

> We used to stand up with a reader in our hand and we will be given, each person will be given a paragraph to read. And when it came my turn I picked up the, the reader and turned to a page where I was supposed to. And other students took turns reading their paragraph. And then when it came my turn, I got up and I started to read the paragraph and I got down a little ways and I come across a word that I could not pronounce and I stopped, because I could not pronounce the word, I didn't know what to say.
>
> [The teacher] had a long wooden pointer, they used to point to the blackboard and she had it in her hand. And she said, "Read!" And I was very frightened and scared as a young, young boy. You know, then she took that pointer and pointed it at me and said, "Read! Read! Read!"
>
> She was shouting at me and I, I couldn't 'cause I was afraid and she had that pointer, she came closer, then she took that pointer and I raised my hands and she broke the pointer over my arms. And in doing so, I dirtied my pants; I shit myself because of

fear. And in doing so she seen what happened, and she said, "You filthy little boy. Get upstairs and go to bed."[422]

Traumatized by her experiences at schools in Ontario and Québec, Mary Lou Iahtail had difficulty learning. Her inability to speak in class led a teacher to single her out for humiliation.

> I was afraid I didn't know that word, and the teacher thought I was, I was just doing that, so she got mad at me, that I was just showing off. I really didn't know the word, and I was feeling so bad because so many people were staring at me. She, she brought a big, big yardstick ruler, yardstick, and she came after me, and I was afraid of her. I really was scared. She scared me so much, and I was afraid of the big stick. So, what I did is I run out of the classroom, and she ran after me, and I ran to next, next door, where our dorm is, our dorm was very close to the classroom.[423]

Leona Agawa never felt comfortable in the classroom at the Spanish school. For much of her time in school, she was frightened or intimidated.

> I could hear [the teacher] say my name, but I couldn't hear her what, what she was asking me, and that happened all over. I, I just, I was just a person that couldn't hear anybody talking to me, or asking me questions. My mind would go blank. So, I never did have any, really any schooling. I would hide behind a girl, or who's ever behind, in front, I'd hide. And somebody would say, "Leona." I'd hear my name, but I never got to answer. I stood up, never got to answer what they were saying when they sat me down. And I'd get a good slap after, after you, you leave there for not being nice in school.[424]

Dorothy Ross recalled her time in the Sioux Lookout school classroom as being one of fear and punishment.

> I remember the, the classroom. It was kind of dark, dingy-looking place. And I sat there, and holding a pencil, practise my name. She would write my name on a piece of paper, and the ABCs. It took me a while to understand those letters, the numbers. Like, I didn't, I guess some of them were hard for me. I couldn't pronounce them right, and I would, I would cry again if I do it again, make me do it all over again, over and over, and she would hit me. This is my first time that I experience. She had a, she had a, a stick, a ruler kind of, it was long, eh, a ruler stick. And if I didn't, if I, if she didn't like my, the way I was supposed to write with the pencil the first time, and this is where the first time ever being hit, right on my head. She would hit me three or four times across, over here, with that ruler, and my head would go down, and I would try to write at the same time, and she would hit me again.[425]

Margaret Paulette recalled that at Shubenacadie, there was a boy who could not read due to a stutter. Physical abuse and public humiliation did not help him. "The nuns put a piece, a wedge about this big in his mouth and he hadn't eaten all day and he was drooling and all that and then later on in the day they took it out and told him to read, 'Now you can open your mouth. You'll be able to read.' Poor guy wasn't able to read. And today that guy still stutters."[426]

Clara Munroe felt she received a very limited education at the Roman Catholic school at Kamsack, Saskatchewan, with the biggest focus on religion. "It was always prayer, praying, singing hymns in Latin, something we didn't even understand. That's how that school was operated."[427]

Mary Courchene described a similar education at the Fort Alexander school in the 1940s.

> The first few years we were there I never had a teacher, a real teacher. The nuns that taught us weren't teachers; they weren't qualified. They had no qualifications what- soever to, to, to be able to teach. Their only mandate was to Christianize and civilize; and it's written in black and white. And every single day we were reminded.[428]

At the Hobbema school in Alberta in the 1950s, Flora Northwest said, students were provided with a minimal education. The language training was compromised by the fact that neither teacher was a fluent English speaker. "And the English that I learned from there was ... it was really hard for me to speak the English language because of the teaching that was passed on to us through the teachers with their French accent, so I had difficult— difficulties with my English language."[429]

Some students said that the limits of the education they had received in residential school became apparent when they were integrated into the public school system. Victoria McIntosh, who had attended the Fort Alexander school, said that when she entered public school, she discovered that "I could hardly read and write. And I knew that I wasn't, you know, like, stupid, or, or dumb, or anything like that, it just, I didn't know how to read and write, and I didn't get a lot of these things. And I remember the teacher asking me where did you go to school? And I didn't know how to answer her."[430]

Tina Duguay had always done well academically at residential school in British Columbia, but when she went to a public school for Grade Seven, "I was lucky just to be able to pass. So that told me something right there that they weren't teaching us, the best academics possible."[431]

Many students said there was no expectation that they would succeed. Walter Jones never forgot the answer that a fellow student at the Alberni, British Columbia, school was given when he asked if he would be able to go to Grade Twelve.

> That supervisor said, "You don't need to go that far," he says. He says, "Your people are never going to get education to be a professional worker, and it doesn't matter what lawyer, or doctor, or electrician, or anything, that a person has to go to school for." He says, "You're going to be working jobs that the white man don't want to do, that they figure it's too lowly only for them. And you will do the menial jobs, the jobs that doesn't require schooling." I became a logger. I was a fisherman to start with, and I, most of our people do that. That had a lot of, I guess, a lot of things they did, like, teaching us our, like, to not speak our language, getting strapped for it, and telling us that we're never going to be able to take the good jobs and stuff like that, and it

happened. These things happened, and they, we lost so many of our people because of that residential school thing.[432]

For high school, Roger Cromarty lived in the Shingwauk Home in Sault Ste. Marie and attended local public schools. He recalled that he did not receive any guidance counselling.

Roger Cromarty.

> We were all just shovelled into the technical pro-
> gram, technical school program, whether we want-
> ed, we wanted to go in the technical stuff or not.
> Nobody asked us, or nobody showed us the vistas
> of going to the collegiate, and we were in a five-year
> program, or go into a technical program, which is a
> four-year. So, I end up being in a technical school,
> Sault Ste. Marie technical and commercial high
> school they called it.[433]

Lena Small recalled that when she turned sixteen, she was essentially forced to leave the Hobbema school. "We didn't have any future plans for us. The nuns didn't tell us there was a high school. They didn't tell us anything about life. They didn't tell us how to love one another, how to care for our families. We had no parenting, no nothing. All we had was religion."[434]

Nora Abou-Tibbett said that on one occasion, the girls at the Lower Post, British Columbia, school were lined up and asked what they wanted to be when they grew up. Many said they wanted to be nuns or missionaries. She said she did not know yet, but expected to know when she was older.

> They put me up front, and said, "Now, you see, there's this girl, now, how stupid she
> is, and I'm so happy that you kids aren't like her, because she is stupid to, to be say-
> ing, I mean she's the same age as you girls, and she doesn't know what she wants to
> be when she grows up." And so I was labelled stupid and dumb, whatever. But I, I just
> said, "Well, I know I just don't know, because until I grow a little older, I know by then
> what I want to be."[435]

Students also noted that the curriculum itself was racist. Lorna Cochrane recalled an illustration from her Canadian history textbook.

> But I remember what it is like reading history. I think it was social studies that made a
> huge impact on me. We were studying about the 'savage Indian.' There was a picture
> of two Jesuits laying in the snow, they were murdered by these two 'savages.' And they
> had this what we call 'a blood curdling look' on their faces is how I remember that
> picture.[436]

The study of Canadian history led Pierre Papatie to become ashamed of his Aboriginal ancestry. The textbooks he said were full of "images that were telling us that, that the Elders were, savages who massacred missionaries. It was written in, it was in all, we were seeing that in the images in the history of Canada. That's what hurt me. That's what made me hate my father, even my father. Even all the Natives, I hated them all."[437]

Specific teachers were remembered with gratitude. Madeleine Dion Stout, who attended the Blue Quills school, spoke of a teacher who had shown her special attention. "She really affirmed my existence. She affirmed my quest for knowledge, and, and just wanting to learn as much as I could."[438]

When Roddy Soosay lived in residence, he attended a local public school. He credited his high school principal at the Ponoka, Alberta, public school for pushing him to succeed.

> And one of the strangest things that happened in my life was our school principal was Halvar Jonson and Halvar Jonson called me into his office the next year and said, "If you don't—if you don't behave yourself, you don't push yourself to do better this year, then that's it. I don't want you in my school ever again." And I just said, "Okay." And he said, "Condition is, you're going to take drama." And I was like [laughs] "Drama, what are you talking about? Why?" And he said, "For—you'll probably benefit by looking at other people. And you'll probably benefit by pretending to be somebody else that you're not." And he said, "It'll do you some good for your own public speaking, it'll do you some good for your own confidence." And I was just, whatever. Long story short, when I graduated, my highest grades were in law and in drama. And those two things got me through. And I was even more shocked when I graduated and they gave me a scholarship and awards and recognized me for those things. And I forever thanked him for that because, had he not done that, I'd probably would've never, ever, as the saying goes, to walk in somebody else's moccasins. I did that.[439]

Lawrence Wanakamik said that after he got over his initial fears, he did well academically at the McIntosh, Ontario, school. "I used to be the, one of the top three students, you know, get 100s, get 95s, and no, no less than 90 in, in the marks, you know, 9 out of 10, or, you know, stuff like that." He had fond memories of one of his teachers. "Her name's Nancy, and she, she was nice, I liked her, everybody liked her, 'cause she was, she was friendly, and she was good to everybody. But the nun teachers, those were the ones that hit you with the ruler on your hands if you weren't listening, or you weren't behaving."[440]

Alice Quinney never forgot the positive impact that her Grade Four teacher at the Blue Quills school had on her life.

> It was, it was so nice to have a teacher that really believed in, you know, in you, that you could, you know, that told you you were smart, and that you were doing good, and, and not to hear anything negative from her, you know, like the nuns always hounding you about this, "Do this this way, do this that way," you know. I, I was so thankful to have a, a teacher who really cared about me. And that teacher, she moved to California a few years later and we wrote to each other still when she was in California. Yeah, I didn't stop writing to her until I left school, when I was in Grade Nine.

And I never forget her. Yeah, she was the first, first nice person in that school that made an impact in my life.[441]

Martha Loon said that at the Poplar Hill, Ontario, school in the 1980s, there were staff people who befriended and helped her and her siblings.

> We had staff members who took us under their wing. And one, over the years, started to recognize us as, like, younger siblings. So in a way, he was, like, protecting us, and other staff knew that, so other staff didn't really say or do anything against us because of that. So, sometimes I'll tell people, you know, when, they're talking about their experiences, I'll tell them, you know, this is what, this is what I went through, this is what my siblings and I went through. And I think that's what, how we didn't have those same experiences as some other students that went through a negative, bad experiences.

There was one staff member to whom she could tell all her problems. "I could say anything to her, and we'd go for walks sometimes. So, I could tell her anything and she wouldn't, she wouldn't say anything to other staff members about it. So, in a way, that's, you know, gave me a chance to express my frustrations, and the things that I didn't like."[442]

Other students were able to concentrate on their studies. Frederick Ernest Koe said that at Stringer Hall in Inuvik, he devoted all his energies to studies and work.

> You kind of develop a protective mechanism on the shell that you didn't rat on anybody, you kind of behave, you followed orders and things would go smooth.

> And what I did like is we had a study hall, and that study hall I was able to put a lot of time in there and get on with my studies and developed that discipline to work, and this is discipline that gave me to complete my studies to achieve my professional designation. I'm a professional accountant and have a degree in management.

> I helped a lot of the other kids because a lot of other kids had trouble in math and spelling and whatever, and I used to help the big boys, the bigger boys, because everybody was bigger than me then. But I used to help them.[443]

Helen Hanson thought the discipline in the classroom at the Sechelt, British Columbia, school was too strict in her early years there. She did, however, come to enjoy her schooling.

> I like learning, and I liked the challenge of learning, spelling and stuff like that, getting that golden star. And so throughout my school years, seven years that I was there, I actually kind of enjoyed it because of the schoolwork and the friends that I made there. I guess maybe in my grown-up years, like, in the last five years when things started coming up with the residential school issues, that, that I started thinking about what I had missed going to school there.[444]

Eli Carpenter, who said he was physically abused at the Presbyterian school in Kenora, did credit the school with providing students with an educational advantage. "At the residential school, it gave us a jump-start I think you know, 'cause I'm not, I know people are looking for the bad, the negative things on the reserve but I think it gave us a start anyway, you know. They taught us English and I think kids went to Grade Eight at that time that was high enough to find a good job."[445]

Every fall, William Antoine had always pleaded with his parents not to send him back to the Spanish boys' school. They had comforted him by telling him that he could quit when he turned sixteen. However, by the time he turned sixteen, he discovered he wanted to continue his education and he had no options for high school other than at the Spanish residential school. He said the school "was getting better. You know they didn't bother you as much, they didn't, you know, wasn't as disciplined as they were when you were in the smaller grades. And, yeah, you had more free time to yourself."[446]

Madeleine Dion Stout succeeded academically at the Blue Quills school. But she did not credit the school for her success.

Madeleine Dion Stout.

It's not residential school that made me a good student. My, the fundamental values and good example I had before I went to residential school by my grandfather and my parents, and all the old people on the reserve where I grew up are the ones who made me a good student. Residential school had nothing to do with it, I swear by that. And the reason why I swear by that is because I would watch my grandfather work, and he made everything from scratch, and he didn't say do this, do that, it's, you know, memorize this or anything, he would just do what, what he had to do to survive, because in those days, there was no welfare. People were very self-reliant, and they worked very hard to be self-reliant. So that I was successful in school, and that I'm successful today academically, people might say, is not because I went to residential school; it's because I had, from a very early age, I was taught by example and through oral tradition how to live my life.[447]

Regimentation

"Only the devil writes with the left hand."

Left-handed students were subjected to additional stresses. It was common in schools in Canada and Europe to force left-handed children to learn to write with their right hands. This can be attributed to both a superstitious distrust of left-handed people and the actual difficulty that left-handed people experience in writing languages that read from left to right.[448] Forcing children to change dominant hands has been associated with the onset of developmental problems, including stuttering.[449]

In residential schools, it appears the ban on left-handedness was strictly and harshly enforced. At the Spanish boys' school, William Antoine was told that he had to write with his right hand. "The teacher I had was really, really, really mean; and, very strict. And every time I was using my left hand to write, he would hit me with the ruler. With the ruler, right, you know, not flat but, that way that really hurt my hand. And, you know, I couldn't write. He'd tell me, 'use your right hand,' and I would."[450]

Several students recalled that the ban on the use of the left hand was given religious overtones. At the Blue Quills school, Louise Large was told not to use her left hand to write. "I was a lefty. And the nuns used to hit my hand saying, 'You know, this is the devil's hand. You can't use your left, you're gonna go to hell.'"[451]

Archie Hyacinthe said that at the Roman Catholic school in Kenora, one teacher would hit him across the knuckles for writing with his left hand. He was told, "Don't write with your left hand ... only the devil writes with the left hand."[452]

Doris Young recalled being disciplined for writing with her left hand at Anglican schools in Manitoba and Saskatchewan. She recalled one teacher as being particularly harsh.

> She would make me stand up in, in front of the class, and make me write, and so of course I would write with my left hand, and, and she would take my hand, and she would, she would make me hold my hand behind my back, my left hand behind my back, and if I, if I try to pull it away, then she would hit me. And, and this one time when I was writing with my left hand, she hit me ... with a ruler, and, and broke my, my little finger here.[453]

Margaret Plamondon was naturally left-handed. However, at the Fort Chipewyan, Alberta, school, her teacher forced her to use her right hand. "I kept still trying to use my left hand, and then she'd sneak up behind me, and hit me on the left. That's when my finger were broken when she hit me on this finger, and she broke my hand, and I'm, well, I just stayed in class like that."[454]

Integration into public schools
"The teachers never talked to me, students never talked to me."

In the 1950s, the federal government initiated its policy of integrating Aboriginal students into local public schools (or in the case of many Roman Catholic students, church-run schools). In some cases, students would live in a residence but attend a local school. Many recalled their reception at the schools as being hostile. Dorothy Ross said the students from the Sioux Lookout residence did not feel welcomed by the non-Aboriginal students in the local school. "They would call us down. They would call us squaws, a dirty Indian."[455]

Shirley Leon attended the Kamloops, British Columbia, school in the 1940s. She was among the first students to be sent to a local public school when the integration policy was implemented. It was just as unhappy an experience as residential school had been. "There we had horrific experiences because we were the savages ... we were taunted, our hair was pulled, our clothing torn, and we hid wherever we could, and didn't want to go to school. So, those kinds of stories are, are just as traumatic as what happened at residential school."[456]

Martina Therese Fisher lived in the Assiniboia residence in Winnipeg for three years. The first year she was there, she attended a Roman Catholic girls' school, at which she did

Martina Therese Fisher.

well. For the next two, lonely years, she took classes at two large Winnipeg high schools. "The teachers never talked to me, students never talked to me. I felt singled out. I was, I was lonely, I was scared. There was nobody to help me with my work. I couldn't wait to be eighteen years old."[457]

When she was in Grade Eight, Emily Kematch lived in the Anglican residence in Dauphin, Manitoba, and attended the local public school, where treatment by fellow students was isolating and racist.

> It wasn't a good experience. 'Cause this was my first time too, going to the white system with the white kids and we weren't treated very well there. We got called down quite a bit. They use to call us squaws and neechies, and dirty Indian, you know. They'd drive by in their cars and say awful things to us. Even the girls didn't associate with us, the white girls, they didn't associate with us.

The following year, she boarded with a local family.

> The first family that I lived with the lady her name was Wilma and Ron Rogers. It seemed like home, they treated us very well. There's three of us girls that stayed there and we got good meals. You know we were treated very well and we bonded with the Rogers. But in the other home, we stayed with a lady, she was a widow and it wasn't very good. She didn't really associate with us. All we did was, we'd eat with her, but we had to work for her. We had to work in her garden, pulling weeds and things like that, hoeing and helping her pull her garden out when it was ready.[458]

Richard Hall, who was abused at the Alberni, British Columbia, school in the 1950s, found respite when he was moved from the school into a boarding program.

> I was put in a home with Bill and Betty Anderson, a Scottish family with one brother, he had one son, one daughter, Gary and Lynn and today they are my brothers and sisters. I'm still connected to them today. Bill gladly accepted me as his son. And he guided me like my grandfather did. He gave me a sense of hope that there's something better but the damage was done but he kept cool and lying down and he kept cool that rage in me. Took me fishing, took me to Long Beach where we can run, play in the waves. He later, many years past died of cancer. Both of them did, but I stayed connected to them.[459]

Annie Wesley was attending the Catholic school in Kenora when the integration policy was put in place.

> I returned with my sister to St. Mary's to complete Grade Twelve. But when we got to St. Mary's, we were informed of very devastating news; the government had a policy of integration. We were being sent to white, a white residential school to be integrated. There was three of us. We were devastated by the news. We had created a bond of friendship between us. We got along well. We were starting to enjoy social activities at high school. And this government policy meant that we were going to be separated and integrated into the white society.

She was sent to a Catholic girls' boarding school in Pembroke, Ontario. She felt she and the other Aboriginal students were not welcomed by the other students. "We were outcasts in this white residential school."[460]

Truancy
"I never went back."

Many students said they ran away to escape the discipline of the school. Ken Lacquette attended residential schools in Brandon and Portage la Prairie, Manitoba. He found the discipline so harsh that he and his friends regularly ran away. "They used to give us straps all the time with our pants down, they'd give us straps right in the public. Then ... this started happening, after a while when I was getting old enough I started taking off from there, running away."[461]

After being subjected to ongoing sexual abuse, Anthony Wilson ran away from the Alberni school.

> I barely even remember how I made it home, but ... I got bits of pieces of how I made it home, I took off from residential school in Port Alberni, and I hitchhiked from Port Alberni to Nanaimo, and I made it as far as where the BC ferries were. And when I was a young child, and I was so messed up after the abuse, I didn't know what to do, and so I was hiding.[462]

Anthony Wilson.

When she returned to the Qu'Appelle school after being sexually abused by a fellow student the year before, Shirley Brass decided to run away. She did not even bother to unpack her suitcase on the first day at the school.

> I took it down to the laundry room and everybody was taking their suitcases down to wherever they kept them. I took my suitcase down. I told the nun, I said, "I have to do my laundry," I said so I took it to the laundry room. I hid it there and that night this other girl was supposed to run away with me but everybody was going up to the dorm and I went and I asked her, "Are you coming with me?" And she said, "No, I'm staying." So I said, "Well, I'm going." So I left, went and got my suitcase and I sneaked out. I went by the lake. I stayed there for I don't know how long. I walked by the lake and I sneaked through the little village of Lebret, stayed in a ditch. I saw the school truck passing twice and I just stayed there. I never went back. I hiked to—I had an aunt in Gordon's Reserve so I went there. I had a brother who was living—a half-brother who was living with his grandparents in Gordon's and he found me and somehow he got word to my mom and dad where I was and they came and got me. My dad wouldn't

send me back to Lebret so I went to school in Norquay, put myself back in Grade Ten. I didn't think much of myself. I quit when I was [in] Grade Eleven in Norquay.[463]

In the 1940s, Arthur Ron McKay regularly ran away from the Sandy Bay school. "I didn't even know where my home was, the first time right away. But these guys are the ones; my friends were living in nearby reserve, what they call Ebb and Flow, that's where they were going so I followed." He said he was physically abused for running away, and that

> my supervisors they'd hit me, like a man hitting somebody else, like a fist and all that. So this went on and on and on, I don't exactly know how to say. And then one time the principal threatened us, "If you run away one more time, we're going to send you to a reform school in Portage, boys' reform school." The boys' home, they call it a re-form school, "If you run away one more time that's where I'm going to send you and take you down there." I was thinking about that and I said, oh it's better to go away, maybe it's better down at the reform school.[464]

Ivan George and a group of his friends ran away from the Mission, British Columbia, school when he was eleven years old.

> Got as far as Abbotsford, and they recognized our clothes, or whatever, and hair cut, I guess, and said, "Where are you guys going?" I says, "Chilliwack." He said, "Okay." He picked us up, drove us right around, right back to here. He gave us a warning. Next time you get the strap.

> So, I stayed for another month or so, and I took off by myself. Got as far as the free-way, and the police picked me up, took me back. This time they made me take my pants down, and strapped me. So about two months later, me and this other guy decided to run again.

This time, he got as far as his home in Chilliwack. Indian Affairs officials sent them back.

> That guy was getting the strap first, my best friend, and he said, "You again." I says, "Yeah." He was just gonna strap me, and I took the strap, and I threw it down in the dormitory. He said, "Go pick it up." And I says, "You go pick it up." He gave me extra strappings for that, what I did to him. So, I stayed the whole year.[465]

Muriel Morrisseau ran away from the Fort Alexander school almost every year she was at the school.

> I ran away for, I don't know, just to make the nuns angry, the priests angry I guess. I didn't get anything out of running away, more punishment. I remember one time when the priest come and got us, me and this girl that I was close to, we went home for a night and he'd come and get us the next day. Nothing good became out of it any-way. I remember running away again trying to cross the river and it started freezing up, we all got scared, we had to come back again with a tail under our legs.[466]

In most cases, the motives would be mixed: the desire to return home was coupled with the need to escape punishment or bullying. Josie Angeconeb ran away on numerous occasions from schools in Sioux Lookout and Kenora. In part, she simply wanted to see her family. "It is a long year, only time we came home was summertime. We never went home for Christmas or we never went home for Easter." But she also wanted to get away from bullying at school. "I remember getting bullied by kids, and I remember getting abused by former students." She and her sister were always caught, returned, and punished. "I remember getting straps on the hand. I remember my sister getting a strap too when she ran away with me."[467]

Students might run away for an adventure and then return. William Garson left the Elkhorn, Manitoba, school in the 1940s. "I went to Brandon; jumped on the freight train, ... trying to get away from school. I jumped on the freight train and went to Brandon for [the] circus." When the circus was over, he returned to the school on his own.[468]

In some cases, students ran away even though they had no expectation of making it to their homes. They simply could not bear residential school life any longer. Walter Jones attended the Alberni school in British Columbia. He ran away several times and was harshly punished in front of other students on his return. "We were all thinking we're not gonna cry when that happens. Come to my turn, too, all three of us, one after the other, I cried, they cried, and all the other ones cried." Despite this humiliation, he continued to run away. "We knew it was, we might not be able to get where we come from, but we didn't think of that, you know, we're just running away because we were, wanted to run away, you know, 'cause we were, didn't, we couldn't stay there."[469]

Marguerite Wabano, who was born in 1904, was the one of the oldest former students to provide a statement to the Commission. While she could recall little of her own time at the Fort Albany school, she had a strong memory of three boys who were never found when they ran away. "Yes they did run away for good. And they went missing for good. Yes and they didn't talk to anybody though they saw them."[470]

Even when it was not fatal, running away was frightening. Isaac Daniels ran away from the Prince Albert, Saskatchewan, school with two older boys. Their escape route involved crossing a railway bridge. Partway across, Daniels became too frightened to continue and turned back.

> And it was already late, it must have been about 11:00, 12:00 o'clock. So, I said to myself, well, I'll go back, I'll go back, follow this track all the way, I'll go back to residential school.

> So, so that, that was already the sun was coming up by the time I got back to the residential school. And I was just a young fella, you know. So, anyway, I couldn't get in. Dormitory locked, doors were locked, so I went around the corner, and I slept on the, by my window there. I just have a window, and I used to sneak in and out from the, through the window there. So, I must have sat down there, and I must have fell asleep.[471]

Dora Necan ran away from the Fort Frances school with a friend.

> Then we ran away to, me and a girl, we, by Fort
> Frances, it's, you know, the States is on the other
> side of the tracks, so we were crawling there just to
> run away, that was in the springtime. There was a
> lot of ice, and there was river flowing down, down
> there. There was a train coming behind us, so we
> were crawling to go past this bridge. And it's a
> good thing my friend had long hair, that's where I
> grabbed her, was so she wouldn't slip into the river,
> yeah.

Dora Necan.

They made it to the United States and stayed there
for three days before returning to the school.[472]

Nellie Cournoyea was sheltered by Aboriginal
families along her route when she ran away from an Anglican hostel in the Northwest
Territories after a confrontation with a teacher. "It was late Easter time so there was a lot of
camps along the way so everybody said, you know, welcomed me and then, you know, and
we have a lot of love among our people."[473]

When Lawrence Waquan ran away from the Fort Chipewyan school in 1965, there was
no one along the way to support him.

> I walked from Fort Chipewyan to Fort Smith, 130 miles. It took me about five days. I
> was only about sixteen. And I just ate berries and drank water to survive. But at that
> time I knew my brother was living in Fort Smith. Simon Waquan, he was living there
> that time. That's when he took me under his wing, in 1966.[474]

There were many students who considered running away but, in the end, decided
against it because they had no place to go. Roy Denny, for example, carefully prepared his
escape from the Shubenacadie school.

> It's been like, I tried running away once; and I saved all my lunch, I hid it away. And
> one night I went down and tried to make a run for it. I went downstairs, I was at the
> door, big door, I opened it, it was around midnight, after midnight I think. And I stood
> there; I'm thinking where in the hell am I going to go? Didn't have family; the only I
> have is my grandmother. So I went back in, I went back to my bed. I felt so helpless or
> I couldn't, I don't know the feeling I had and I didn't want to leave my sisters there;
> that's another thing too. I couldn't take them with me 'cause they're, they're on the
> other side. So I said I might as well tough it out.[475]

Richard Morrison and his friends regularly tried to get away from the Fort Frances school.

> We ran and they always caught us because the town, the town people knew the res-
> idential school was there and they'd always report us. They would phone the police

right away and the police would just surround us as we were young Natives walking around town, they already knew, they would just bring us back to the school.[476]

When Beverley Anne Machelle and her friends ran away from the Lytton, British Columbia, school, they had to contend with the school's isolated and mountainous location.

It's a plateau region, and the residence was here, and then we walked up onto the road, and then the road goes along, and then it goes a little bit up, and then, and then there's a great big hill going down, and it was halfway down this big hill, and then from there you could see town. And we got halfway down there, and we were all feeling, like, woo-hoo, you know, and we got out of there, and, and we're gonna go do something fun, and, and then we got halfway down, and then we realized, well, we have no money, and we have no place to go. There was no place to go. There was no safe place to go. And that was really weird to me because, because where the residential school was and where I lived just before I went into the residential school, I lived on the reserve just, like, it was, like, less than a mile away, and yet I had no place to go. Yeah, so we were very sad, and we all agreed that we had to go back because we had no place to go, so we went back.[477]

One student even flew away from school. Doug Beardy left the Stirland Lake, Ontario, school for good, shortly before his two years at the school were completed.

There was a plane that, that used to come there with, I think, with fish, tubs of fish that they, they would drop them off there, and they were thrown off to a truck, a semi-truck. And so this plane landed, and I went down to the plane and stood around until the pilot was ready to go, and, you know, he was right about ready to close the door, and when he was ready to close door, I jumped into the plane. This, this pilot was in Round Lake for many years, and he has since passed away. He didn't ask me anything. He didn't ask me why I jumped into the plane. He just looked at me when I jumped into, into the plane, he just looked at me and didn't say anything, and he just took off. And, and that's how I left the school.[478]

Doug Beardy.

Discipline
"I saw violence for the first time."

Many students were caught by surprise by the violent nature of the discipline at the schools. Isabelle Whitford said that prior to coming to the Sandy Bay school, she had not been physically disciplined.

> All my dad have to do was raise his voice, and we knew what he meant. So, when I first got hit by the nuns, it was really devastating 'cause how can they hit me when my parents didn't hit me, you know? Never did I ever get a licking from my parents. It was just ... my dad raising his voice. And, and, we knew what he meant. We had our chores to do; we would do them.[479]

Rachel Chakasim said that at the Fort Albany, Ontario, school,

> I saw violence for the first time. I would see kids getting hit. Sometimes in the classrooms, a yardstick was being used to hit. A nun would hit us. Even though our hair was short as it is, the nuns would grab us by the hair, and throw us on the floor of the classroom.... We never knew such fear before. It was very scary. I witness as other children were being mistreated.[480]

Ricky Kakekagumick said that students at the Poplar Hill, Ontario, school were often disciplined at night.

> You try and sleep, you just hear that noise of somebody crying. I don't know how long, maybe a month later, that's when I finally found out what was going on. Whoever was bad, didn't listen, well, the, the ones they wanted to punish, they'd come and get them in the middle of the night, when everybody's asleep, that's what they did, that's why I kept hearing this whimpering and crying at night. They came and got them at the night, took them down, wherever they wanted to strap them, and they brought them back.[481]

Ricky Kakekagumick.

Dorothy Jane Beaulieu said that at the Fort Resolution school in the Northwest Territories, harsh and abusive discipline was administered in a seemingly random fashion.

> There's three of us, we were washing the floor, and the water was getting dirty, you know, so I asked, I said, "Sister, can I change my water?" You know she never said

nothing. She was just looking around. So again I asked her. You know the other girls changed their water. I said, "Can I change my water?" I guess I asked her too many times, and she took the pail, and threw it over my head, and just pounding me with, you know, with a mop on my, you know, while that pail was on my head, you know. Yeah, I think that's when Nora came out of the kitchen. I remember the old kitchen that used to be there.[482]

Stella Marie Tookate never forgot being called to the principal's office at the Fort Albany, Ontario, school.

There was a priest there, standing, and the sister standing, a nun. And then, they were two in the office. And at that time, I remember, they were strapping me five times—five times on my hands and five times the other hand. And that's where, that's where I stopped going to school because I was … I showed my dad my hands at that time, and then he took me away from school. It was hard for me to continue my school at that time. It was hard to feel that stripes on my hands…. My hands were red at that time—painful. Sometimes, I could, I could tell, sometimes how I was feeling. I feel that pain sometimes. And I stopped going to school after that.[483]

Fred Brass said that his years at the Roman Catholic school at Kamsack, Saskatchewan, were "the hellish years of my life. You know to be degraded by our so-called educators, to be beat by these people that were supposed to have been there to look after us, to teach us right from wrong. It makes me wonder now today a lot of times I ask that question, who was right and who was wrong?"

Brass described a school dominated by a violent regime of punishment.

I saw my brother with his face held to a hot steaming pipe and then getting burned on the arm by the supervisor. And I took my brother, tried to get him out of there. And I saw my cousin get beat up to the point where he was getting kicked where he couldn't even walk and then it was my turn. I got beat so bad that I wet my pants. Fears I lived with day and night to the point where at nighttime when you want to go to the bathroom you can't because there is someone sitting there with a stick or a strap ready to beat on you if you try to go to that bathroom. And the only choice we had was to pee in our beds. That's not a nice feeling to have to sleep in that kind of a bed.[484]

According to Geraldine Bob, the staff members at the Kamloops school she attended were not able to control their tempers once they began to punish a student.

And from the beatings, because I didn't cry, they went berserk; you know the two nuns. They would just start beating you and lose control and hurl you against the wall, throw you on the floor, kick you, punch you and just laid you; they couldn't stop. You know, they were insane, yeah. And they were not able to control themselves at all.[485]

Joanne Morrison Methot told the Commission that noisy behaviour was punished severely at the Shubenacadie school.

> I used to count. One girl got strapped forty-five times, I was counting, yeah, and then it came to my turn, I got a beating, and I wouldn't cry. I just let her beat me and beat me, and I wouldn't cry. I just let her do that because, well, sometimes I would pretend I'm crying just so she'll stop, but then other times I just didn't cry, 'cause I knew I was talking, maybe it was my fault, so I just let her beat me, and then next one, then after we'd go to bed.[486]

Alfred Nolie said that corporal punishment at the Alert Bay school was strict and painful.

> There was one big staff there. He used to lay me over a desk, big square thing there. I think because I used to work up at the farm up here, there were horses up here, they had those big leather straps, big leather, heavy ones, about that thick, I guess, I'd lean over a desk, take my pants down, and hit me in the bum with that strap, and that hurts really bad. Every time I get caught talking our language that's when it's usually big staff, was 300 pounds, really big guy.[487]

Ron Windsor had strong memories of being punished for laughing at the dining-room table at the Alert Bay school. "I didn't know what he was gonna do. He grabbed my hair, put his knee in my back, and held me right on the floor, and I tried to tell him my neck is sore, and I was crying. And he caught me off guard, I didn't expect that. Now, why would you do [that] to a little boy like me at that time?"[488]

For crossing into the girls' playground at the Sioux Lookout school, Ken A. Littledeer was grabbed by two staff members. One of them then beat him on the hands with branches from a thorny bush. "I was crying. Never cried hard before. I never felt this sharp pain before, and anger build up, and resentment build up, that if I grow bigger I would get this person back. I knew that I was small, and I can't hit him back."[489]

Ken A. Littledeer.

Doug Beardy said that at the Stirland Lake, Ontario, school, the principal punished him with blows administered with "a hockey stick, a goalie stick ... that was cut off like ... a paddle."[490]

As a punishment at the Alberni school, Frances Tait said, she was once dressed in a pair of overalls and hung on a hook in a closed and darkened cloakroom.[491] For laughing in church at the Roman Catholic school in Aklavik, Alphonsine McNeely said, she was shut in the school's cellar.[492]

Mervin Mirasty said that at the Beauval, Saskatchewan, school, boys caught throwing snowballs were punished with blows to their hands from the blade of a hockey stick. "There was about thirty of us. Every one of us got ten smacks. Every one of us cried except one, one guy, and he refused to cry, but it hurt so much. That was for playing with the snowballs, being a kid, just playing around."[493]

For going to the washroom in the middle of the night at the Sault Ste. Marie residence, Diana Lariviere said, she was sent "down to the basement, and I was in the basement practically all night, scrubbing the cement floor, on my hands and knees, and that was my punishment for that night. Now it, it was a, a scary, a very frightening situation because of all the creaks and the noises that were going on in the basement."[494]

Lynda Pahpasay McDonald said that on one occasion, she was placed in a closet as punishment at the Roman Catholic school in Kenora. "There's just a little bit of light coming through that door, and, and I sat there I don't know how many hours. It felt like a long time. And that's where they put any child that acted up, into the closet. I remember my sister going there a couple of times, too, my younger one. She would go in there also."[495]

Extended periods of kneeling were another form of discipline. Wesley Keewatin said that at the Qu'Appelle school, students might have to kneel in front of a statue of the Virgin Mary for half an hour to an hour. Keewatin also recalled that at the Qu'Appelle school, a teacher he had thought had always treated him well slapped him so hard that he "went flying." He attributed his deafness in one ear to this incident.[496]

Inez Dieter felt that her hearing was damaged by the punishment she received at a Saskatchewan school.

> I was speaking out of turn and there was a male
> supervisor, I was about fourteen, maybe thirteen.
> He was a male supervisor, he was big, he came up
> to me and instead of talking to me in a nice way, he
> just ploughed into my ear like this.

Wesley Keewatin.

> Today I wear hearing aids. Today I can't hear, I can't hear well enough. And that really
> hurt because there was nobody there to say, "I'm sorry," because everybody was
> scared. Nobody wanted to say anything but I felt it. I felt the blow and again I cried.[497]

Delores Adolph also said that the punishment she received at the Mission school impaired her hearing.

> The nun slapped me across the face, and, and I had too much soap in my hair, and
> my ears, and I was trying to get the soap out of my ears and my face, and she gave me
> one good slap, and, like, and all I saw was stars. And so I didn't know that my eardrum was broken at that, at that point. So, after a while, you know, they were getting
> mad because I, I couldn't hear what they were saying.[498]

Many students spoke of teachers punishing them by pulling their ears. At Sioux Lookout, Dorothy Ross said, "There's one time me and this other girl were, we were, were fooling around, we were teasing each other in our own language, we got, I got caught. She pulled my ear so hard. She took me to the corner, and I stood there for a long time. I don't know why."[499] Archie Hyacinthe recalled that in the classrooms of the Roman Catholic school in Kenora, "every time we didn't listen, they would tug us behind the ear, or behind the neck, or on the elbows."[500] Joseph Wabano said that at the Fort Albany, Ontario, school, the staff would hit students with a one-inch-thick board. "And there was a lot of times I got hit, me too, for some reason. They had a board, one by three, like one inch thick, and it was cut like that, they use it for the board, and that nun used to hit my head, wanted to hit my ears. She said, 'I'm gonna hit your ears.'"[501]

Edmund Metatawabin spoke of how he and other students at the Fort Albany school had been punished by being placed in what students referred to as the "electric chair." According to Metatawabin, this was a metal-framed chair with a wooden seat and back. After being buckled into the chair an electric current from a hand-cranked generator was run into their bodies. The chair had been constructed by Brother Goulet, the school's electrician, and had apparently been initially used as an entertainment. It came, however, to be used as an instrument of punishment. Metatawabin said he had "sat on the electric chair three times."[502] Simeon Nakoochee was another student who was put in the chair.

> To them it's, like, entertainment, like it was just, like, "Who wants to get in?" There wasn't, it was like a selection. I never wanted to get in that chair, you know. I saw that chair. I could even describe it, that thing too, you know. That thing just right out of my mind, I could, I could describe it, you know, what the, what the chair looked like, you know, what, what they use. Then they, well, I never volunteer, or raised my hand, you know, and I just, and then she called my name, the nun, you know, "Just sit on that chair." It was almost like a crack, you know. She wouldn't let me get off there until, and then I, I probably cried after that, you know, and she wouldn't let me get out after this. People thought it was, kids were laughing asking why I cry, you know.

He said he thought the chair was later destroyed.[503]

Jonas Grandjambe recalled how the nun in charge of the boys' dormitory at the Roman Catholic school in Aklavik gave the students what he called a "rough time."

> A strapping, grabbing us by the ear, and pushing us against the corner to kneel down. Sometimes we had to kneel down all day. And if we spilt something, she would do the same thing, grab our ear and twist it until we, make us get down on the floor, and whatever we dropped there we have to eat it or lick it. I don't know.[504]

Margaret Plamondon, who attended the Holy Angels Residential School in Fort Chipewyan, Alberta, said she once saw a nun push a student down a flight of stairs.

> It was one of my, one of my friends, and we were lining up to go to the bathrooms before school was, was to start, and I don't know what happened, and one of the nuns, one of the nuns that were looking after us, not the teacher, and then she, as, as I turn around, I see the nun push that girl down a flight of stairs, and she never got up, and

we were chased away, down to go away from there. I don't know what happened, but she never came back for months.

And when she came back, she was kind of crippled. She was never the same after that. She even likely, she had a broken back after. She came back, and she was almost gone a year before I see her again. They didn't tell us what went wrong.[505]

Noel Starblanket recalled being constantly "slapped on the side of the head" at the Qu'Appelle school. One teacher struck him in the face and broke his nose.

My nose started bleeding, I ran out, I went to the bathroom, was wiping my face with cold water, and it took a long time to stop it, and I plugged it with toilet paper, and toilet, paper towel, whatever I could find. I went back in class, and everybody was teasing me, bugging me, and ha-ha-ha, look at, look at him, you know, all that, humiliating me. And, and so, anyway, it started swelling up, getting blue under here, and I wondered, gee, you know, is there something wrong? I was sore here. So, a couple of days after it started going down, and I remember waking up in the middle of the night, and my nose would be bleeding, and I'd have to run to the bathroom, and wash it and plug it again.[506]

Adam Highway recalled a beating that he witnessed the principal of the Sturgeon Landing, Saskatchewan, school administer in the 1920s.

The priest grabbed him, grabbed him by the hair, threw him down. Now, that was a cement floor where we played. And here he kicked him repeatedly. There was no stick. He had brand new boots, leather. I was sitting not too far away. I wasn't very big. I still can't forget to this day. It's like I'm still watching him. It must have been ten minutes. These were brand new boots. On the thighs and the buttocks. He bounced his boots off him as he kicked him. And the brother that looked at him. Now the principal said to him. "George," he said, "you will kneel there until six o'clock," he told him.[507]

There are also reports of group punishment. Earl Clarke recalled how at the Prince Albert, Saskatchewan, school, many of the boys would start fooling around when the lights went out in the dormitory. Eventually, he said, the supervisor would come out and line up the boys he suspected to have been making noise. He would then "take them down to the end of the hall, and would get out a, a leather strap, just like a conveyor belt type of material. And the kids would come hopping out, crying, bawling, you know, little, little ones 'cause the little ones would get forced to go first."[508]

Ernest Barkman, who went to the Fort Albany school, said that, on one occasion, all the boys were punished for the actions of one student. "We all stood in rows (three or four rows, all the boys, and we had to stand there for an hour) one hour and we were told not to move, and if we moved we got hit, that's one thing I remember."[509]

At the Norway House school, Shirley Ida Moore recalled:

When, when something would happen, like one of the girls would get into trouble or somebody would, or somebody, or somebody would get into trouble, they'd haul us all down to the playroom and we'd stand in these lines, we had to stand at attention. And you would walk around, we would, we would be forced to stand there until somebody, whoever did what confessed. And, and I guess the, the memory that I have is like, we stood there for so long, I saw girls falling; that's, that's how long we had stood there. So I guess it was really a battle of wills.[510]

Gerald McLeod recalled being subjected to group punishments at the Carcross, Yukon, school.

And another place where, where we used to play downstairs, they call it the play area ... where they make us stand up in line, and if one guy got in trouble, all of us would have to stand there 'til we confessed who did, like, stole candy from the candy place, or whatever went wrong, or something, we always all got punished for it.[511]

Students might also be punished if it was felt they were withholding information about the activities of other students. Eli Carpenter recalled that the principal of the Presbyterian school in Kenora in the early 1940s was very strict. On one occasion, Carpenter was strapped because the principal believed he was not revealing information about the destination of a boy who had run away. Carpenter said the boy had not shared his plans with him.[512]

Mary Vivier saw her brother publicly flogged at the Fort Frances school.

I don't know what my, what my brother ... what he did. All I know is that it was, we were all in the dining area when they brought him in, when they brought them in. They had, I don't know, I was just pretty small, but it looked like a big, long rod to me, maybe it was smaller. That's when they were hit in front of all the students. Maybe it was a lesson for us, or scare tactic, I'm not sure, but I was, I cried. I had one of the nuns holding me down, so I don't go running to my brother. They had another one by my sister. I remember that day. I cried, I cried and I cried.[513]

Mary Vivier.

Daniel Andre was disciplined in front of other students at Grollier Hall, the Roman Catholic residence in Inuvik.

All I remember is being singled out, and the centre of attention, and being abused physically. And when he couldn't make me cry, or, or weaken me that way, he would get all the students to call me all different kinds of names, and, and laugh at me, forcibly make them laugh at me so that I cried, and I cried every single time when it happened. I couldn't help it.[514]

Not only were runaway students often punished as a group, but they were also often disciplined in front of the entire student body and subjected to punishments that were clearly intended to humiliate them and intimidate the rest of the students.

When a group of runaway girls were brought back to the Sioux Lookout school, they were punished in front of the assembled students. According to Nellie Ningewance, "We were all lined up. Boys on one side, girls on one side, to watch them being punished. Their pants were pulled down right to bare butt, they were strapped with a belt; bent over. And all the boys and girls were watching that."[515]

Boys who ran away from the Spanish school also were punished in front of their fellow students. William Antoine said,

> What they did to them, they cut all their hair off. And ... they got all the boys to look at what is happening to this boy, what they were doing to him because he ran away.
>
> They cut all his hair off and they pulled, pulled his pants down and he was kneeling on the floor, and holding onto the chair. And they were, whipping him, with this big belt. I mean hard too. They were hitting him, for I don't know how long. He, he started to cry after; it was hurting so bad eh. But I don't know how many times they hit him, but they hit him lots of times. And those boys that got whipped that time, was, there was two of them, they, they couldn't sit down for two months; that's how bad it was. That's how bad they got beat because they ran away. And that's what the priest said, "If any of you boys run away, that's what you're going to get."[516]

According to Lawrence Wanakamik, students who ran away from the McIntosh, Ontario, school were subjected to a similar punishment.

> When they got caught a couple of days after, they'd, they'd haul them into the, into the playroom, and they told us, you know, gather around. There used to be benches along the walls in the playroom, and everybody would sit down, and we'd sit down there, and we knew, we knew it was those kids got caught, and we didn't know where they were though. We didn't know what happened. But then after everybody was gathered, you know, they'd bring them in, wherever how much they were, two, three, sometimes four. And they, one of the nuns brought in a big strap, real big strap, about two feet long. It was one of those hard rubber conveyor belt type of rubber. They'd bring that out. They'd tell the kids to put their hands out, and they did pow! pow! I don't know how many times.[517]

According to Eva Simpson, students at the Catholic school in The Pas had their heads shaved if they ran away. "And they used to get their head shaved; their hair. My cousin was like that; the boys, their hair was all shaved. And the girls, their hair was just chopped up to here."[518]

J.G. Michel Sutherland recalled the public punishment of boys who ran away from the Fort Albany, Ontario, school in the 1960s.

So, all the boys were lined up, and at the west side of the building where the sun side was, they were lining up these four boys that had been caught, that ran away. I'm six years old, and there was about twenty-five of us, you know, you know starting, and then the Grade Ones. There was another twenty-five of them, so there was quite a few of us, six, seven years old. And the brothers in black robes were standing there. There was about five of them. And there was some nuns. So, we were there to learn a lesson. They stripped the four boys naked. They tied them up on this big, big thing, and it looked like a wheel, it was, well, they, they, they got 'em by the hands, and they started whipping them one by one.[519]

Doris Young recalled that runaways from the Anglican schools she attended in Manitoba and Saskatchewan were punished in front of the assembled students.

They both were brought back into the dining room, where we witnessed them getting their head shaved. And, and then they had to remove their clothes, they'd remove their clothes, and they strapped them in front of all of us. And we all had to go into the dining room, where, where the, where usually the, the boys' and the girls' dining rooms were separated, and but we, we were all taken into the dining room, and we were, we had to witness this beating, and I thought, oh, I hope it's not one of my brothers, but, but it wasn't, and still they, they were boys and girls that, the boys and girls, and everybody, the, the supervisors were all standing there witnessing this, these horrible beatings that these boys were getting because they ran away from school.[520]

Even when the students were not disciplined in public, they were subjected to invasive and humiliating punishment. Once, Violet Beaulieu and her friends slipped out of the Fort Resolution school in the middle of winter. "I don't know why I did that. So, we planned it all out. And it was a really, really cold winter night, blizzard." They were quickly caught and accused of attempting to get into the boys' dormitory.

They got the father there to, took us each our turn in the room, and really gave it to us. "Better tell the truth. Lay down there, pull your pants down." Whack, whack. "What did you do?" "Nothing." Again, whack. Holy smokes I was just bruised. And they tried to make us say that we saw somebody. Who did we see? All that stuff, just for a dare, you know. And they put us in penance for, like we were, we were forbidden to do anything, go anywhere. Like, they'd have Sunday movies, stuff like that, and we were, shut us out, and they tried to get us to say we did something.[521]

Dorothy Ross and a friend ran away from the Sioux Lookout school.

We ran as fast as we could. Down the lake, along the shore, we followed that girl, through the bush. I remember the tracks. I just followed, you know, and that, there's the tracks, a train. We didn't get too far. We ran on the tracks, the side of the tracks, and I could see lights coming, lights coming, eh, and people running, chasing after us.

They were caught, returned to the school, and sent to the principal's office. There, she was told to pull her pants down so she could be strapped on her bare bottom.

> "Pull your pants down," he would yell at me, but I won't, I won't let him. So, he grabbed me by my collar, took me to the, the desk. It's a long desk. Put me against that desk. "Pull your pants down," I remember him saying that all the time, "pull your pants down" and I wasn't gonna give in. He had to force me. He forced me to pull my pants down. He had to do it; I didn't do it. So, he put me against that desk, and he whacked me with that, I remember the strap, it was a big thick strap, brown, that, and he hit me on my bum. I started crying, that's how much it hurted. "You're a bad girl. You don't run away again, or you will, you're gonna get it again."[522]

When she was at the Lestock, Saskatchewan, school, Clara Munroe joined a group of girls who were running away.

> One evening they said, "Come with us," and I said, "Okay." I thought, okay, I'll go with them. Here I didn't know they were planning to run away. There was twelve of us. So that's what I did, I followed them. Next thing I knew there was a wagon, team of horses, picked us up like a bunch of cattle, throw us in the wagon, brought us back. Didn't say nothing, they just, and we used to line up, we used to get in line and we were on our way to the dormitories, bedtime, who do they call? They called me. They called on another girl there. The two of us and I was blamed for that and I didn't even know a thing about it, so they wouldn't listen to me. So what did they do? They took us to the principal's office. The principal was there, there was three nuns there, and not a word, they just pulled my pants down [pause] and the priest, the father principal, gave me a strap. And yet it was I know I was so ashamed I start laughing and that nun said, "She's laughing," and he strapped, strapped me harder and longer. I was so embarrassed.[523]

Some students said they tried not to show any signs of pain when they were being punished. Once, when Tina Duguay and her friend Sandra were about to be punished at their school in British Columbia, Tina told herself, "This time they're not breaking me. I don't care what, they're not gonna break me." She recalled receiving 100 strokes on each hand without crying.

> So after she sent us out of her office, walking down the stairs, and Sandra says, "Man, you're tough," and I said, "No, I just stopped it," and I says, "Now I'm gonna cry." So, I ended up crying. We went in the bathroom, and let, just let it out, and I said, "There," and I said, "That's it. She didn't see me do it though."[524]

Percy Tuesday refused to cry when the boys' supervisor at the Fort Frances school strapped him.

> The boys' supervisor, I remember him giving me a strap, and I don't know for whatever reason. But I, you know, he, he, he strapped me all the way up my arm, but I, I refused to cry. I mean I think he was, he was trying to break me, but I refuse. I just

stood there and I let him hit me, and trying to hit me harder and harder and harder and harder, and I could see he was going nuts, so I, so I pretended to cry to, to keep him from driving himself crazy, you know. So that's what I remember about Fort Frances and boys' supervisor.[525]

Joseph Ward told how, when he was strapped at the Shubenacadie school, "I put my hand out and he hit me so hard, that the strap went right up here and it stuck out, the red. And I didn't say anything, I just, just the tears were welling up. He said, 'Go back in line.' So I was kind of like a hero, like with the kids after, like." But whether or not the boys cried, the punishment hurt. "So we were all smirking and whatever before we got the strap but we weren't smirking after. You know, everybody was hurting."[526]

Percy Tuesday.

To their frustration, some students were not able to convince their parents of the severity of the punishment at the schools. Noel Knockwood found it difficult to get his parents to believe that he and his fellow students were being harshly punished at Shubenacadie in the 1940s.

> And when we would tell our mothers and fathers and when, when Mother and Father will come and visit us on, on, on the Sunday, they usually have visiting days on Sunday, we would all go into the, the, to the room where we would meet and I would tell my mother and father that we seen some boys and some girls getting beaten. Some of them were whipped; some of them were beaten with a leather strap. And Mom and Dad, they always said, "Oh no, the priests and nuns wouldn't do that because they are the people of God." My mother and father were very strong Catholics.[527]

Faron Fontaine said he was not able to make his grandfather believe that the discipline at the Fort Alexander school was too strict. "He said, 'You guys probably deserve it,' he said. So, I quit trying to tell anybody. If you can't tell your own family, you know, they don't believe you, who, who is gonna believe you, especially when it comes to the priests and that? So that went on for a long time, man."[528]

Lena McKay thought she and the other children at the Fort Resolution school were treated roughly by the staff. "Our mother never did that to us, you know, pulling hair, ears, I seen a lot of that, and hitting. Seeing kids getting hit with a ruler, and some of them under the teacher's desk, a lot of them, I saw that." But she never complained about the treatment to her mother.

> She always said they're Sisters of Charity, and she tried to put that into our heads, like, they were doing all this for nothing, they were working for God, and whatever we did, you know, we're doing wrong, that's why they're punishing us, you know, 'cause

that's what they were told, too. And so, I always thought I was the bad one, bad one all the time, eh, even though it wasn't much that we did, you know.[529]

Students recalled that some staff members were clearly uncomfortable with the harsh disciplinary regimes that prevailed at so many schools. Eugene Tetreault was an Aboriginal man who worked as a boys' supervisor at the Fort Frances school. It was his job to discipline students who had been referred to him by one of the nuns at the school. He said, "It's not my thing to do that kind of work." He said he would tell boys, "'I'll take the slap, I'll, I'll slap on the, on, on my desk, and you scream.' And I'll say the boy was really happy about that, so I, I slap on the table, and the boy screamed 'Ow, ow, ouch!,' and that was the end of it."[530]

Eugene Tetreault.

Once, at the Anglican school in Onion Lake, Ula Hotonami was strapped by the laundry superintendent for joking with a student in the hallway. The principal encountered her shortly afterwards and asked her why she was crying. When she explained what happened, the principal told her to go into his office.

> And he put me in his office, and he had told me, "You wait there," and so I, I waited in his office. We were never allowed in his office, like, not, and he, he went down to the laundry room, and must have went and talked to her. Within two weeks she was gone, anyway. So, I don't know. His name was Mr. Card and that. And so he told me, "You can miss school 'til the swelling goes down." So, I was thinking what's going on here, like, you know, why, why do I have to miss school now? I can't go to work. I can't go to school. And so I asked him, "Well, what am I gonna do? Like, I have to go to school and that." And he told me, "Well just, you, you can't do anything, anyway. You can't hold anything in your hand," he said, "they're all swollen." Like, my hand was just puffed up, like, from the strapping that I got.[531]

Roger Cromarty said that at the Sioux Lookout school, different staff members were allowed to discipline students in different ways. While teachers might use a yardstick, dormitory supervisors used a strap.

> This would be a strap about one and half inches wide, quarter-inch thick and about twelve inches long, that they, those, they would use that on, on us boys either open hand, or in some cases if the principal is there, they would strap them in the bum, bare bum with, with the principal as a witness.

> Now when you got punished by, if the punishment was being done by the principal, he had a, a longer strap. That's about fifteen inches long, and it's an inch and a half wide, and a quarter-inch thick, and he was the one, he didn't have to have a witness.

I never saw him, when he hit me with it, he never, there was no witness, and you're supposed to have a witness.[532]

Strict discipline bred animosity. Roy Johnson said that at the Carcross school, students came to hate their supervisors.

But I remember hating. It's, it's, it's really something to behold to hate a person. You look them right in the eye, and say over and over, you know, you're going down last day, which means you can go to hell last day, over and over. Then when you're getting strapping, you keep, you try to keep that frame of mind burning, that hatred burning in, in you, until finally you can't take it anymore.

On one occasion, Johnson said, the older boys went on a "rampage" in response to the school discipline.

They were upstairs and downstairs, locked themself in the dormitory, or whatever, but the supervisor was chasing them, and the principal. And I was looking up from the playroom, and from the fire door, a tin garbage can came flying down, and got me here. I think a boy was taking off running. He was, he was hollering back, "Sorry, Roy." You know I was holding my head. I had Kleenex. I had to be taken to dispensary. I guess those, they were dealt with when they were all caught.

And there's another boy from here, fire hose was used on him. But his older brother would get in a fight with his, with the supervisor. They would fight up in the, up in the dormitory, they fight there, and then again in the kitchen. I think then again in the playroom. The kitchen one was sort of a ... whose who, who is tougher, I guess, I don't know. But that boy grab a pot of mashed potatoes, and just lift it up and put it over the supervisor's head, and they were fighting, wrestling around for a while. That's funny, it wasn't funny to me, but it was, you know it was, that's how life was there.[533]

Mollie Roy recalled fighting when a teacher at the girls' school in Spanish tried to punish her.

[The teacher] was tall, and she was mean, and she'd grab us by the cheeks, and just twist, just turn, and she'd do this every time. Well, I guess one day I was her victim, and that was the last time. She turned, she put her finger, and I bit on it, and bit it just about to the bone. There was blood pouring down. She was just freaking out. "Let go." And I kept shaking my head ... and that was the last time she ever touched anybody's cheeks. But we'd have big marks on our cheeks all the time.[534]

Larry Beardy recalled how, at the Dauphin school, the students eventually rebelled.

But one of the saddest things that I, I want to share is in the, in the dormitories we were in, young boys, we started to notice a lot of my colleagues running away, and, and every time somebody ran away, the whole dorm would get physically strapped by the principal of that school, and also the supervisors. And this kept continuing, and it escalated so bad, a eight-year-old, a nine-year-old, ten-year-old, we ransacked the whole dorm. We went violent.[535]

Abuse

"I thought that I was the only one that it was happening to."

The mandate of the Truth and Reconciliation Commission specifies that the Commissioners

> shall not name names in their events, activities, public statements, report or recommendations, or make use of personal information or of statements made which identify a person, without the express consent of that individual, unless that information and/or the identity of the person so identified has already been established through legal proceedings, by admission, or by public disclosure by that individual.[536]

In keeping with this instruction, this report does not identify or name alleged perpetrators of sexual or physical abuse. In instances where Survivors spoke of individuals who have been convicted of abuse, those names have been included.

While reports of sexual abuse were common, it was far from being the only type of abuse experienced by students. In many cases, a single student described many different types of abuse they experienced. Jean Pierre Bellemare, who attended the Amos, Québec, school, said he had been subjected to "physical violence, verbal violence, touchings, everything that comes with it."[537]

Andrew Yellowback was at the Cross Lake, Manitoba, school for eight years. "During that time, I was sexually, physically, emotionally, and mentally abused by both the sisters and brothers."[538] Some students were abused at more than one school.[539] Students reported assaults from staff members of both the opposite sex and the same sex as themselves.[540] For many students, abuse, fear, and violence dominated their school experience. Sheila Gunderson recalled there being "a lot of physical abuse and sexual abuse" at Lapointe Hall, the Roman Catholic hostel in Fort Simpson, Northwest Territories, in the 1960s.[541] Given the power relations in a residential school, no sexual relationship between a staff member and student could be considered consensual. Many former students spoke of having been raped at school.[542] Stella Marie Tookate, who attended the Fort Albany, Ontario, school, said, "I didn't enjoy myself when I was in school because I was too much abused. I didn't learn anything; that's what I was feeling."[543] Her words echo the experiences of many former students.

Stella Marie Tookate.

While some sexual abusers carefully recruited their victims, providing them with treats and small favours, others made use of threats and physical force. At the Fort Albany school, one of the lay brothers cornered Josephine Sutherland in the school garage.

> I couldn't call for help, I couldn't. And he did awful things to me, and I was just a little girl, not even thirteen years old yet, and he did something to me that the experience as having a horrible pain. You know he got me from the back, and he was holding me down with his, covering my mouth, and, you know, and, and I couldn't yell out. I was so stunned, I couldn't move, I couldn't.[544]

One former student said he was sexually abused by a staff member of the Blue Quills school when he was five years old. His abuser told him that if he did not submit, "he's gonna smack me, you know, he was gonna strap me."[545]

Marie Therese Kistabish said she was sexually abused in the church confessional at the Amos school. "The priest was there. He told me to kneel down. I knelt, and then he began to raise up his, his robes, his tunic, it was a long black tunic, and when he started to raise the tunic, I started shouting and crying, yelling, so he let me go."[546]

As a student at the Fort Frances school in the 1960s, Richard Morrison said, he was called into a change room by a staff member. Once he was in the room, a bag was put over his head and his clothes were removed.

> I remember that he had struggled with me really, really hard and I fought back and fought back and I don't know how long it was, I just fought and pretty soon he just, I don't know what he did, he had restrained me somehow. And when that happened, he had sexually abused me, he penetrated me and I was just, all I remember was just a pain. A pain was just strong. It was really hurtful and I remember that day after that I was a very, very angry kid.[547]

At the Qu'Appelle school, Raynie Tuckanow said, he witnessed staff committing sadistic acts of abuse.

> But I know what they did. I know what they did to me and I know what they did to others, too. Looking up here, just like that up here, I watched the young man. They tied him. And I know him today, I see him today. They tied him by his ankles and they tied him to the [heat] register and they put him out the window with a broomstick handle shoved up his ass. And I witnessed that.[548]

Leonard Peter Alexcee was abused at the Alberni school. The abuse began one night when a staff member tapped him on the shoulder and told him it was time for him to take a shower.

> Middle of the night. So, I thought that was one of the things going on there. I'll go back a bit. First morning, he woke us up about 6:30. Take us down to the playroom and this big, big guy. I was a small, very small, but you know and he start pushing me around, pushing me around, slapping me. "Come on! Let's fight," he said. "I'm the boss here." There was no kids in the playroom. They're all looking through the little

window outside, so I just fell down and cried, and cried, and cried. Finally, he left me alone. And then we went into the dining room.

Later, Leonard was told to take his clothes off. "The next thing I know he had all his clothes off too. He said, 'I'm gonna wash you.' He washed me down. He started fooling around with my part—private parts and then he took his—he took my hand and put it on his private parts. And then I started crying."[549]

In some cases, students said that discipline was mixed with sexual abuse. Mary Vivier told the Commission about her experience at the Fort Frances school.

> And there was a priest, I'm not sure what he, what he was, I don't know, but he was the head priest at the time, the principal, I don't what they call it. He had a chair. Whenever, whenever we were brought up to his office to get our strapping, he, there was chairs outside his office, and then there was, like, a leaning chair, I guess. It was low enough for us to, from here on down. He'd remove our, our unders, our pants, our underpants. He would strap us, and he would rub us, saying. "You shouldn't have done that, you shouldn't have done this." Another strap, another fondling. Where, where I was, we were exposed. I think I was, when I was younger, I only got five, but as I grew older I got more and more.[550]

Donna Antoine was exposed to ongoing harassment from a staff member at one of the Roman Catholic schools she attended in the interior of British Columbia.

> He was [the] maintenance person, he would come over, and he, he would stand in my way. He did that for a while, and then he just, and other times he would tap me on the backside, and that felt very uncomfortable. And then when I was go, when I'd go by, 'cause he'd stand right by the table and we had to squeeze by him in a little, little area, he made sure that he stood in the way, and he grabbed me by the backside. And so I told my sister about it. I was afraid to tell the sister because she might think I was an evil person; I didn't want to displease her. So and the next time, he, he found me carrying up a load of laundry in my hands, going up the stairs, and then he took that opportunity to put his hands between my legs. And I thought why, why is that happening? What did I do to deserve to be treated like this?[551]

Female students spoke of how some staff members took advantage of their innocence, rubbing against them sexually while they were sitting on their laps.[552] Vitaline Elsie Jenner said that a bishop used to seat children on his lap when he visited the Fort Chipewyan school.

> I just went and sat on his lap, but when I sat on his lap, he, he was holding me, you know, holding me around like that, and pressing me against his, his penis, and, you know, like, kind of like moving me up and down, and I could feel, like, a hardness of his penis underneath my bottom, and I didn't know what to do. I became scared.[553]

Louisa Papatie said that at the Amos school, the head of the school once summoned her upstairs. "'Come.' That's what she said, 'Come with me.' She gave me a, a kiss on the mouth.

And at one point she started caressing my back, and I fought back, and I tried to get away, but I didn't have the strength, because I was just a child, and she was bigger than me."[554]

Ricky Kakekagumick said that one of the supervisors at the Poplar Hills, Ontario, school used to invite him into his room every weekend.

> When he would start changing, taking his church clothes off, he kept his underwear on though. He would just stand there only in his underwear, every Sunday that was me in there. I didn't like being in there. I was so uncomfortable. It's a smaller room, just enough for his bed to fit and a drawer and a chair. So every Sunday I had to go in there. I felt violated, I was so uncomfortable. I didn't, like he liked me being in there, him standing there, 'cause he didn't put his pants back on right away, he just stands there, talks to me, in his underwear. He made me feel uncomfortable, 'cause usually you can see the bulginess of, of that underwear. I think he was getting his thrills like that. I don't know if he wanted, I don't know if he wanted to violate me, physically. I just kept on ignoring him, try and look away. That still bugs me this day.[555]

Students recalled being humiliated because staff, sometimes of the opposite sex, would watch them when they showered. In some cases, they say, staff members would touch them inappropriately at these times.[556] Doris Judy McKay said that at the Birtle, Manitoba, school, the principal would come into the girls' shower area. "And then we'd have our, we'd go and have our showers, and when we were in the shower, he'd come there, walk around, check us out, and as we try and hide ourselves we'd crouch into a corner of the shower and try and hide, and he'd be walking around there, check, just back and forth, checking us out."[557]

Doris Judy McKay.

At the Beauval school in Saskatchewan, Mervin Mirasty was told to take a lunch pail to a priest's room. He had not been warned that boys who were sent on such errands were likely to be abused, as Mirasty was in this instance. When he returned, he felt that boys who knew what had happened to him were mocking him. "The boys looked at me, and some of the older ones, they were all smiling." He warned his own brother to never take the lunch pail to the priest. "And to this day, I don't know why he didn't listen to me, like, he, he went up there I guess the next day, or soon after, he come back crying."[558]

Students were particularly vulnerable when they were alone. Flora Northwest said that she was victimized by both staff and fellow students at the Hobbema, Alberta, school. To protect herself, she said, "I always tried to make sure that I was not alone. I'd try not to be alone."[559] Aaron Leon said he was abused by supervisors at the Mission, British Columbia, school. The abuse generally took place on the weekends when there were fewer students and staff at the school.[560]

Certain dormitory supervisors used their authority to institute dormitory-wide systems of abuse. Arthur Plint was eventually convicted for abuses he committed while he was a dormitory supervisor at the Alberni, British Columbia, school. Richard Hall was one of his victims. According to Hall, Plint coerced a group of older students into assisting him in imposing a regime of abuse upon the rest of the students in the dormitory.

> And there's times when that, the bullies, I called them goons, I called them. They chased me, get me and bring me to that pedophile so he could molest me, have his way with me. And you would live in constant fear. You'd watch for these guys all the time. You'd be running all the time because I was in a group of boys that I was one of the smaller, a runt of the boys, I guess you would say but I was aggressive. And that's probably one of the reasons they moved me really quick because I was aggressive. I did learn to be aggressive. And times, at night, these boys under his thumb would get their ways and do things to the kids. I could hear the kids and those fears were also in me that you'd be urinated on and they had an ointment called Winter Green that they used to put, at night, used to reach under the blankets of the young boys and wipe it all over their genitals and it would burn. And if you added water it will burn even more, and they laughed about it. They got what they wanted. If the dorm was punished these boys got the food, they got to do what they want. And for some of the behaviours, Plint, I think also gave them alcohol. These boys would also in the night travel to other dorms. I know because they asked me to be part of it but it wasn't in my nature.

The experience of abuse changed his life immediately. "I went home for the summer. I went home a different person back to Bella Coola for the summer. I was twelve years old. At twelve years old I began drinking alcohol to forget."[561]

Frances Tait was also sexually abused by staff and students at the Alberni school. In this case, several supervisors might have been involved in the abuse.

> I was taken out night after night after night. And that went on until I was about twelve years old. And it was several of the male supervisors plus a female. And it was in the dorm; it was in their room; it was in the carport; it was in his car; it was in the gym; the back of the crummy that took us on road trips; the public school; the change room.[562]

Abuse often took place at night, when supervisors might summon a student to join them in their room or a private location. Many students spoke of the fear and anxiety that spread across many dormitories in the evenings. Timothy Henderson, who attended school in Manitoba, said he recalled the tension he felt lying in bed. "I know nobody was sleeping, 'cause he hadn't picked anybody yet. So you'd be under your covers; I know I was. You know right under them. I could hear light footsteps."[563]

At night in the Sioux Lookout dormitory, Nellie Ningewance said, "the supervisor would sneak in, in the dark; take one of the students out. I'd freeze when they would come in; wondering if I was going to be the next one. I was never able to go to sleep. Wondering where they were taking her; what was happening. Then she would come in by, then the student would come in by herself."[564]

Students were particularly vulnerable to abusive staff members who sought to win their trust through what initially appeared to be simple kindness. Marlene Kayseas recalled that at the school she attended, the principal began focusing extra attention on her. "I don't remember if he did that to other kids, but he used to let me stay up when they used to have movies, sometimes, if the sister was in a good mood, I guess. We watched a movie on TV and if the kids, some kids went to bed, if they didn't listen they were sent to bed." This favouritism, however, was the prelude to a sexual assault that left her scared and confused. "'Why is my friend doing this to me?' I trusted him. And I just started to feel really, not good."[565]

Andrew Captain recalled being well treated by a female staff member at a school in northern Manitoba. Having won his trust, she would order him into a room and demand sexual attention. "I thought that's how much she cared for me in a different way, but I didn't know it was coming in the wrong way.... This kept on for a long time. But like I said, I didn't know if it was right or wrong."[566]

Shortly after one student's arrival at the Chapleau school, one of the staff members became closely attentive to his needs, encouraging him in sports and telling him to let him know if anyone was bothering him. One night, this particular staff member escorted the student into a small room and hugged him. In later encounters, the staff member attempted to fondle him.[567]

Fred Brass said that on one occasion at the Roman Catholic school at Kamsack, Saskatchewan, a nun, who he thought was consoling him after he had been beaten up by other students, "made me put my hands down her panties and made me feel her up and this went on for a long, long time. That was supposed to be the one that was supposed to comfort me and help me. But she used me in that way for her own self-gratitude."[568]

Elaine Durocher recalled that the staff at the same school took advantage of the children's simplest needs to coerce them into sexual activities.

> And then after church, there was a little canteen in the church, and the priest would sell us candies. Well, after they got to know us, they started making us touch their penis for candy. So not only were we going to church to pray, and go to catechism, but we were also going to church 'cause they were giving us candy for touching them. We didn't have money.[569]

According to John B. Custer, one abusive staff member at the Roman Catholic school near The Pas "would give us little gifts, like bananas and oranges, and I had no choice but take them, because we were always hungry."[570] At the Blue Quills school, Louise Large said, students were sexually abused by staff who offered them money to buy candy.[571]

Shortly after Ben Pratt started attending the Gordon's, Saskatchewan, school, the residence supervisor, William Starr, asked him if he wanted to work in the school canteen. He agreed, since it was a way of making some extra spending money. However, after a short time on the job, he was invited into Starr's office.

> And I remember after that evening, he took me into his office, and there was about five or six of us boys in there, and he started touching us boys. Some would leave, and some would come back, some would leave and come back when we're watching TV in, in the back of his office. He had a couch in there, and a TV. And we'd all get ready to go to bed, and he made me stay back. And at that time, I didn't know what was gonna happen. I was sitting there, and I was wondering how come I had to stay back, and I was watching TV there, and then he start touching me, and between my legs, and he pulled my, my pyjamas down. And the experience that I went through of him raping me, and I cried, and I yelled, but it didn't do any good, 'cause he shoved the rag in my mouth, and he was much stronger than me, he held me down, and the pain and the yelling that I was screaming why are you doing that to me, there was no one to help me. I felt helpless. And after he finished doing what he did to me, he sent me back to my room, and I was in so much pain I couldn't even hardly walk, and I could feel this warm feeling running down the back of my leg on my pyjamas and on my shorts. And I went to the washroom. I tried to clean myself up. This was blood.

Starr organized a variety of extracurricular clubs to justify taking students on field trips. According to Pratt:

> We went all, all over, Saskatchewan, and dancing powwow, and going boxing, be different places, cadets, but it still continued to happen. As we were travelling in the vehicle, we always had big station wagons, or a van, and he fondled us boys. All of us boys knew what was happening, but none of us ever spoke about it, or shared anything what happened to us. We were too ashamed, too, too scared.[572]

Percy Isaac, who also lived in the Gordon's residence, recalled how Starr would first win the confidence of the students he intended to abuse.

> Like paying us off, paying us off when we worked the canteen. Paying us off when we'd work the bingo. Paying us off to do any kind of things which he had. Like he had a boat, he had skidoos, he had all these different kind of gadgets, cars, let us drive cars when we were underage, we were driving a car.

He too recalled how field trips were both rewards and opportunities for abuse. "Abused, abused in hotels, motels, all over the damn place. Toronto, Ottawa, you name it. Finland, went to Finland, got abused over there, you know. I was just constantly abused, sexually abused from this man. It was horrible."[573]

In 1993, Starr was convicted of ten counts of sexually assaulting the Gordon's residence students.[574]

Most students came to school with little knowledge or understanding of sexual activity, let alone the types of sexual abuse to which they might be subjected. As a result, their experiences were not only painful and humiliating, but they were also bewildering. Eric

Robinson said, "As a little boy, you don't know a whole lot. When you are a five-year-old boy and you are placed in this place, and the priest takes a liking to you, and then things start happening, and then you don't realize it at that age, but you are being sexually abused, in fact, you are being raped."[575]

Many students thought they were the only children being abused. Clara Quisess said she was abused by a staff person at the Fort Albany school.

> There was no support, no one to tell that this is all happening in this building. A lot of girls must have experienced it, what the priest was doing and you're not to tell anybody. I always hate that priest and then I had to live like that for two years, even though I didn't want to. It's like I had no choice, put myself in that situation. Him, putting his hand underneath my dress, feeling me up, I felt so disgusted. Even though I didn't have no words for what I was feeling.[576]

This confusion made it difficult for students to describe or report their abuse. Lynda Pahpasay McDonald said she was sexually molested by a staff member of the Roman Catholic school in Kenora.

> And this woman, what she did to me, and how she molested me as a child, and I was wondering why I'll be the only one being taken to this room all the time, and to her bedroom and stuff like that. And I thought it was normal. I thought it was, you know, this is what happened, like, to everybody, so I never said nothing.[577]

Helen Harry did not speak to other students about being abused at the Williams Lake school. "I thought that I was the only one that it was happening to. I always felt like it was just me."[578]

Abusers often told their victims never to speak of what had happened. Larry Roger Listener, who was abused when he attended residential school in Alberta, said a priest told him that "'God's going to punish you if you say anything.' I always fear God. All these years I never said anything. I still kind of fear God because I never forgot what that priest told me. He going to punish me."[579] Mary Vivier, who was abused at the Fort Frances school, was told she would "be in purgatory" for the rest of her life if she spoke of her abuse.[580] The staff member who sexually abused Elisabeth Ashini at the Sept-Îles, Québec, school, told her she could never speak of what he had done to her. He said "'You have to keep it to yourself, because little Jesus will be angry, he won't be happy.'" As a result, she did not report the abuse.[581]

In some cases, school officials took immediate action when abuse was reported to them. Norman Courchene said he was sexually abused by a supervisor while he was on a field trip from the Fort Alexander school. When he told the principal about the abuse, the supervisor was fired.[582]

For many other children, however, the abuse was compounded by the disbelief they met when they spoke about what had been done to them. Amelia Galligos-Thomas said she was sexually abused by a staff member at the Sechelt, British Columbia, school. "I didn't know it was wrong. I always thought I did wrong, so I didn't tell people right away. So, I held it in. I just went to the dorm and cleaned up."

Eventually, she told a staff member she trusted, who arranged for her to see a doctor. "But nothing got done because no one would believe me or her. So, that went on for years of me being sexually assaulted."[583]

When he went home for the Christmas break, Ivan George told his father he was being abused at the Mission school. "And he'd say, 'What did he do? What he'd been doing to you?' And I told him, 'He was kind of drunk.' He says, 'No, you're going back. You're just making that up just to stay out of there.'" The following year, he ran away and refused to be sent back to the school. "I never did return ... and I was glad of it. I was put into foster homes, group homes after that. I didn't go back."[584]

When Dorothy Jane Beaulieu told an aunt she had been abused by a priest at the Fort Resolution school, she was told, "'Don't make up stories. You're just making it up. They work for God, and they can't do things like that.'"[585]

Lorna Morgan said she was sexually molested by a female staff member at the Presbyterian school in Kenora. The molestation took place at night, when the staff member would take her into the school dispensary. When she tried to tell her family about the abuse, she was told, "'Don't talk about people like that, that are looking after you, you know. You shouldn't say stuff like that, you know.'"[586]

In Ben Pratt's case, a laundry worker at the Gordon's residence realized that something was wrong and asked him what had happened. Pratt initially resisted telling her, but then he explained how William Starr had abused him. "The look on her face she was angry, but she never said nothing."

When he was an adult, Pratt told his mother about the abuse that he and other students were being subjected to at Gordon's.

> And she screamed, and she started crying, and I continued telling her what was happening when I was there. And the look on her face, the anger and the rage that came out of her, she screamed and yelled, and she went quiet for a long time, and this is the first time I ever had talked to my mother. She went calm for about fifteen, twenty minutes. And she said, "My boy," she said, "the school I went to, when I was a young girl," she said, "I, too, was sexually abused," she said, "by the fathers." And I asked her, "What school did you go to, Mom?" She said, "St. Philips." I didn't know where it was. And the things she told me that happened to her as a girl, from the fathers that run the school or worked there, the anger that came up inside me was so painful. I bent over, and I couldn't sit up straight, how much anger and rage I had inside when she was telling me what happened. We talked for a good half-hour to an hour, me and my mother. Then it's the first time I ever heard my mom tell me "I love you, my boy."[587]

Some students never reported abuse for fear they would not be believed. Michael Muskego said he was sexually abused by a staff member at the Roman Catholic residential school near The Pas in the 1960s. "I couldn't say anything, I couldn't tell the priest or the police 'cause if I did, the priest won't believe me."[588]

In some cases, students who reported abuse were told that they were to blame. Josephine Sutherland started attending the Fort Albany, Ontario, school in the late 1950s. After being attacked by a male staff member on several occasions, she went to speak to one of the nuns who worked at the school. "I told her something just happened to me, somebody did something to me, and she said, 'You must have been bad again.'"[589]

Shortly after he was enrolled at the Sturgeon Lake school in Calais, Alberta, Jimmy Cunningham was sexually assaulted. When he told one of the nuns what had been done to him, he was strapped for lying.

> I told the sister what happened. She didn't believe me. She strapped me for lying.
> So, I went to see the priest, Father Superior ... and he says there's nothing he could
> do. Sent me back to the boys' hall and then the first thing you know the phone rang.
> The old crank phones. The sister answered it and it was Father telling her that I had
> been there complaining about what happened. She immediately took me again and
> strapped me again for doing that without her permission.[590]

Others simply felt too ashamed to ever speak of the abuse. One of the supervisors at the Assiniboia school in Winnipeg attempted to rape Violet Rupp Cook in the school gymnasium. She was able to beat him back, but the event left her shaken. "I didn't know what to do. I was, I was afraid, I was just shaking, I went, I went back to the dorms. I didn't tell anybody I was so, I felt so ashamed. I didn't tell my supervisor, I didn't tell anyone. I didn't tell any of the girls that were there." From then on, she was always afraid and unable to concentrate on her school work.[591]

Violet Rupp Cook.

Elizabeth Good said she was abused during her years at the Alberni school. "I won't get into detail about the abuse, because it was so violent. I had three abusers, two men and one woman. I was also the youngest one in the residential school at the time." She wondered if that was one of the reasons she was targeted by one of the abusers. "There was a couple of occasions where he had mentioned that I was the baby in the residential school, and he always told me that I was gonna be a no good for nothing squaw. All I'll be good, good for is having babies, and they're gonna be worthless, and he is so wrong today."[592]

To the extent that they could, many students tried to protect themselves and others from abuse. At the Gordon's school in Saskatchewan, the older children tried to protect the younger ones from abuse at the hands of the dormitory staff. Hazel Mary Anderson recalled, "Sometimes you'd get too tired to stay up at night to watch over them so nobody bothers them 'cause these workers would, especially night workers would bother the younger kids. The younger kids' dorms were next to the older girls' dorms."[593]

Peter Ross said that a staff member of the Roman Catholic school in Aklavik attempted to sexually abuse him when he attended the school in the 1940s. "It just happened a couple of times with me, but I stayed away from the, the lay brother that was trying to bother me, but he never got anywhere with me. Because a lot of my friends were there for me and I was there for them. And we sort of looked after one another."[594]

Some students ran away from school in an attempt to escape sexual abuse. Hazel Mary Anderson and her sister found the atmosphere so abusive at the Gordon's school that they ran away so often that they were transferred to the Lestock school.[595] Wayne Reindeer was abused while attending the Roman Catholic hostel in Inuvik. He had been placed in residential school by his family because his mother was ill and his father could not care for all his children. He ran away from the school several times. On one occasion, he returned to the family home in Inuvik. "I hid under the house for two days and my sisters fed me, until the hostel contacted my father and he said, 'Wayne has been missing.' And my dad found out from my sisters and he dragged me back, kicking and screaming all the way. I wanted to stay home."[596]

Students also fought back. Ken A. Littledeer was sexually abused by Leonard Hands, a member of the staff of the Sioux Lookout school. Initially, he submitted to the abuse because he feared Hands "might get mad, and hit me, and spank me, or something like that, or punish me." But when Hands approached him a second time, Littledeer punched him and ran away.[597]

Sphenia Jones said that when a staff member attempted to abuse her one night, she fought back.

> I grabbed her, and I, boom, I went like that to her, and she went flying, and then all the kids in the dormitory woke up when I started screaming. She crawled back out the door, and she didn't come back in the dormitory for, gee, for maybe a week or two after that, right, but she never bothered me again.[598]

Many of those who fought back were overpowered. Lawrence Waquan said that he was sexually abused by male and female staff at a residential school in northern Alberta. He told the Commission that he eventually concluded, "Nothing you can do. You can say no, and the more you fight back, she'd slap you over and over again. Finally, you can't cry, you know, you are shaken, scared."[599]

In some cases, students fought back en masse. At the Edmonton, Alberta, school, students deliberately barred the doors to the dormitory in order to stop the abuse during the nights. Mel H. Buffalo said he was one of the organizers of the protest. He told the Commission about how the students had

> backed up the, the ... dressers that were full of clothes and stuff, and put it against the entrance to the dorm, and at 4:30 in the morning the people were, I guess they were

doing the checks, couldn't ... couldn't open the door. And this time they were really furious. They got the bigger boys from the other areas to come help them try to break down the door, but they couldn't.

Eventually, he said, the police were called.

We threw our shoes and stuff out at them, and yelled ... some guys knew how to swear, I didn't, they were swearing at everybody. We threw a list of demands down to the principal; we wrote on there that we wanted better food, we wanted certain staff people fired that we were suspicious of, and we wanted our clothes back that we came with when we, we got to school. Because they confiscated all our clothes and gave us government-issued clothes ... we finally decided, well we better do, what needs to be done.

When the protest ended, he was called into the principal's office. "I went down to see the principal, and to my surprise there was my grandfather, sitting there. And the principal said, 'Mr. Buffalo, your son is here ... we can't handle him, we'd appreciate it if you could take him back, and good luck in raising him.'"[600]

Student victimization of students
"You had to watch out."

Statements from former students from across the country indicate that student victimization of other students was a common problem. The statements highlight the difficulties that some students had in getting staff to address bullying, and help explain why other students did not raise the issue with staff. In their statements, many former students recalled how bullies contributed to the atmosphere of fear and violence that prevailed at many of the schools.

William Garson recalled that at the Elkhorn, Manitoba, school, "we were always like hiding in the corners; you know away from any abusement. From other, older, from older, elder boys, students."[601] Percy Thompson said that at the Hobbema, Alberta, school, "one bully used to come at me and he'd pretend he was going to talk to me and all of sudden hit me in the belly. And of course I gag, gag, and he'd laugh his head off and, you know, to see me in such a predicament."[602] Alice Ruperthouse spoke of "the cruelty of the other children" at the Amos, Québec, school. "It was, you know, like in a jungle. Like in a jungle, you don't know what's going to come out but you know you had to watch out."[603] Albert Elias felt that the classroom at the Anglican school in Aklavik "was the safest place to be in 'cause that's where nobody could beat me up. I dreaded recesses and lunches and after school, I dreaded those times."[604]

Bullying might start shortly after arrival. In some schools, all new male students were put through a hazing. Denis Morrison gave the following description of arrival at the Fort Frances school.

> It's almost like every kid that came in, the new kid that came in, like, you almost had, that's like being a new, they call us new fish, eh, the new fish and coming into the tank. They used to initiate you, like, they would beat the hell out of you, the other kids would. It wasn't anybody else, it was the other kids, the older ones, eh. It's like they, it was like the normal thing to happen. You were the one that had to get beat up now, eh, and so you, you went through the getting beat up.[605]

Denis Morrison.

Timothy Henderson said that the boys at the Fort Alexander school were forced to fight.

If you didn't fight, someone fought you. And the loser was always put in a steel locker, the kind you have in high schools, even university, but they were long, like, they're not, they weren't half a locker, they were a full locker. So, the older people, I know who they are, would pick who was fighting today. And you'd be in the bathroom, in the basement, every day. Let's say you won your last three fights, maybe you, you weren't picked that day, 'cause maybe your hands were sore, or where you, you had some bruising. But I can remember staff coming in and out of there just to kind of make sure that no one was getting seriously hurt, but I knew they knew.[606]

In some cases, the schools encouraged these fights. Joseph Maud recalled that at the school at Pine Creek, Manitoba, students were forced to fight one another.

It seems to me that there was also a lot of boxing, like, boxing matches between the boys. We had to box against another boy, and, you know, until one of us cried. So, I don't know if that's, like it just seemed like I, I picked up some of those habits from, from that supervisor. It seemed like he liked that. He got a kick out of watching another boy beat up another boy, just like that, you know that, there's a word they call that, like being kind of, like, sadistic, like enjoying pain, inflicting pain, and you know, like, you were the loser, you know, of course he would be crying. And I know I lost my, my share of, of boxing matches. And you know, like, and no-body could really help you. Like, sure, my brothers were there, and 'cause I know they were made to fight, too, other boys, so it was like a no-win situation. Even if you did win, just like, just like another boy would challenge you anyway, like, if you did win your fight, and just, like the supervisor liked that, and he enjoyed it, you know, watching boys pound each other, give each, give each other bleeding noses, or making each other cry. It almost seemed like that, that supervisor enjoyed that, and it almost seemed like I picked up some of those habits later on in my life.[607]

Joseph Maud.

Bob Baxter recalled that there were student gangs at the Sioux Lookout school. He was beaten up and knifed on one occasion. He had a vivid memory of people tying him to his bed and throwing hot water over him.[608] Clara Quisess said that at the Fort Albany school in Ontario, older girls would threaten the younger ones with knives.[609] Louisa Birote recalled that the girls at the La Tuque, Québec, school all formed themselves into hostile groups. "We hated each other. So, this little gang didn't like the other gang. That's the way at the school, that's what we were taught, fears, and we were scared, and I went to hide in what we called the junk room, the junk closet."[610]

Such violence bred violence. David Charleson said that at the Christie, British Columbia, school, the students were "learning how to hurt each other."[611] Students were quickly hardened by the violent atmosphere of the schools. Victoria McIntosh said the Fort Alexander school reminded her of a "prison yard."

> If you didn't have older siblings to protect you, you're on your own, so you learned how to, to fight, anger, and not trusting anybody, and just being hard, you know, and you weren't gonna cry, and if you cried then that was not a good thing, and it was a sign of being weak. But I always felt, like, inside that I hated, I hated all of that. I never wanted to intentionally hurt anybody.[612]

To survive at schools in northern Ontario in the 1960s, one former student said she made herself "tough" and began "picking on those younger than me." She said she was "trying to look out for me since nobody else was."[613]

At school in Prince Albert, Saskatchewan, Leona Bird grew up fearful and angry.

> They are girls from Manitoba, girls from different places. They weren't too friendly with me. I learned to fight. The hatred that built up in me, I learned to fight my way out of everything that I can, whether a beating or not, I didn't care, as long as I fought back. That's how hatred was building up so big there inside my whole body. I couldn't do nothing.[614]

Louise Large described herself as "the leader of the pack" at the Blue Quills school.

> Nobody could bother the Crees, or … they would have to deal with me. And so I ended up, I beat anybody. And it came to the point where the boys would try and, you know, even when we started playing with the boys slowly, but even the boys would come fight with us, and I, and I would always beat them all up.[615]

Don Willie said that the Alert Bay school had a bully system. "It started out with the senior boys, and it just worked its way right down." He said he "used to get punched every day by one of them." Eventually, he fought back.

> I end up fighting him back, and then he's saying, "No, the only reason you're fighting is the girls are watching." And so all the girls rushed to the window when we started fighting. But I said, "Okay, well let's go upstairs and fight then." So, we went upstairs, and he just backed right off, but he didn't bother me again after that, and I thought one of the other bullies were gonna come after me, but they didn't, so. But it was that system that, I don't know, kind of really bothered me after, and I know it bothered my brother.[616]

Mary Stoney recalled being bullied in residential school in Alberta. "We were so afraid of them we didn't dare report them. Until one day a group of us girls got together, took them on verbally, we put them in their place in a good way. A group of girls fell apart, the bullying stopped. This incident made me angry for years."[617]

During her early years at the Lestock school, Geraldine Shingoose and other young girls were attacked by older girls. "When I got into the senior dormitory, we, we got those girls, we got them back, and they stopped, they stopped doing that to us, and we got all the, some older girls too, to go after them, and they stopped doing that to us."[618]

In their statements, former students rarely made reference to attempts to report episodes of bullying to the school administration. The statements of those who did make such reports suggest that they found it difficult to get staff to believe them, or take them seriously. Eva Bad Eagle, for example, felt she was not believed when she reported the abuse to the staff.[619]

Janet Murray had a similar experience at the same school.

> I thought here I would have an easy life but the kids picked on me and abused me. So where the little kids were between seven and five years old, that's where I was. That's where I was placed. And the supervisor was old, very old. He couldn't look after us, so he asked these two seniors to come look after us, help us out. Comb my hair and to teach us how to make our beds, I guess. And that's when the abuse started.... There were three of us, and things were always done to us. Seniors. These girls—young women—were big that came there to look after us. They combed our hair. I don't know if it's a wire brush or something. They used to hit us on the head like this until we had scabs. We had to have a brush cut because we had scabs all over our heads. And when we went to school, the boys, young men laughed at us because we had bald heads. Sometimes they stabbed us in the face, and we had bruises but they say we were so clumsy they said we banged our face into the wall, that's what they said. And one time they came and woke us up in the middle of the night. They told us to take our panties off. They told us to spread our legs and they used that brush between our legs and they even put a cloth in our mouths so we couldn't yell or cry. For two weeks we couldn't go to school because we couldn't walk. There were scars all over there. Sometimes they would come to our bed and spread our legs just to see what damage they had done to us, and they'd laugh like if it's funny.

When she tried to get help, she was punished again. "But that time I couldn't talk English. Even now. I was trying to speak for myself. Talking Cree I was trying to tell the supervisor. Instead I was hit for talking Cree."[620]

The most important source of protection against bullying was another family member. Daniel Nanooch was bullied and beaten by other students at the Wabasca, Alberta, school.

> Everybody was fighting me, beating me up because I was alone I had no brothers ... everybody else had their brothers with them but I had nobody there to protect me So I was fighting, I was getting beat up so when I think back as a little child in the mission, I remember all those crying for somebody to see they're getting beat up by the nuns, or by the other kids, because they knew I was there alone so they could hit me and there was nobody to protect me.[621]

Eva Bad Eagle felt protected by her older sister at the Brocket, Alberta, school. When her sister left, she said, other students began to abuse her.[622]

When Gordon Keewatin attended the Portage la Prairie and Birtle schools in Manitoba, he depended on his brother to protect him from school bullies. He said that "the next thing I knew there were older boys there that used to, used to pick on the younger ones, and I was starting to get picked on. But I always ran to my brother, always looked for him, especially if somebody come and start poking me."

In later years, he looked after his younger brother. He gave him the same advice his older brother had given him: "not to ask questions, and to just go with the flow, to follow orders, do what he was told. I told him I'd protect him if he, somebody tried to fight him or whatever."[623]

Students could not always protect their siblings. In some cases, all they could do was watch them being bullied and humiliated. Mary Rose Julian remembered seeing her brother bullied at the Shubenacadie school.

> And one time I was working in, in the refectory, I was cleaning up in there, and I saw my brother cornered. There was about four, four or five boys, you know, that cornered him in there. There was the chapel and the, the refectory, and he was cornered, and I went like this, you know, I was gonna see him getting beat, he got, he was getting beaten up, and he was just cornered, and these guys were going after him. All of a sudden, I saw somebody grab those boys and throw them off one by one, and they scattered, and he went and picked up my brother, and when he turned around, I recognized him, it was Albert Marshall from Eskasoni. He was, like, friends from our same community, eh. And oh, my God, I was relieved, and I was there screaming, and I was going like this, you know, you know I was just screaming inside, I couldn't do nothing, helpless and everything. I didn't want my brother in, in that kind of situation.[624]

In some situations, students were obliged to punish their siblings. Harvey Behn recalled how students who ran away from the Lower Post, British Columbia, school were forced to run the 'gauntlet.' He said that

> for you people that don't understand what the gauntlet is, it's a row of people standing with weapons in their hands, their fists clenched and the offending students were made to run through this group of people and get hit and get beat. And if they didn't participate, then they were forced to run through this gauntlet. So I, myself, was made to run through and was hit and beaten and my brother ran through it and I had to hit him and I had to beat him.[625]

In some schools, there were conflicts between students who came from different communities and First Nations. Roger Cromarty said that at the Sioux Lookout school, students from one First Nation dominated the others. Those who dominated made other students bring them extra food.[626] Louise Large recalled how at the Blue Quills school, "we used to fight, the Chipewyans and the Crees."[627] Students from the same communities often stuck together. Of her time at the Moose Factory, Ontario, school in the 1960s, Nellie Trapper recalled that students at the school came from communities from all over northern Ontario and Québec. In the face of bullying at the school, students from the same community would stick together.[628]

At Stringer Hall, the Anglican residence in Inuvik, Angus Havioyak said, he was physically abused by both fellow students and residents of Inuvik. He fought back.

> At the same time, I was abused by an Indian for who I am. I'm an Inuk, and they're the Indians, and they go against me for some reason. They tease me, tease me for who I am. So, I tried my best, you know, not to be scared anymore, so I grabbed his neck. I was tired of his, his bullshit and that, and his buddy standing around us. I grabbed his neck and put him down, and I got a scar yet from that, I still have it right now.[629]

There could also be conflicts between students who lived in different residences in the same community. Allen Kanayok also lived in the Anglican Stringer Hall in Inuvik. He said he was sexually assaulted by a group of boys from Grollier Hall, the Roman Catholic residence.[630]

Les Carpenter also lived at Stringer Hall. He described it as "a hierarchical society and you had to exist, function and survive within that society itself. And, for the most part, we made it through." What did stand out in his mind was the religious animosity that was instilled in the students: "I was taught to hate Catholics." This created problems for him, since his best friend from his home community was Catholic. "When we got home in the summer after not having any kind of relationship through the ten months, it was hard to come together again and be friends again."[631] Paul Andrew, who lived in the Roman Catholic Grollier Hall, recalled things from the other side of the religious divide: that students were taught to dislike Anglicans. He related a friend's recollection: "'We'd go to Grollier Hall,' she said, 'and then by the springtime when we're going back on the same plane, those cousins of ours, we hated them, we didn't talk to them all the way back home because they were Catholics and we were not,' you know?"[632]

Alphonsine McNeely used to try to talk to the students from the Anglican school at Aklavik when those children went for walks near the Catholic school she attended. "The sister used to tell me they're evil, they're no good, they're not Catholics, and they're no good. And, and then they used to get some of the girls to throw rocks or whatever at them. They taught us hate, to, to hate other religion."[633]

Edwin F. Jebb.

Edwin F. Jebb said that when he was growing up in The Pas, there was ongoing hostility between Roman Catholic and Anglican Aboriginal children. When the students returned to the nearby residential school in the fall, they told the Oblates who operated the school that they had been picked on by the Anglican children. "They told us, 'My child, or my children, get on your knees,' they said. So we got on our knees, I didn't know what was going to happen. They said, 'Pray for them, they're going to hell.'"[634]

In some cases, students were able to overcome these barriers. Martina Therese Fisher went to the Assiniboia residence in Winnipeg in the 1970s. She was the only student from the Bloodvein Reserve at the school.

> I was harassed by these students from up north; they were from God's Lake. And they said, "You're not going to, you won't be able to stay here one year." And I said, "Why?" And they said, "We chased all the Saulteaux girls away before you came." But because they said that to me I made up my mind, 'I'm going to stick it out here this year.'

She did and, eventually, she and the other girls became friends.[635]

Noel Starblanket said that at the Qu'Appelle school, he and his friends would have to "give this bully our bread, or our butter, or whatever, that, that was our payment to him for not bullying us, and, and then we'd eat whatever we had left then."[636] Dorothy Ross said that at the Presbyterian school in Kenora in the 1960s, the older students "would take our candies, whatever you had, food, candies, chocolate bars. We weren't allowed. We had to pass them on to the bigger, the older. Or if you had money, they would take that money from you."[637]

Lydia Ross recalled being bullied by older students at the Cross Lake, Manitoba, school. She said the bullies would "take everything away. They'd hit you on your back as you were walking." If a student did not obey them, "you'd get hit, anyway, or pull your hair, or taking your belongings, your barrettes, or from your petticoat pocket. So, they were mean older girls that were there."[638]

Some bullies demanded money, rather than food. Isaac Daniels said that at the Prince Albert school, an older boy robbed him of money that was intended for his sick brother. "He said, 'You got any money?' I said, 'No.' 'Let me see it,' he said. 'No,' I said, 'I don't have no money.' Well, he beat the heck out of me, threw me down right in the washroom there, took my wallet, took all my money."[639]

In other cases, students sought protection from bullies by giving treats to older boys. Gordon Keewatin, who attended schools in Manitoba, turned over his oranges in exchange for such protection.[640]

At the Beauval, Saskatchewan, school, an older boy was assigned by the school to help Albert Fiddler adapt to the school. However, the boy soon insisted that Albert give him his dessert at dinner.

> So, I had to go out there, and sneak, and give him my, my sweet stuff, yeah, that's how I was paying him for that. That's how they were, they were doing that I guess. They had this little racket going on that they were, they get all the dessert from the small boys, or otherwise they will, like, it was more of a, they're gonna protect us, or whatever.

In this case, bullying became increasingly sinister: eventually, the bully began to sexually abuse Fiddler.[641]

Fiddler was one of many students who were sexually abused by fellow students. Many more students reported such abuse in their statements.[642] The assaults ranged from being forced to kiss someone, to being forced to simulate a sex act, to being raped. While, in some cases, victims were given small treats to encourage them to be silent, in other cases, they were told they would be killed if they reported the assault.[643] Agnes Moses recalled being molested by older girls at a hostel in northern Canada. "I never quite understood it, and it really wrecked my life, it wrecked my life as a mother, a wife, a woman, and sexuality was a real, it was a dirty word for us."[644] The experience of being abused at a British Columbia school by a group of boys left Don Willie distrustful of most people. "The only, only friends I kept after that were my relatives."[645]

Ilene Nepoose felt that poor supervision of the playground at the Blue Quills school helped pave the way for sexual abuse at that school. "The nuns would be by the sidewalks near the buildings of the school and the playground is huge. They would just stay there, they wouldn't like look around or they wouldn't supervise properly. They just stood by the building and observed from way over there."[646]

As with the case of Albert Fiddler, some new students were victimized by older students who had been assigned responsibility for initiating them into the life of the school.

The younger students could also be confused or uncertain about what was being done to them. In describing the abuse she was subjected to by a fellow student, Alphonsine McNeely said, "I'm just a little girl. I didn't know what she was doing to me. She was touching my private parts, and used to push her hand way into me, and, and she used to tell me, 'Don't say anything.' And I don't know what is going on, I don't know, I don't, I didn't know that what she is doing is not a good thing."[647]

Wesley Keewatin said that when he attended the Qu'Appelle school, he found the routine strange at first, but soon adapted. But then older boys started coming into his bed at night.

> And then they'd, they'd make me feel them and then they'd feel me, me up and then, it started, they started, oh how can I put this, is there any way to put it?
>
> They started sexually molesting me. They were, screwing my bottom and when, when it started happening, you know like I'd, I'd, I was confused, I was confused there because, you know like I had older brothers there and I said, "Okay, you know, I'm going to get these guys for doing that to me." But they, they used to tell me ... "Yeah, I know your brothers, you know, if you tell them, they'll get a licking too," you know. You know it went on like that for a long time.
>
> And I used to tell and I used to tell the nuns that this was going on, this was happening to me. And what they'd tell me was, "Go pray; just go pray." And, and that, oh that, that really confused me even more you know. It's like they knew that it was going on

but they, like who would, who would they believe? You know, like would they believe me or, or whoever I was pointing my, my finger at? You know because these older boys, they could certainly, most certainly deny it.

Keewatin told his parents of the abuse, but they continued to send him to the school. "It must have happened to them too because they'd always bring me back and, I figured, 'Okay, you know, this is normal.'"[648] Gladys Prince recalled that her mother did not believe her when she told her of the sexual abuse of students at the Sandy Bay, Manitoba, school.[649]

Students who were seen as being different were often particularly vulnerable to bullying. Gordon James Pemmican said he was the subject of regular bullying when he was a student at the Sioux Lookout school.

> So, they used to beat me up quite a bit, and they teased me because of my voice. I was born prematurely, and I sounded different. And I too, also as a result, I had, probably had bladder problems, like peeing the bed, and so I got teased for that. The kids were really mean there, and I never understood that, eh. And I got beaten up quite often, almost every day. It was hard for me to find moments, you know, where I can actually just relax and have fun with some, you know, some other, other little kids, eh. If we got too exposed, and the other kids seen me, then they came over and, you know, they would take me off and beat me up.[650]

It was a world in which he felt completely powerless. "This was their world. Their rules. And nothing I said mattered, so let them do whatever they want. I was sexually abused there for a long time, more than once. And then I got sexually assaulted by a senior boy, one of my own kind. So this confused me too."[651]

Students found it difficult to speak about what had been done to them. Bernard Catcheway was sexually abused by a fellow student at the Pine Creek school. "I couldn't tell anybody. Like it was a hush-hush thing to staff members."[652] Some students had been told by their abusers they would be killed if they ever spoke about the incident.[653] Those who did report an incident

Henry Bob.

of abuse rarely received the sort of help they needed. Henry Bob said that when he told a staff member of the Mission school that he had been sexually assaulted, "I was given a strap."[654] When Alphonsine McNeely told a staff member of the abuse she was undergoing from another girl, "the girl told her that I was lying, so I got the licking."[655]

In other cases, complaints were taken seriously. When she was attending school at Yellowknife, Northwest Territories, Mabel Brown was assaulted by a fellow student in the school darkroom. "I reported that to the principal's wife. And oh boy she, she, she, sure didn't like that and she dealt with it and he was sent home."[656]

One student was raped by three fellow students while living in Grollier Hall in the Northwest Territories in the 1970s. One of the staff members could see she was in distress. However, the student could not bring herself to tell her what had happened. "I felt so ashamed, you know, and I thought it was my fault. And then I quit school; and I went home, you know."[657]

The younger siblings of abusive students reported that on some occasions, they were abused during the holiday period or when their sibling left school.

Within a week of being placed in a Manitoba residential school, Greg Murdock was raped by a group of older boys. That assault represents a failure on the part of the residential school system to protect him. But the failure did not end there. Murdock told school officials about the assault the day after it occurred.

> They said, "Don't worry, Greg, we will look after it."

> The next night it happened again, I got raped again. I remember getting beat, putting my hand up, "Don't hit me, stop hitting me." No, they did it again.

> The next day I went again, but this time, the second day I couldn't speak so loud, my voice was a little smaller now. "They hurt me again," I said.

> "What did they do?"

> But at that time I was only seven, I didn't know what it was, so I just said, "Well, they hurt me."

> Well the next night it happened again. This time they said, "You really going to get it if you speak, you are really going to get it."

When school staff asked him the next day if anything had happened, he said, "No, nothing happened." His mother brought him home, where he told her:

> "Don't send me back there no more."

> She said, "Greg, I have got to send you back."

> I said, "I don't want to go there, they are mean to me, Mom, don't send me back."

> She sent me back. Again I was being beaten. Again I went home. This time I thought, no, I gotta do something different, I know what I'm going to do. I got up early in the morning on Sunday and I cleaned up the floors, I washed the floors, I washed the windows, I washed all of the dishes.

> I said, "Mom, look what I did, I cleaned the house for you, don't send me back. If you, if you don't send me back, I will always look after the house, Mom. I will always keep it clean. They're mean to me. Don't send me there."

> "I gotta send you there my son," she said.

> I said, "No, Ma, don't, they are mean."

She sent me in the taxi and I remember I jumped out of that taxi and I ran away, I was running away down to the bush. And I could hear this man chasing me and he picked me up, put me under his arm and he carried me. I looked in the taxi and I could see my mom crying, and me too I was crying. But they took me.[658]

Medical attention
"We never saw anybody."

Former students spoke of the limited medical and dental attention they received in the schools. Bernard Catcheway, who attended the Pine Creek, Manitoba, school, and Doris Judy McKay, who attended the Brandon and Birtle schools in Manitoba, were both critical of the medical attention available to students in the schools. Catcheway said, "And I remember when we were sick we were never taken to a hospital, never."[659] Robert Malcolm could not recall receiving any medical attention while attending the Sandy Bay, Manitoba, school. "Well, you would tell, you would tell the, the, the supervisor, and the supervisor would either do something, or I don't ever once remember going to see a doctor in the time that I was there. If I was sick, then you just had to tough it out, I guess."[660]

Robert Malcolm.

Georgina Harry said that a playground injury at the Sechelt, British Columbia, school was not properly treated. "I got damage on my leg, and I think it's from that fall that never got addressed when I was, when they brought me to the hospital. They didn't address my leg. Because to this day, I have a split, that what they call it, a split muscle, and I don't like it."[661]

Roger Cromarty said he had no memory of a doctor visiting the Sioux Lookout school during the seven years he spent at the school.

> Even though a lot of times once somebody caught something and it spread in the whole school like wildfire, and they would just more or less, we had to live out whatever it is that we caught, whether it's measles, mumps, sores, bedbugs, all that kind of stuff, we just had to live with it. We got some stuff from the matron. We used to have a matron that sort of acted as a nurse as well. So a medical doctor we never saw.

Georgina Harry.

He said students did not receive dental care until the Indian Affairs hospital opened in Sioux Lookout.

Now, the dentist, again, we never saw anybody until, I think it was when the, the Indian hospital was opened at Sioux Lookout, in the town of Sioux Lookout in 1951 and '52. The doctor there came up to the school, and did the dental work, and he wasn't a dentist. And it was, it was really ironic how he did it. He, and all of us, everybody had to go to the senior classroom and line up, and one by one, he'd look in their mouth. If you didn't have any cavities, he'd shove you on and go onto the next guy. But if you had to have a tooth pull out, he did it right there, and there was no ether, or ether, or any kind of, what they call that when you freeze, freezing. He didn't have that. He just go ahead and pulled that. I saw lots of kids there cry.[662]

Lydia Ross said the dental care at the Cross Lake, Manitoba, school was limited and painful. "There was no anaesthesia. There was no tools like the dentist tools. They used ordinary pliers. He use, he used to be the one to pull the teeth. He used the pliers, and pulled my tooth, just put Kleenex in there or something, and there's no pain pill, you have to suffer, but I got over it, anyway."[663]

Sarah Cleary had a similar memory of the dental treatment at residential schools in the North. "I still remember the dentist. We were all lined up in the hospital to have our—I don't know what. I can't remember much of it but I know I was really nervous, crying and shaking. That was the worst experience."[664]

Marie Brown, who attended one residential school in northern Manitoba and another in northern Saskatchewan, said she never received proper medical attention.

I had this grippe. It's some kind of a cold that affects your bones, and I was in bed, bedridden for about three months. And, and then I felt that, you know, as I went, as I, when I was, we became older, I realized that they should have come given me, taken me to the hospital because I almost died, eh, of that disease.[665]

When schools were hit with infectious illnesses, they were often placed under quarantine. Students said these were particularly lonely times. Martha Minoose recalled that the Roman Catholic school at Cardston was once under quarantine for six to eight weeks. "It was some kind of an epidemic but I don't know what it was. During the night they woke us up and they gave us a pill [and] a drink and we went back to bed. In the afternoon we [had] a rest period and ... but I didn't know what it was so we never saw our parents during that time."[666]

When Shirley Waskewitch came down with a contagious lung illness, she was in the infirmary in the Onion Lake school for at least a week.

Being locked up in the infirmary was one thing I never, never forget. In a small room, must have been about this small, a little bit bigger, and I was locked up in there for, oh, a long time, maybe I'd say about a week, two weeks, I would say, by myself in the infirmary in the high dormitory, and I used to hear somebody coming up the stairs, and the keys would be jangling, and they open the door, and they just put a tray in there, and lock me up there again. I was sick and, I was sick, and I don't know what was wrong with me, but I was sick, and I was there for a long time in that little room.

I don't remember getting any medicine at all, maybe I did, I'm not too sure, but I had headaches all the time from all the coughing.

The isolation, I, I remember that, being locked up in that room all the time. Created, created a silent fear to be in there, nothingness, nobody to talk to, just, just to lie on the bed. It used to be so quiet, and I don't know what I did to myself, just lie there on the bed, that's it, had nothing in there.[667]

Hospitalization was also a difficult experience. Children sent to sanatoria were often confined to their beds. Many found this forced inactivity difficult to bear. Vitaline Elsie Jenner was diagnosed with tuberculosis and sent to a sanatorium for a year.

And in those years, anybody that developed TB weren't allowed to get out, get out of bed. So, what I did, I was only nine years old, I was a young girl, you know, very active, and, and, you know, energetic, and to lay in bed all day, all night, bedpans were brought, brought in, couldn't get out of bed even to go to the washroom, so I one day I went, I went sneaking out of the room. And one of the nuns caught me when I was supposed to be in bed, and what she did, she stuck me in the operating room. And in those years, and the, the operating room, they didn't really, all the sterilized equipment was in, in view, you could see all that stuff, like I seen it before, and I thought, oh, my God, they're not gonna do anything to me, and I seen that great big lighting overtop, you know, to the operating, and the table was right there, and she stuck me right in the corner in total darkness. They shut the light off, after I had seen all the, I had seen all the instruments exposed on trays, sterilized, they were sterilized. And once she shut the door, that was my penance. I was being punished for getting out of bed, so they stuck me in there, and, and once they shut the light off, in total darkness, oh, my God, the fear. I just thought are they gonna come back, and they're gonna do something with me. Oh, my God, are they, are they gonna cut me up? You know I was thinking of all these thoughts of fear, and I just started to cry and cry and cry. I don't know how long I was left there. I betcha I was left there for a couple of hours. Finally, I guess, they decided to come and pick, to come and get me, and put me to bed. And then once they put me in bed, what they did, the nun did was tie, she tied my, my arms, stretched out like that, tied my, my wrist onto the, the bedpost, tied my two feet, my ankles, you know. I was spread out like that, and then what she did, then she covered me up.[668]

When Forrest Kendi, an Anglican, became ill, he was sent to a hospital in Fort Smith. To his alarm, he was placed in a Catholic hospital. His religious instruction at the Anglican hostel had made him fearful of Catholics.

So when they gave me my bed and took my clothes and gave me pyjamas, I spent the whole week crying, every day. And the nuns were trying to find out why I was crying or other peoples were trying to find out why I was crying. I wouldn't tell 'em. All the time I was picturing that my mother told me, "You keep staying around the Roman Catholic they're going to steal you and we'll never see you again."[669]

Students who were hospitalized sometimes never returned. Greg Rainville recalled a friend passing out in church next to him. "I didn't know where he went, because he never come back to school. I haven't seen that guy ever since. I don't know if he died, or he went to Fort Qu'Appelle, where there's a hospital, 'cause a lot of times we should have been put in the hospital."[670]

The death of a fellow student left a deep and bitter memory. Ray Silver said that he always blamed the Alberni school for the death of his brother Dalton.

Ray Silver.

> And I always blamed the residential school for kill-
> ing my brother. Dalton was his name. I never, I nev-
> er, I never ever forgave them. I don't know whether
> my dad and mother ever knew how he died, but I
> never found out. But I know that he died over there.
> They allowed me to [go] and see him once before he
> died, and he didn't even know me. He was a little
> guy, laying in the bed in the infirmary, dying, and I
> didn't know 'til he died. You know that's, that was
> the end of my education.[671]

Mary Coon-Come attended the La Tuque, Québec, school in the 1960s. One of the other girls at the schools was Juliet Rabbitskin.

> She had a handicap, she was small for her age, and she was our baby. We treat, we
> treated her as our baby. We used to dress her up. Brush her little rotten teeth, and
> comb her dry hair. Anyway, to us she was beautiful. One night she, she was sick. They
> came to wake me up. So, I had said that I stayed with her, with her little teddy bear,
> and I sang a lullaby that my grandmother used to sing to us to put us to bed. I knew
> she wasn't feeling, she had a fever, and she fell asleep, so I went back to sleep again.
> Then again, they woke me up, and told me she's not feeling good. So, I went to see
> her, and I knew there was something wrong. So, I woke up one of my friends, and
> I, I told her, "We have to take her to the dispensary. There's something wrong." She
> wasn't crying, but she was looking at us, smiling the kind of smile that we knew that
> something was wrong. So, I wrapped her up like a little baby, with her teddy bear.
> While the other girl ran downstairs to get the nurse, and there was a chair just before,
> beside the door of the clinic, I sat there, and I held her, and I sang to her. [crying] The
> girl that was with me, who ran down, she said, "She's coming, the nurse is coming." I
> don't know how long we waited there. I felt underneath her, she was wetting herself,
> and I, I told that girl, "Go get the nurse. I think she's dying." We, we could see her eyes
> go up, up and down. She ran down again to get the nurse. A few minutes after she
> came, she, she had her nurse uniform on, you could see she took her, shower her and
> everything, and when she saw the little girl, when she saw Juliet, she, she told me,
> she told me to put her on the bed in the, in the infirmary, so I did. She didn't even
> come, and she, the ambulance came, the doctor came, and I still can remember that

doctor.... When they took her down, I held her hand to the door, when they put her in the ambulance, and that was the last time I saw her.

That day, after dinner, they called us, all, all of us to go in our rooms, and I knew that there was something wrong. So, I asked Candy, the lady that looked after us, we used to call her Candy because she always gave us candies, and she, she's dead, and she didn't want to say anything to me. And I ran after her, she ran into her room, and I ran after her, and said, "Tell me." She, when she closed the door, I, I went in her room, and I told her, "Tell me she's dead." She didn't want to tell me. So, they put all us in one room, and they told us she died. When they brought the body back, the tomb was near the church, they didn't even open it for us to see. I wanted to see it. I wanted her to, I, I felt she wasn't there, that everything was just lies.

She helped carry the casket to the church. "We're going to bury her, were only five people there. The parents weren't even there. They didn't even invite, invite the parents to come. Even to this day, I can't go to the cemetery, knowing that I'm gonna see a little plate with just a number on it."[672]

Alex Alikashuak said that when he attended the Churchill, Manitoba, school, one of the students, Paulosie Meeko, was killed by a polar bear.

Alex Alikashuak.

In the fall time when bears are migrating and they're coming through Churchill, they used to come, come through our campus, eh, and when they come through during the daytime, all of us kids would go out and start chasing them, 'cause we're kids, like, you know obviously they're running, there's a whole bunch of us chasing them. And then one day, I guess a whole other, bunch of other kids were chasing a bear, and a bear had happened to hide behind a rock, and when one of the kids jumped, jumped over, he, he slapped him to death, and that was a kid was in my classroom, and he was my best friend.[673]

The death of a child often prompted parents to withdraw the rest of their children from a school. One former student spoke of how, when her sister became ill at the Anglican school at Aklavik, her father made a special visit to the school. "He cried over us. He took me home. He put her in a hospital, and she died."[674]

Disability

"I was so helpless."

Former students with disabilities spoke of not receiving needed care at residential schools. Stella August's grandmother eventually removed her from the Mission school because she felt Stella was not receiving proper medical attention for her hearing problems.[675]

Marjorie Ovayuak, who had a hearing disability, said that older students at Stringer Hall in Inuvik would mock and tease her. She decided to confront them when she was in her second year at the school.

> I said, "Okay, I work hard." I'm fed up with it! "I work hard! Okay which one of you is going to take me on?" I said, "I'm not scared no more. I'm not taking this bullshit no more." So I went like this, and they're big girls, they're big girls; about this much taller than me but, I, I, I took a chance on taking them on, but I guess they figured I'm not going to back away. I'm not going to take this bullshit no more. So from there on they never bothered me.[676]

Marjorie Ovayuak.

At the Carcross school, Gerald McLeod was hit in the head by a supervisor when he was trying to break up a fight.

> I didn't realize he broke my eardrum right there and then, 'til a few days later my ear started running and everything, and so I started complaining about it, and nothing got done about it. They checked it. They say, "Oh, you just got a running ear, running ear." They kept saying "running ear." I always had trouble with my left ear then. And finally, I lived like that through the whole school, so I, I was nine years old when that happened, and I had to go through school not hearing as well as other kids. So, I complained about it, but nothing was done about it. So, I ended up going through school without listening right, or hearing right, and had troubles, and I was getting more trouble for not listening, or I was not listening, I was not hearing, I couldn't hear proper.[677]

Clara Quisess felt that her vision problems led to her being bullied by other students at the Fort Albany school.

> No one didn't want to be my friend or didn't want me to be part of the team because I'm being blamed because I participated in the beginning to do Phys Ed, play base-

ball and other stuff but I was getting the team, lose their team because it was my fault. "You could have catched the ball, why didn't you catch the ball?" So scared 'cause it hit my nose, landed on my face and they calling me, "How stupid you are. You should, put up, raise up your glove and you could have catched that ball" rather than me hitting it on my face, but they don't even know that I have a visual problem. When they found out I could, can't see, they don't want me to be a part of their team. Every time when there was outdoor games, I would go hide in the tall grasses 'cause I don't want to be part. I have to hide there and I don't want the sister to find me hiding. I don't want them to put me in that team. I didn't want her to tell me, "You have to be on this team, you can't go hide there." "I don't want to be punished, but I don't want to be part of the team either, I just want out."

She felt that the school staff members were equally hard on her.

If I dropped something, "You're bad." If I didn0't do something right, "You're bad." That's all I learned that I am bad. 'Cause I always grew up believing that I am bad. I was so helpless that I can't even see that I try my best to see what they wanted me to see. "Can you see this? How 'bout this? How 'bout that?" "Can't you see anything!" The nun is shouting at me, I can't see and they're telling me that "Don't pretend that you don't see 'cause I know you can see!"[678]

Warm memories
"I learned some fine things at the school."

Although their overall description of their residential school years was largely negative, many students also pointed to benefits they received from their schooling, activities they enjoyed, or staff members they remembered with affection.

Paul Johnup said his two and a half years at the Stirland Lake, Ontario, school were both positive and negative.

Paul Johnup.

> I learned things there. I knew, I got to know people that are, people from other communities. I got to learn, I got to know some people from the States. That's where the staff was from, eh, mainly from the, from the States. And I learned some academic courses too, and I learned carpentry, mechanical, electrical.[679]

Monique Papatie, who attended the Amos school and went on to teach, was positive about much of her residential school experience.

> I learned some fine things at the school. When I began working at the school, I was never late. It was very rare that I was late. This, that's what I learned in residential school and to be ready to teach. That's why this morning you see me walking with a book, I'm still that way today, I'm still an educator. That's what I learned in the residential school, and to tell the truth as well, that's what I learned.[680]

Although Lillian Kennedy had problems with academics in the higher grades of the Fort Alexander school, she said she

Lillian Kennedy.

> enjoyed being at the residential school. I think I learned lots from the nuns that were there. And I got along with everybody. I had lots of friends, and then I helped at the kitchen or wherever, whenever they did work, I did, I did, like housekeeping work, making bread, helping the old lady that made bread every day. And then we learned how to knit and sew embroidery. Whatever they had I enjoyed doing it. I, I helped with everything in the school.[681]

Jennie Thomas recalled a teacher at one of the schools she attended in British Columbia who encouraged her to read.

Jennie Thomas.

> There was a whole set of those, I don't know, Spot and Jane books, and then little blue books that went up from there—read all of those books, went down to the grade-level books, read all of those; and then, there was, I think, there was a yellow colour, too. So, these are really old books, and they're school books. And I remember reading through all of those, and that's what kept me going. I don't know if those books are still around, but that just came back to me. And that was really … I guess that's what kept me sane.[682]

Shirley Ida Moore had positive memories of a supervisor named Mrs. Saunders at the Norway House school. "She made these chocolate, Easter-nest type things. She took us down to the kitchen and she, we made them. That was my, my, my one food I liked."[683]

Geraldine Shingoose had positive memories of the Lestock school principal. "But one of the things I wanted to share about Father Desjarlais was that I really, I really liked him. He was, he treated us good. He was, he was the principal of the school and that, and I know that he, he meant it in his heart to take care of, of the kids, just the staff that were working there didn't."[684]

Jeanne Rioux found the Edmonton school to be a respite from an unpleasant family situation.

> My mother didn't really seem to know how to show affection physically at all so there's a kind of cold atmosphere and my father was absent a lot and he was working. I mean I sort of understand that was necessary because there were so many of us and, but it was not really the most loving circumstance so anyway that's just kind of a bit of a framework. I went to … I was sent to boarding school when I was fourteen. And that was 100 miles away from where we lived. I lived in Red Deer at the time. And I was sent to boarding school in Edmonton and for me that was a pleasure to be in boarding school. There were a lot of people in the school that were trying to run away constantly but I was happy to be there because it was less hurting and less anger and yeah.[685]

Martha Minoose had strong memories of the friendships she formed with some girls at the Roman Catholic school in Cardston. Like many others, she described her friends as her residential school 'family.'

> I had three friends, they were my best friends and I was the fourth one and we hang around together. We became so close. I think we took each other as a family. We were so close so one day we said let's really try our best so we won't get punished so we

can go to the show. We have to watch everything we do so we are really trying our best. Next thing we got our name again, for some little thing and we couldn't go to the show and ... but we remained close and that has kept us going and in our little group we always laughed, we always shared stories, we always talk Blackfoot, that made us feel better.[686]

Alphonsine McNeely said that on the weekends, the students at the Roman Catholic school at Aklavik used to go for school picnics. "Then we'd play outside. We go sliding. We play all kind of games on the lake, and, oh, we'll just have fun."[687]

According to David Charleson, the only time he had fun at the Christie school was when he was "out of the school building. When we were in the woods, we felt free, or we were down on the beach by the water, collecting food that we were used to eating."[688]

Like many other schools, the Spanish boys' school had regular movie nights. William Antoine said that "the best thing that we all liked was the movies. They had movies on Sunday, on Sunday night; and oh that was the one thing that we looked forward to, back then, it was the movies."[689]

At the Presbyterian school in Kenora in the 1960s, Saturday night was the highlight of the week. Donald Copenace recalled, "They'd bring a box of old comic books and the kids would all, we'd grab whatever comic book and read that and that was it."[690]

Even those students who were abused at school could identify certain, qualified benefits of their school experience. Amelia Galligos-Thomas, who was sexually assaulted at the two schools she attended in British Columbia, spoke of the trips that the school organized for students.

> The one thing I could say that came good out of boarding school is we got to travel. I got to learn to play different instruments. I got to meet Pierre Trudeau. The farthest I've travelled was Disneyland. I've met Bob Barker. I learned how to Scottish dance. I learned how to play "Star Wars" on an instrument.[691]

Robert Malcolm, who was sexually abused while attending the Sandy Bay school, said there were positive aspects to the residential school experience.

Amelia Galligos-Thomas.

> I guess it, it wasn't all, it wasn't all bad, like, even though I received an education, I actually did fairly well in, in my studies when I was there. Like, I'm thankful that I was able to be involved in sports, when those sports weren't part of my home environment before. I was able to play hockey, and baseball, and stuff like that, basketball.[692]

Mary Rose Julian valued what she learned at the Shubenacadie school.

> I learned English. And that's why I want to make this statement, because so much negative came out of it, but I can see a lot of positives. I learned English; that was my

objective for going there in the first place. My brother learned English; that was my second objective, for him to learn English. And, and then I learned more prayers. I learned Latin, and I, I learned, like, there was Sunday school every Sunday, so you learned your Bible. I know my Bible inside and out. I know my Latin. I can read Latin. And, and I know, and another thing I learned was I learned how to take care of kids. I already knew how to take care of kids. I had a little bit of experience with my brothers and sisters, but over there I learned when I had a charge, I would look after my charge no problem at all. And then I learned to sew. Already I, I already knew, when I went to residential school, I already knew how to sew, and it was on those pedal machines. I could even thread the needle, I mean bobbins and stuff, and I could do all that.

Mary Rose Julian.

Julian said she never experienced physical abuse at the school. "I was there a year and a half; a nun never laid a hand on me. And lot of people that I've listened to, you know, talk about this ordeal every single night, or every single day, you know, they were being strapped, or something was happening to them. Nothing like that ever happened to me."[693]

For Percy Tuesday, who attended the Roman Catholic school in Kenora, the only positive memories of schooling came from when he stood up for himself.

This friend of mine and I used to play guitar a lot together. So, we used to play, jamming, you know. One day that, that boy's supervisor took my guitar away, took it from me, and I felt, I guess there was nothing I could do. So I went, I went storming up to the principal's office, and I told him, "This guy took my guitar, I want it back now." And I was, I was mad. I had it back within ten minutes. That's the only time that I remember standing up for myself, everything else, I did what I was told, 'cause obedience was the highest virtue, you know.[694]

Sports and recreation
"This gym was a saviour."

The opportunity to participate in organized sports was limited in residential schools. Many schools didn't have a gymnasium, a skating rink, or a playing field. Equipment was often in short supply or poor repair, or was improperly sized. But, where it existed, many students seized the limited athletic and recreational opportunities presented to them. Many students claimed that sports helped them make it through residential school.

Christina Kimball attended the Roman Catholic school near The Pas, where she experienced physical, sexual, and emotional abuse. She believes that it was only through her involvement with sports that she survived. "I was very sports-oriented. I played baseball. Well, we play baseball, and even hockey. We had a hockey team. That was benefited, benefited me in a way 'cause I loved playing sports. Well, that's one way, too. I don't know how I did it but I was pretty good in sports."[695]

Noel Starblanket said that at the Qu'Appelle school,

> I had some good moments, in particular in the sports side, 'cause I really enjoyed sports. I was quite athletic, and basically that's what kept me alive, that's what kept me going was the sports. When I was forced to go back after holidays, or things like that, the only thing that I wanted to go back for was for the sports, nothing else. I didn't want to go back for the teaching, for the teachers, for the, the Christian indoctrination, or, or the strapping, or any of the other abuses. I wanted to go back for the sports. That was the only thing I went back for.[696]

At the Lestock school, Geraldine Shingoose took refuge in extracurricular activities.

> One of the good things that I would do to try and get out of just the abuse was try to, I would join track-meet, try and be, and I was quite athletic in boarding school. And I also joined the band, and I played a trombone. And, and that was something that took me away from the school, and just to, it was a relief.[697]

Paul Andrew spent seven years at Grollier Hall in Inuvik. One of his strongest and most positive memories related to school sports. At a Truth and Reconciliation Commission of Canada public dialogue in the school gymnasium in the Inuvik school, he recalled that he

> ran around this gym a lot of times, and this gym was a saviour for a lot of things because we were good at the physical stuff, we were good athletes, we were good at the sports. I don't know about people, I didn't do very good in classrooms because I didn't have the basics, the background in education. And there was times when I was called dumb and stupid and there were times when I felt dumb and stupid. But put me in a gym, there was not too many people better than I am. There were

some, but not too many better than I. And so I loved it in the gyms. I loved it all in the cross-country trails, I loved it on the hockey, hockey arenas because they made me feel like I'm part of, they made me feel good. But in the education it wasn't quite the same.[698]

John Kistabish was another of the students who took refuge in sports. "I really liked to play hockey. I liked a lot because we helped each other, you weren't alone, because I wanted to win. And, we had fun because we helped each other a lot.[699] In some cases, the coaches took the pleasure out of sports. Pierre Papatie played goalie for the Amos school team. He said that "When we were losing, we were getting beaten with a ruler. We always had to win. We didn't know how to lose. It was always, win, win."[700]

Aaron Leon spent seven years at the Mission school, where he was sexually and physically abused. School sports were among the few positive elements of school life that he could recall.

> And the positive stuff I got out of it was I learned how to play in a band, I learned gymnastics, soccer, baseball, you know, physical part of me. Another positive, I guess, would be being amongst a big group of different people I didn't know, and it felt good to be amongst my own people not knowing who they are.[701]

Participation in athletics gave students a sense of accomplishment. While she was at the Blue Quills school, Alice Quinney looked forward to sports days. "Track and field day was a day when your, your parents got invited to come and watch you perform in your track events. Even my mom and dad would come."[702]

Alice Quinney.

Mel H. Buffalo recalled playing hockey, football, and soccer as well as participating in track-and-field activities at the Edmonton, Alberta, school. "I won the provincial city championship for the two mile and came in second in provincial for the—actually for the same distance as well. So I learned to run long time."[703]

One of Albert Fiddler's few positive memories of the Beauval, Saskatchewan, school revolved around sports. "I was a good athlete, I was a good hockey player, I was a good runner, I was a good jumper, so that I guess I started getting patted on the back. I started getting a little, a little bit of recognition as a, an athlete, so because I could outrun anybody, out-jump anybody. I was good ballplayer, so." When Fiddler got into trouble at school, the priest who coached the school team spoke up on his behalf. "He didn't want to lose his hockey player, he didn't want to lose his runner, because we get, we'll lose points if we want to compete."

Fiddler said the boys would often use department-store catalogues for shin pads, but a new principal had a greater interest in sports.

We started having new skates, start having good, good socks. We starting having bought, what you call, Toronto Maple Leafs and the Canadiens, those were the two, so we, we had two set of sweaters. And Maple Leafs, we used them at home, and then when we go out and play out we have to be Canadiens, so but none of those things, just toques, that's all, no facemask, nothing, no, no. We had little, finally we got those things, too. So, he bought all that stuff for us. So, we start getting bigger, better hockey players, too. We started competing. We came, we came and compete in town, in Meadow Lake. We had, they, they call us bush hockey players, but we, they couldn't beat us because we were, we were, we had a good coach, so we started winning.[704]

Orval Commanda recalled that sports played a positive role in his life at the Spanish, Ontario, boys' school, and that the opportunity to play sports was used as an incentive to get the students to do their school work.

So anyway in, when I came here, in '52, there was a lot of sports going on, and, and I was into sports, you know. I played hockey, and basketball, and at the time they played softball, like, and also played pool, because I started playing pool when I was seven years old....

And I liked playing sports. You know if you wanted to be on a hockey team, you had to have your work done, you know?[705]

William Antoine was one of the students who credited Jesuit Father Maurice for the extensive sports program at the Spanish school.

The one thing I liked over there was the sports. Oh, there's, there's any sport you wanted to play. You know, there's basketball in the fall of the year, you know. And then hockey, you know, in the winter time. And, summer time there was softball, baseball, lacrosse. Lacrosse was my, my favourite sport; I really loved that sport and I was good at it too. A little ball you threw around to get in the net, yeah. I really liked that sport. And I was good at running; you know I was fast, I was skinny. You know I was pretty agile, that's why I loved that sport.

Under Father Maurice, there were also sports banquets to honour student and team accomplishments, and annual field days.

You know, running, jumping, pole vaulting, high jumping, and shot put. All those games, you know we played those games and that was a real fun time, fun day you know. It was for one day and it was all day; and, and whoever won, well they got, they got, a medal of some kind and it showed that you, you know, you were, you were good at what you did, you know. So that was so, very rewarding.[706]

Joseph Maud learned to skate at the Pine Creek school.

And I remember, I remember some of the activities that we would, we'd, we would do, like, there was a skating rink outside, and my brother Marcel taught me how to skate. And once a week on Saturday evenings, we would have a skating party, where the girls would join the boys, and we would skate maybe from, like, from 6:00 o'clock 'til 10:00 o'clock every Saturday. So that was, that was probably one of the happier times at the residential school.[707]

In 1967, when the city of Winnipeg hosted the Pan American Games, Patrick Bruyere was attending the Assiniboia residential school. He and nine of his fellow students were selected to be among those running with the ceremonial Pan Am Games torch. The boys thought they would bring the torch into the stadium.[708]

It took us, we left Sunday morning, Minneapolis, and we, the last leg was from St. Norbert to the stadium. So, there was, we ran a ways, and then the last couple of miles two guys ran, and then eight of us were taken to the stadium, and we brought in the pattern flag, and we brought in the Canadian flag into the stadium, so we had to fold those flags and hand them, handed them over to the, the officials, the head guy for the Pan Am Games, I forget his name again, and I think the prime minister, I think. I don't even remember who it was, you know, back then. But anyway, they were there, eh. So, we hand them over, and we came outside, and we thought we were gonna bring in the torch, and then one of the Indian Affairs fellas says, "Thank you very much, boys. There's breakfast waiting for you around the corner there, Pancake House." And then they, they gave this torch to this athlete, eh, and he took it in, and that was it. So, we didn't think anything, eh. Like I said, in boarding school you did as you were told and that was it, you didn't ask questions.[709]

Many years later, Bruyere and his fellow students' experience became the subject of a film. Bruyere appeared in the film, playing a grandfather and speaking in Ojibway.[710] When the Pan Am Games were held again in Winnipeg in 1999, the surviving runners were invited back, and received an apology.[711]

Not all students were athletic, and not all athletic experiences were positive. Roddy Soosay recalled that one of his physical education teachers at the Hobbema school was particularly sadistic.

All I remember about him is grabbing the dodge ball and making me run and throw-

ing it and hitting me in the head and thinking it was funny, and sent me flying. I remember him picking me up by the throat and holding me up in the air and I remember him dropping me and I was like—I don't know, thinking back, no more than three feet tall. And dropping me, and he's probably, what, six foot two, six foot three, somewhere around there. And holding me up in the air saying, I'm probably dropping from, you know, four or five feet over, and landing on my head. And all I remember is trying to stand up and getting kicked in the butt there from him. And this hockey stick—his broken hockey stick that everybody knew—he called it Hector.

Roddy Soosay.

And he'd hit me and made me stand up. And I remember clearly because I wasn't able to straighten out my head. My head was on my shoulder like that and I couldn't straighten out my head. And I couldn't understand why I couldn't straighten out my head. It was a long time before I was able to stand up straight.[712]

Even for successful students, sports might provide only limited comfort. Fred Sasakamoose, who became the first Treaty Indian to play in the National Hockey League, attended the Duck Lake, Saskatchewan, school in the 1940s. He said that the priests who ran the school were from Québec and loved hockey. During the winters, the boys had the opportunity to skate every day. But the school staff employed the same sort of discipline in sports as they did in every other aspect of school life. According to Sasakamoose, "The priests never talked twice. The second time, you got the strap. But Father Roussell had a dream. He told me, 'Freddie, I'm going to work you hard, but if you work hard, you're going to be successful.'"[713]

He was correct: Sasakamoose was the star player on a team that won a provincial championship.[714] But he had also been seriously abused at the school. He left it as soon as he could.

> I said, "I'm going home to my mother." I was fifteen years old. "I'm going home." My gosh, I felt good. I felt that the world had changed, had opened a gate for me. There was no more wall on the other side of these girls that I never seen that were there for last ten years. We were segregated from them; you couldn't talk to them, even my own sister.[715]

When a priest brought a hockey scout to his family's home, Sasakamoose hid, convinced he was going to be taken back to school. It was only with coaxing that he agreed to play junior hockey in Moose Jaw.[716] Although he was a good player, he never felt that he fit into the world of professional sports: "I look at myself sometimes and say, 'How in the hell did I ever get there?' I didn't want to be an athlete, I didn't want to be a hockey player, I didn't want to be anything. All I wanted was my parents."[717]

Some students found refuge in the arts. Again, opportunities were limited and discipline often strict. The Kamloops school dance troupe, run by Sister Leonita, became well known through British Columbia. Students joined the Kamloops dancers for various reasons: some valued the fact that dancers got to miss the early Mass; others thought it was "a way to get something out of this place." Some joined for self-esteem, and some for the respect that outsiders gave the dance company.[718]

Jean Margaret Brown had mixed feelings about the Kamloops dance experience.

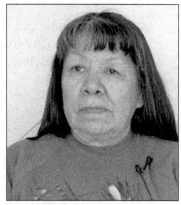

Jean Margaret Brown.

We were forced to learn Irish and Spanish and I was in a Jewish group dance. We had to sing all kinds of folksy music, which was okay I guess, but, didn't have nothing to do with our, our language or our traditions or our culture.

I did learn that, from different walks of life that, being in a dance troupe I was made to feel special. But the work that we did to be in that dance group was really, really harsh. The discipline from the nuns that were teaching us, often used their knuckles and rulers on the back, on our back; on our shoulder blades or, right in the base of our head with a ruler.[719]

Wilbur Abrahams recalled when a young staff member brought rock and roll to the Alert Bay school.

He was some kind of a, I don't know, a musician I guess you can call him, and he put, hooked up loudspeakers in the basement, and played music, you know, the rock and roll music at that time of the year, in '53, maybe '54. That year they were, they called it the jive. And I remember dancing in the basement. It seemed like a time in my life where I could just dance and forget about my abuse. And pretty soon he opened up, we had a little hall, and he opened that up, and the boys and girls got together. And this one girl pulled me up, and kind of showing me how to dance and to jive. I remember catching on really quick, and I really, I really loved dancing, 'cause you know when I danced, I, I forgot about where I was for, for an hour or two. Like when I danced, I gave it my all, you know, I didn't, I didn't care, it was 'cause I was dancing to forget, and it worked, those couple of hours.[720]

By the 1960s, Aboriginal artists were being brought into some schools to give lessons. Henry Speck was born in 1908 and attended the Alert Bay school for two years. He had begun to receive public attention for his paintings and carvings in the 1960s. He became the artistic director of the Kwakwa̱ka'wakw Big House project at Alert Bay in the mid-1960s.[721] During this period, he gave art classes at the school there. Former student Don Willie recalled Speck's classes:

Don Willie.

Like I was talking about out there, is that, Henry Speck came in through the day school, and he did a drawing on the board, Thunderbird, and one of the things that I really liked to do when I was a young boy was to draw out of comics, just draw. Started off with the simpler ones, I guess, and then I did the Marvel comics and the superheroes and stuff like that, so I kind of knew how to draw a bit. So when Henry Speck came by, and did this drawing on the blackboard, I end up becom ing, well I learned how to draw from him. So, he had this book, and I don't know, all the kids kind of knew that I was, they liked my drawings 'cause I did a good job of copying Henry Speck, I guess, so they, so they used to ask me to start to draw for them, so I started to draw for them, and end up drawing, end up having a carving class in St. Mike's. And the Joseph boys that came in, their, their dad teached us, he was our, was the layout teacher, how to carve. Anyhow, he got me to draw all bunch of designs around this carving room, so I did, and he had this book out of Henry Speck's drawings, copied all of them on the walls.[722]

Cadets

"I've learned and heard something stronger than this."

Many of the boys who attended residential schools participated in cadets, a military-sponsored training program. Cadet training was part of the drill at the two Anglican residential schools that Michael Cheena attended in the 1960s. "While I was in the residential school I also—I was also a member of the Army Cadets. I used to go to Army Cadets once a week on Thursday nights. I kind of liked that because it was something to do, you know, during the week, other than sit around and do nothing."[723]

Earl Clarke also participated in cadets, and recalled it as being highly regimented.

> And the others were, they were cadets. We, we join, we had to join the 590 squadron. We'd march around for hours in that building, and you had to stand still for a long time. If your nose itched, or whatever, you know, you couldn't, or else you'd be kneeling with your arms out, or running around, discipline, army discipline I guess they call it.[724]

One of Ray Silver's strongest memories of the Alberni school during the 1940s was military drill.

> I learned how to march. See, the war was on, and they took us out on route marches. And you can imagine going on a route march thirsty and hungry.... We were little guys. When we got a little, well, later on we even had the little wooden guns that we packed and marched, and sang songs, "London's burning, London's burning, look over yonder." I never, never forgot that. "And there will always be an England, England shall be free," and we're gonna free England, that's what they taught us.[725]

Students sometimes went from the cadet corps straight to the army. Thomas Keesick said that in the 1940s at the McIntosh school in Kenora, six boys were recruited. "It was later that they found out these six boys were sent off to war, Second World War, and only one returned, his name was Albert Stone and I was there at his burial in Grassy."[726]

Noel Knockwood joined the Canadian army after attending the Shubenacadie school in the 1940s. "I spent 413 days in combat in Korea. And I served in 1952 and '53."[727] Alan Knockwood said that life at the Shubenacadie school prepared him for the Canadian navy.

> I went to navy boot camp. Standing in line and doing PT in the morning, or what have you, and having the chief petty officer, or drill sergeant in some cases, holler at me. I would stand there at attention and look at them and say, "You ain't got nothing on Sister Claire or Brother Sampson. I've learned and heard something stronger than this."[728]

Larry Roger Listener also enjoyed his participation in the cadet program.

> The government didn't realize, you know, these guys are getting good in the cadets. That's when AIM [American Indian Movement] and all this was going on. So they cut the cadets off because maybe to them they were making us warriors, but no, they helped us. Every time we shot a gun there was a target there. That's where most of us learned how to go hunt, is by shooting those guns.[729]

Improvements
"There was a lot more freedom."

In 1969, the federal government restructured the residential school system. The schools usually were divided into two, separate entities: a government-run school and a church-administered residence. Beginning in the 1970s, agreements were reached under which Aboriginal organizations took over the operation of several of the institutions. Greg Rainville attended the Qu'Appelle school while these transformations were taking place.

> I've seen the, where the priests and nuns controlled the school. I was there when Indian Affairs took control of the residential school, and was there when Native Control started. But the most, the nuns there, when the nuns and the priests were there, there was, things got better after they left. They weren't perfect, but there was still abuse when Indian Affairs control. A lot of things were, weren't addressed, or, or made known to people, 'cause it was always hush-hush.

Rainville said the change from church to Indian Affairs administration brought about an improvement in personal freedom and food at the school.

> When the nuns were there, we were just like a jail. There was a big fence all around. You couldn't leave. Yeah, we had black and white TVs. We had, we didn't go no place. Everything that we had was either outside in the yard, or in the gym. But when Indian Affairs got there, we, we were allowed to go maybe downtown to the hardware store, where we would have pop at the, in the café there in Lebret. You were allowed to do that. Before you weren't even allowed to go. You know if you're caught downtown, you were in trouble. But there was a lot more freedom. We used to get to go to drive-ins, movies.

> When the nuns were there, everything was just, I don't know, everything was hamburger-based. Everything was we ate the whole year was either mush, hamburgers, whatever, maybe the odd chicken, or odd ham. But with Indian Affairs, our food started, like, we had pork chops, we had boiled potatoes, stuff you could identify. Like, then when Native Control came to be, again we were back to hamburger, like, you know, from hamburger to steak, to hamburger again. That was, that's the only way I could describe the different times people were there.[730]

Ronalee Lavallee attended the Grayson, Saskatchewan, school in the 1960s and 1970s, and then worked at the school for twenty-two years as a child-care worker. She recalled a change in attitude at the school when it came under band management. "When our First Nation took over the boarding school, and the nuns were no longer there and the priest, and I could see that difference. It was, like, it was so much lighter, and I could see that in the children. They were so much freer."[731]

Velma Jackson was placed in the Blue Quills school after the death of her grandmother. She came from a different community than most of the other students at the school, and felt she was treated as an outsider. By then, many members of the supervisory staff were Aboriginal. In her opinion, they tended to favour their relatives. She also said the supervisors used to bring alcohol into the school on weekends. "And these were our own Native people that were running the school. It was, I just felt so totally lost there.... That's where I became an alcoholic was at Blue Quills, 'cause it was brought there all the time. I bet you, you can go there and check in the bird sanctuary, and it'll be filled with beer bottles."[732]

Velma Jackson.

Amber K. K. Pelletier, who was the youngest Survivor to provide the Commission with a statement, attended the residence operated by the Marieval Community Education Centre on the Cowessess First Nation from 1993 to 1997. She said that a number of the long-disliked policies were still in practice at the residence. For example, the school had retained the policy of cutting students' hair when they first arrived, and assigning them numbers. According to Pelletier, in the 1990s, "We could tell when the keepers were mad because they would, they would use our number to call us or to talk to us. In breakfast line or supper, dinner line, if we were acting up they'd say, 'Number 20.' And then you just stopped whatever you were doing."

She also felt that the behaviour of some staff members was objectionable.

And then the keepers, some of them would come around and tuck you in and they would give you a kiss on the cheek and they would say, "I love you." I remember the first night I was just lying there and they were doing that. And I, I was thinking, that lady's going to come and, that lady's going to come around my bed. So by the third, fourth day I figured out that if I threw my blankets over my head and looked tucked in, then you know, all the work was done. And then I would just have to listen to their steps, 'cause it would take one, two, three steps to get to my bed from the next bed. And I could just peek and say, "I love you, goodnight." And they wouldn't have to, they wouldn't kiss me.[733]

Amber K. K. Pelletier.

The end

"The doors are closing for good."

Most students left residential school when they turned sixteen. Some students, however, contrived to leave earlier. At the end of one summer, Roy Denny hid in the woods so he would not be returned to school. When the Indian agent came to visit his grandmother, she told them he would rather be at home helping her. According to Roy, "They said, 'okay,' and jeez, I was real glad; real happy."[734]

Rebecca Many Grey Horses's parents successfully withdrew her from the Anglican school in Cardston after another student broke her collarbone. "I was taken to the hospital and spent a few days there, my parents came, and so, it was at that time that I asked that, you know, not to be put back in there."[735]

Many of the students in the hostels in northern Canada in the 1960s and 1970s were well over the official school-leaving age. But they had come from remote communities to finish high school or take vocational training. As they grew older, some found the curfews and limits on personal freedom difficult to accept. When she was in her late teens, Lena McKay snuck out of Breynat Hall, one of the Fort Smith residences in the Northwest Territories, to spend an evening with a friend. She was caught sneaking back in later that night. The event left her frustrated with the limits on her freedom. "I was just sick of it, so I said no, it's not for me. I can't stay. So, and I said, 'I'm not gonna sneak around, and yeah, I'm not gonna do that again.'" As a result, she left.[736]

Many students could remember their day of discharge. Roy Johnson was glad when the day came when he could leave the Carcross school. "And when I left, I was, you know, well, abused, psychological damage, illiterate. I was very happy the last day came along when I left Carcross. Jump on that bus, that's your angel is the bus driver, 'cause he'd be taking you home, really."[737]

William Francis Paul vividly recalled the day he was discharged from Shubenacadie. He said he was woken up in the middle of the night and informed that he was going home. He was driven to the local train station and placed on a train to his home community. While on the train, he befriended an Aboriginal woman with a son his age. Instead of continuing on to his home, he got off the train and lived with them for a while. Eventually, the Indian agent located him and returned him to his family in Membertou, Nova Scotia.[738]

William Francis Paul.

For some students, the last day of school was also the last day that the school itself was open. Rose Marie Prosper said she would never forget the day the students were told that the Shubenacadie school was going to be closed. One day in early 1967, her teacher, Sister Charles Marie, came into the classroom.

She went up to her, her desk there, and she just stood there, and she, she was looking at us, like we were all just talking among ourselves, and she was just standing there looking at us. And, we were like, 'Okay, she's going to flip out pretty soon. She's going to snap her yardstick on our desk and tell us to be quiet or something.'

And she didn't say anything. And I was sitting at my desk and I was looking at her. I wasn't talking because I, I get strapped for everything, so I kind of learned, not to talk. So, I was sitting there and I was looking at her and she was standing there. She had her hands like this up to her mouth and she was looking at all of us. And, she said, "Okay," she said, "I want everyone to quiet down." So we were sure we were all going to start our work.

Rose Marie Prosper.

So she sat on her desk in the front there. She said, "I have something to tell all of you." And she said, "After I tell you," she said, "I want you all to stay in your desks, stay in your chairs, and not to make any noise; to be very, very quiet." So we didn't know what was going on or anything. And then she said, "When you leave here in June, you're not coming back." She said, "The doors are closing for good."

It was the happiest news; it was the happiest thing we ever heard. I mean, at the time you're not supposed to touch a boy or nothing, but we had boys in our classroom, and when she said that nobody was coming back in June, that you'll never see each other again; you'll never see any of the nuns again, you'll never see the school again, nothing. She goes, "When you go home, you're staying home for good." When she told us that, we all jumped out of our chairs, we banged our desks, our books went flying, we hugged each other, we grabbed the boys. And we were crying, we were laughing; it was the best thing we ever, ever heard.[739]

Dorene Bernard was also at the Shubenacadie school when it closed in 1967.

Remember my last day walking out of the residential school at the end of June 1967, and we were the last ones to leave because we were getting on a plane, so we had to be, we were the last ones to leave that school, me and my brother and my sisters. My mom was going to meet us at the airport in Boston. We were waiting for a drive to come take us to the airport. And it was just like an evil place, it was empty, you hear your echoes walking through and talking, like this place, you could hear your echo everywhere you went.

And I could remember getting into the car, looking back, and Sister came running down the stairs, and she said, "You forgot something. Dorene, you forgot something," and she passed me that Bible missal. And I took it and I threw it, I threw it away and told her to keep it, "I don't need it where I'm going."

And my sister was even scared when we were getting ready to leave. "Don't do that. Don't say that," she said. I said, "What can they do to me? They're not going to do anything to us now. We're outta here."[740]

Bibliography

The endnotes of this report often commence with the abbreviation TRC, followed by one of the following abbreviations: ASAGR, AVS, CAR, IRSSA, NRA, RBS, and LACAR. The documents so cited are located in the Truth and Reconciliation Commission of Canada's database. At the end of each of these endnotes, in square brackets, is the document identification number for each of these documents. The following is a brief description of each database.

Active and Semi-Active Government Records (ASAGR) Database: The Active and Semi-Active Government Records database contains active and semi-active records collected from federal governmental departments that potentially intersected with the administration and management of the residential school system. Documents that were relevant to the history and/or legacy of the system were disclosed to the Truth and Reconciliation Commission of Canada (TRC) in keeping with the federal government's obligations in relation to the Indian Residential Schools Settlement Agreement (IRSSA). Some of the other federal government departments included, but were not limited to, the Department of Justice, Health Canada, the Royal Canadian Mounted Police, and National Defence. Aboriginal Affairs and Northern Development Canada undertook the responsibility of centrally collecting and producing the records from these other federal departments to the TRC.

Audio/Video Statement (AVS) Database: The Audio/Video Statement database contains video and audio statements provided to the TRC at community hearings and regional and national events held by the TRC, as well as at other special events attended by the TRC.

Church Archival Records (CAR) Database: The Church Archival Records database contains records collected from the different church/religious entities that were involved in administration and management of residential schools. The church/religious entities primarily included, but were not limited to, entities associated with the Roman Catholic Church, the Anglican Church of Canada, the Presbyterian Church in Canada, and the United Church of Canada. The records were collected as part of the TRC's mandate, as set out in the Indian Residential Schools Settlement Agreement, to "identify sources and create as complete an historical record as possible of the IRS system and legacy."

Indian Residential Schools School Authority (IRSSA) Database: The Indian Residential Schools School Authority database is comprised of individual records related to each residential school, as set out by the IRSSA.

National Research and Analysis (NRA) Database: The National Research and Analysis database contains records collected by the National Research and Analysis Directorate, Aboriginal Affairs and Northern Development Canada, formerly Indian Residential Schools Resolution Canada (IRSRC). The records in the database were originally collected for the purpose of research into a variety of allegations, such as abuse in residential schools, and primarily resulted from court processes such as civil and criminal litigation, and later the Indian Residential Schools Settlement Agreement (IRSSA), as well as from out-of-court processes such as Alternative Dispute Resolution. A majority of the records were collected from Aboriginal Affairs and Northern Development Canada. The collection also contains records from other federal departments and religious entities. In the case of some records in the database that were provided by outside entities, the information in the database is incomplete. In those instances, the endnotes in the report reads, "No document location, no document file source."

Red, Black and School Series (RBS) Database: The Red, Black and School Series database contains records provided by Library and Archives Canada to the TRC. These three sub-series contain records that were originally part of the "Headquarters Central Registry System," or records management system, for departments that preceded the current federal department of Aboriginal Affairs and Northern Development Canada. The archival records are currently related to the Department of Indian Affairs and Northern Development fonds and are held as part of Library and Archives Canada's collection.

Library and Archives Canada Archival Records (LACAR) Container and Document Databases The LAC Records Container and Document databases contain records collected from Library and Archives Canada (LACAR). The archival records of federal governmental departments that potentially intersected with the administration and management of Indian Residential Schools were held as part of Library and Archives Canada's collection. Documents that were relevant to the history and/or legacy of the Indian Residential School system were initially collected by the Truth and Reconciliation Commission, in conjunction with Aboriginal Affairs and Northern Development Canada, as part of their mandate, as set out in the Indian Residential School Settlement Agreement. The collection of records was later continued by Aboriginal Affairs and Northern Development Canada, based on the federal government's obligation to disclose documents in relation to the Indian Residential Schools Settlement Agreement.

Truth and Reconciliation Commission Databases

National Research and Analysis Database: NRA
Audio/Video Statement Database: AVS

Books

Haig-Brown, Celia. *Resistance and Renewal: Surviving the Indian Residential School.* Vancouver: Arsenal Pulp Press, 1988.

Marks, Don. *They Call Me Chief: Warriors on Ice.* Winnipeg: J. Gordon Shillingford, 2008.

Robinson, Laura. *Frontrunners = Niigaanibatowaad: a play in two acts.* Port Elgin: Brucedale Press, 2008.

Book Chapters and Journal Articles

Bruyere, Patrick. "Introduction" to *Frontrunners = Niigaanibatowaad: a play in two acts*, by Laura Robinson. Port Elgin: Brucedale Press, 2008, 4–5.

Lewis, Ruth. "The Psychological Approach to the Preschool Stutterer." *Canadian Medical Association Journal* 60, 5 (May 1949): 497–500.

Mandryk, Murray. "Uneasy Neighbours: White-Aboriginal relations and Agricultural Decline." In *Writing Off the Rural West: Globalization, Governments and the Transformation of Rural Communities*, edited by Roger Epp and Dave Whitson. Edmonton: University of Alberta Press with the Parkland Institute, 2001: 205–221.

Radunovich, Heidi Liss, and Garret D. Evans. "Bed Wetting." Department of Family, Youth and Community Sciences, University of Florida/Institute of Food and Agricultural Sciences Extension." Publication #FCS2112. September 2013.

Siebner, H. R., C. Limmer, A. Peinemann, A. Drzezga, B. E. Bloem, M. Schwaiger, and B. Conrad. "Long-term Consequences of Switching Handedness: A Positron Emission Tomography Study on Handwriting in 'Converted' Lefthanders." *The Journal of Neuroscience* 22 (April 1, 2002): 2816–2825.

Websites

Holder, M. K. "Teaching Left-Handers to Write." Handedness Research Institute. http://handedness.org/action/leftwrite.html. Accessed 16 January 2014.

Other

Indian Residential Schools Settlement Agreement, Schedule N, "Mandate for the Truth and Reconciliation Commission."

Indian Residential Schools Settlement Agreement, 8 May 2006, Schedule N, "Mandate for the Truth and Reconciliation Commission [of Canada]," http://www.residentialschoolsettlement.ca/SCHEDULE_N.pdf (accessed 14 March 2015).

Robinson, Laura, Lori Lewis, and Liz Jarvis. *Niigaanibatowaad FrontRunners*, National Film Board of Canada, 2007.

Endnotes

Preface

1. Canada, *Annual Report of the Department of Indian Affairs, 1931*, 60.
2. Indian Residential Schools Settlement – Official Court Website, http://www.residentialschoolsettlement.ca/schools.html (accessed 5 February 2015).
3. Prime Minister Stephen Harper, Statement of Apology – to former students of Indian Residential Schools, 11 June 2008, http://www.aadnc-aandc.gc.ca/eng/1100100015644/1100100015649.

The Survivors Speak

1. TRC, AVS, Bob Baxter, Statement to the Truth and Reconciliation Commission of Canada, Thunder Bay, Ontario, 24 November 2010, Statement Number: 01-ON-24NOV10-012.
2. TRC, AVS, Louise Bossum, Statement to the Truth and Reconciliation Commission of Canada, La Tuque, Québec, 6 March 2013, Statement Number: SP105.
3. TRC, AVS, Thérese Niquay, Statement to the Truth and Reconciliation Commission of Canada, La Tuque, Québec, 6 March 2013, Statement Number: SP105.
4. TRC, AVS, Jeannette Coo Coo, Statement to the Truth and Reconciliation Commission of Canada, La Tuque, Québec, 6 March 2013, Statement Number: SP105.
5. TRC, AVS, Albert Elias, Statement to the Truth and Reconciliation Commission of Canada, Inuvik, Northwest Territories, 1 July 2011, Statement Number: SC092.
6. TRC, AVS, Paul Stanley, Statement to the Truth and Reconciliation Commission of Canada, Deroche, British Columbia, 19 January 2010, Statement Number: 2011-5057.
7. TRC, AVS, Eva Lapage, Statement to the Truth and Reconciliation Commission of Canada, Halifax, Nova Scotia, 29 October 2011, Statement Number: 2011-2919.
8. TRC, AVS, Bob Baxter, Statement to the Truth and Reconciliation Commission of Canada, Thunder Bay, Ontario, 24 November 2010, Statement Number: 01-ON-24NOV10-012.
9. TRC, AVS, Lynda Pahpasay McDonald, Statement to the Truth and Reconciliation Commission of Canada, Winnipeg, Manitoba, 16 June 2010, Statement Number: 02-MB-16JU10-130.
10. TRC, AVS, Mabel Brown, Statement to the Truth and Reconciliation Commission of Canada, Inuvik, Northwest Territories, 28 September 2011, Statement Number: 2011-0325.
11. TRC, AVS, Emily Kematch, Statement to the Truth and Reconciliation Commission of Canada, Winnipeg, Manitoba, 18 June 2010, Statement Number: 02-MB-18JU10-063.
12. TRC, AVS, Piita Irniq, Statement to the Truth and Reconciliation Commission of Canada, Halifax, Nova Scotia, 27 October 2011, Statement Number: 2011-2905.
13. TRC, AVS, Anthony Henry, Statement to the Truth and Reconciliation Commission of Canada, Winnipeg, Manitoba, 17 June 2010, Statement Number: 02-MB-17JU10-086.
14. TRC, AVS, Albert Fiddler, Statement to the Truth and Reconciliation Commission of Canada, Saskatoon, Saskatchewan, 24 June 2012, Statement Number: 2011-1760.

15. TRC, AVS, Doris Young, Statement to the Truth and Reconciliation Commission of Canada, Saskatoon, Saskatchewan, 22 June 2012, Statement Number: 2011-3517.

16. TRC, AVS, Delores Adolph, Statement to the Truth and Reconciliation Commission of Canada, Mission, British Columbia, 19 May 2011, Statement Number: 2011-3458.

17. TRC, AVS, Rosalie Webber, Statement to the Truth and Reconciliation Commission of Canada, Halifax, Nova Scotia, 26 October 2011, Statement Number: 2011-2891.

18. TRC, AVS, Martha Loon, Statement to the Truth and Reconciliation Commission of Canada, Thunder Bay, Ontario, 25 November 2010, Statement Number 01-ON-24NOV10-021.

19. TRC, AVS, Richard Hall, Statement to the Truth and Reconciliation Commission of Canada, Vancouver, British Columbia, 18 September 2013, Statement Number: 2011-1852.

20. Translated words confirmed by Translation Bureau, Public Works and Government Services Canada.

21. TRC, AVS, Noel Starblanket, Statement to the Truth and Reconciliation Commission of Canada, Regina, Saskatchewan, 16 January 2012, Statement Number: 2011-3314.

22. TRC, AVS, Patrick James Hall, Statement to the Truth and Reconciliation Commission of Canada, Winnipeg, Manitoba, 21 December 2010, Statement Number: 03-001-10-036.

23. TRC, AVS, Leona Martin, Statement to the Truth and Reconciliation Commission of Canada, Regina, Saskatchewan, 17 January 2012, Statement Number: SP036.

24. TRC, AVS, Andre Tautu (translated from Inuktitut), Statement to the Truth and Reconciliation Commission of Canada, Chesterfield Inlet, Nunavut, 22 March 2011, Statement Number: SP005.

25. TRC, AVS, [Name redacted], Statement to the Truth and Reconciliation Commission of Canada, Fort Simpson, Northwest Territories, 23 November 2011, Statement Number: 2011-2689.

26. TRC, AVS, [Name redacted], Statement to the Truth and Reconciliation Commission of Canada, Victoria, British Columbia, 13 April 2012, Statement Number: 2011-3978.

27. TRC, AVS, Josephine Eshkibok, Statement to the Truth and Reconciliation Commission of Canada, Little Current, Ontario, 13 May 2011, Statement Number: 2011-2014.

28. TRC, AVS, Isaac Daniels, Statement to the Truth and Reconciliation Commission of Canada, Saskatoon, Saskatchewan, 22 June 2012, Statement Number: 2011-1779.

29. TRC, AVS, Donna Antoine, Statement to the Truth and Reconciliation Commission of Canada, Enderby, British Columbia, 13 October 2011, Statement Number: 2011-3287.

30. TRC, AVS, Vitaline Elsie Jenner, Statement to the Truth and Reconciliation Commission of Canada, Winnipeg, Manitoba, 16 June 2010, Statement Number: 02-MB-16JU10-131.

31. TRC, AVS, Ken A. Littledeer, Statement to the Truth and Reconciliation Commission of Canada, Thunder Bay, Ontario, 26 November 2010, Statement Number: 01-ON-24-NOV10-028.

32. TRC, AVS, Andrew Bull Calf, Statement to the Truth and Reconciliation Commission of Canada, Lethbridge, Alberta, 10 October 2013, Statement Number: 2011-0273.

33. TRC, AVS, Martha Minoose, Statement to the Truth and Reconciliation Commission of Canada, Lethbridge, Alberta, 10 October 2013, Statement Number: 2011-1748.

34. TRC, AVS, Maureen Gloria Johnson, Statement to the Truth and Reconciliation Commission of Canada, Whitehorse, Yukon, 26 May 2011, Statement Number: 2011-1126.

35. TRC, AVS, Paul Dixon, Statement to the Truth and Reconciliation Commission of Canada, Val d'Or, Québec, 6 February 2012, Statement Number: SP101.

36. TRC, AVS, Lynda Pahpasay McDonald, Statement to the Truth and Reconciliation Commission of Canada, Winnipeg, Manitoba, 16 June 2010, Statement Number: 02-MB-16JU10-130.

37. TRC, AVS, Dorothy Ross, Statement to the Truth and Reconciliation Commission of Canada, Thunder Bay, Ontario, 25 November 2010, Statement Number: 01-ON-24NOV10-014.

38. TRC, AVS, Albert Marshall, Statement to the Truth and Reconciliation Commission of Canada, Winnipeg, Manitoba, 17 June 2010, Statement Number: 02-MB-17JU10-050.

39. TRC, AVS, Jaco Anaviapik (translated from Inuktitut), Statement to the Truth and Reconciliation Commission of Canada, Pond Inlet, Nunavut, 7 February 2014, Statement Number: SP044.

40. TRC, AVS, Ellen Smith, Statement to the Truth and Reconciliation Commission of Canada, Fort McPherson, Northwest Territories, 14 September 2011, Statement Number: 2011-0346.

41. TRC, AVS, Shirley Williams, Statement to the Truth and Reconciliation Commission of Canada, Spanish, Ontario, 12 September 2009, Statement Number: 2011-5040.

42. TRC, AVS, [Name redacted], Statement to the Truth and Reconciliation Commission of Canada, Key First Nation, Saskatchewan, 21 January 2012, Statement Number: SP039.

43. TRC, AVS, Leon Wyallon, Statement to the Truth and Reconciliation Commission of Canada, Behchoko, Northwest Territories, 15 April 2011, Statement Number: 2011-0244.

44. TRC, AVS, Anthony Henry, Statement to the Truth and Reconciliation Commission of Canada, Winnipeg, Manitoba, 17 June 2010, Statement Number: 02-MB-17JU10-086.

45. TRC, AVS, Ivan George, Statement to the Truth and Reconciliation Commission of Canada, Mission, British Columbia, 18 May 2011, Statement Number: 2011-3472.

46. TRC, AVS, Cecilia Whitefield-Big George, Statement to the Truth and Reconciliation Commission of Canada, Winnipeg, Manitoba, 17 June 2010, Statement Number: 02-MB-17JU10-030.

47. TRC, AVS, [Named redacted], Statement to the Truth and Reconciliation Commission of Canada, Key First Nation, Saskatchewan, 21 January 2012, Statement Number: SP039.

48. TRC, AVS, Ethel Johnson, Statement to the Truth and Reconciliation Commission of Canada, Eskasoni First Nation, Nova Scotia, 14 October 2011, Statement Number: 2011-2680.

49. TRC, AVS, Dorothy Jane Beaulieu, Statement to the Truth and Reconciliation Commission of Canada, Fort Resolution, Northwest Territories, 28 April 2011, Statement Number: 2011-0379.

50. TRC, AVS, Hazel Mary Anderson, Statement to the Truth and Reconciliation Commission of Canada, Winnipeg, Manitoba, 18 June 2010, Statement Number: 02-MB-18JU10-034.

51. TRC, AVS, [Name redacted], Statement to the Truth and Reconciliation Commission of Canada, Eskasoni First Nation, Nova Scotia, 14 October 2011, Statement Number: 2011-2681.

52. TRC, AVS, [Name redacted], Statement to the Truth and Reconciliation Commission of Canada, Gambier Island, British Columbia, 29 July 2011, Statement Number: 2011-3279.

53. TRC, AVS, Dorene Bernard, Statement to the Truth and Reconciliation Commission of Canada, Indian Brook, Nova Scotia, 12 October 2011, Statement Number: SP029.

54. TRC, AVS, Frederick Ernest Koe, Statement to the Truth and Reconciliation Commission of Canada, Inuvik, Northwest Territories, 30 June 2011, Statement Number: SC091.

55. TRC, AVS, Howard Stacy Jones, Statement to the Truth and Reconciliation Commission of Canada, Victoria, British Columbia, 4 December 2010, Statement Number: 01-BC-03DE10-001.

56. TRC, AVS, Shirley Leon, Statement to the Truth and Reconciliation Commission of Canada, Deroche, British Columbia, 19 January 2010, Statement Number: 2011-5048.

57. TRC, AVS, Marlene Kayseas, Statement to the Truth and Reconciliation Commission of Canada, Regina, Saskatchewan, 16 January 2012, Statement Number: SP035.

58. TRC, AVS, Rick Gilbert, Statement to the Truth and Reconciliation Commission of Canada, Vancouver, British Columbia, 20 September 2013, Statement Number: 2011-2389.

59. TRC, AVS, Alma Scott, Statement to the Truth and Reconciliation Commission of Canada, Winnipeg, Manitoba, 17 June 2010, Statement Number: 02-MB-16JU10-016.

60. TRC, AVS, Leona Bird, Statement to the Truth and Reconciliation Commission of Canada, Saskatoon, Saskatchewan, 21 June 2012, Statement Number: 2011-4415.

61. TRC, AVS, Sam Ross, Statement to the Truth and Reconciliation Commission of Canada, Opaskwayak Cree Nation, Manitoba, 17 January 2012, Statement Number: 2011-0294.

62. TRC, AVS, Benjamin Joseph Lafford, Statement to the Truth and Reconciliation Commission of Canada, Halifax, Nova Scotia, 28 October 2011, Statement Number: SC075.

63. TRC, AVS, Larry Beardy, Statement to the Truth and Reconciliation Commission of Canada, Thompson, Manitoba, 25 September 2012, Statement Number: SP082.

64. TRC, AVS, Emily Kematch, Statement to the Truth and Reconciliation Commission of Canada, Winnipeg, Manitoba, 18 June 2010, Statement Number: 02-MB-18JU10-063.

65. TRC, AVS, Sphenia Jones, Statement to the Truth and Reconciliation Commission of Canada, Terrace, British Columbia, 29 November 2011, Statement Number: 2011-3300.

66. TRC, AVS, John B. Custer, Statement to the Truth and Reconciliation Commission of Canada, Winnipeg, Manitoba, 19 June 2010, Statement Number: 02-MB-19JU10-057.

67. TRC, AVS, Dorothy Hart, Statement to the Truth and Reconciliation Commission of Canada, Nelson House, Manitoba, 22 February 2012, Statement Number: 2011-2586.

68. TRC, AVS, Florence Horassi, Statement to the Truth and Reconciliation Commission of Canada, Tulita, Northwest Territories, 10 May 2011, Statement Number: 2011-0394.

69. TRC, AVS, Joe Krimmerdjuar, Statement to the Truth and Reconciliation Commission of Canada, Inuvik, Northwest Territories, 30 June 2011, Statement Number: SC091.

70. TRC, AVS, Albert Elias, Statement to the Truth and Reconciliation Commission of Canada, Inuvik, Northwest Territories, 1 July 2011, Statement Number: SC092.

71. TRC, AVS, Sam Kautainuk (translated from Inuktitut), Statement to the Truth and Reconciliation Commission of Canada, Pond Inlet, Nunavut, 7 February 2012, Statement Number: SP044.

72. TRC, AVS, Nellie Ningewance, Statement to the Truth and Reconciliation Commission of Canada, Sault Ste. Marie, Ontario, 1 July 2011, Statement Number: 2011-0305.

73. TRC, AVS, Campbell Papequash, Statement to the Truth and Reconciliation Commission of Canada, Key First Nation, Saskatchewan, 20 January 2012, Statement Number: SP038.

74. Marthe Basile-Coocoo, Statement to the Truth and Reconciliation Commission of Canada, (Translated from French) Montreal, Québec, 26 April 2013, Statement Number: 2011-6103.

75. Pauline St-Onge, Statement to the Truth and Reconciliation Commission of Canada, 25 April 2013, Montreal, Québec, Statement Number: 2011-6134.

76. TRC, AVS, Louise Large, Statement to the Truth and Reconciliation Commission of Canada, St. Paul, Alberta, 7 January 2011, Statement Number: 01-AB-06IA11-012.

77. TRC, AVS, Rachel Chakasim, Statement to the Truth and Reconciliation Commission of Canada, Timmins, Ontario, 9 November 2010, Statement Number: 01-ON-4-6NOV10-019.

78. TRC, AVS, Linda Head, Statement to the Truth and Reconciliation Commission of Canada, Saskatoon, Saskatchewan, 24 June 2012, Statement Number: 2011-4442.

79. TRC, AVS, Gilles Petiquay, Statement to the Truth and Reconciliation Commission of Canada, (Translated from French) La Tuque, Québec, 6 March 2013, Statement Number: 2011-6001.

80. TRC, AVS, Mary Courchene, Statement to the Truth and Reconciliation Commission of Canada, Pine Creek First Nation, Manitoba, 28 November 2011, Statement Number: 2011-2515.

81. TRC, AVS, Roy Denny, Statement to the Truth and Reconciliation Commission of Canada, Eskasoni First Nation, Nova Scotia, 14 October 2011, Statement Number: 2011-2678.

82. TRC, AVS, Roy Denny, Statement to the Truth and Reconciliation Commission of Canada, Eskasoni First Nation, Nova Scotia, 14 October 2011, Statement Number: 2011-2678.

83. TRC, AVS, Calvin Myerion, Statement to the Truth and Reconciliation Commission of Canada, Winnipeg, Manitoba, 16 June 2010, Statement Number: 02-MB-16JU10-122.

84. TRC, AVS, Archie Hyacinthe, Statement to the Truth and Reconciliation Commission of Canada, Kenora, Ontario, 15 March 2011, Statement Number: 2011-0279.

85. TRC, AVS, Dorene Bernard, Statement to the Truth and Reconciliation Commission of Canada, Indian Brook, Nova Scotia, 12 October 2011, Statement Number: SP029.

86. TRC, AVS, Ida Ralph Quisess, Statement to the Truth and Reconciliation Commission of Canada, Thunder Bay, Ontario, 24 November 2010, Statement Number: 01-ON-24NOV10-002.

87. TRC, AVS, Vitaline Elsie Jenner, Statement to the Truth and Reconciliation Commission of Canada, Winnipeg, Manitoba, 16 June 2010, Statement Number: 02-MB-16JU10-131. (Translated word confirmed by Translation Bureau, Public Works and Government Services Canada.)

88. TRC, AVS, Lily Bruce, Statement to the Truth and Reconciliation Commission of Canada, Alert Bay, British Columbia, 4 August 2011, Statement Number: 2011-3285.

89. TRC, AVS, Margaret Simpson, Statement to the Truth and Reconciliation Commission of Canada, Winnipeg, Manitoba, 18 June 2010, Statement Number: 02-MB-18JU10-051.

90. TRC, AVS, Lynda Pahpasay McDonald, Statement to the Truth and Reconciliation Commission of Canada, Winnipeg, Manitoba, 16 June 2010, Statement Number: 02-MB-16JU10-130.

91. TRC, AVS, Emily Kematch, Statement to the Truth and Reconciliation Commission of Canada, Winnipeg, Manitoba, 18 June 2010, Statement Number: 02-MB-18JU10-063.

92. TRC, AVS, Verna Kirkness, Statement to the Truth and Reconciliation Commission of Canada, Winnipeg, Manitoba, 18 June 2010, Statement Number: 02-MB-18JU10-033.

93. TRC, AVS, Alice Quinney, Statement to the Truth and Reconciliation Commission of Canada, Winnipeg, Manitoba, 18 June 2010, Statement Number: 02-MB-18JU10-049.

94. TRC, AVS, Lily Bruce, Statement to the Truth and Reconciliation Commission of Canada, Albert Bay, British Columbia, 4 August 2011, Statement Number: 2011-3285.

95. TRC, AVS, Helen Harry, Statement to the Truth and Reconciliation Commission of Canada, Vancouver, British Columbia, 20 September 2013, Statement Number: 2011-3203.

96. TRC, AVS, Ricky Kakekagumick. Statement to the Truth and Reconciliation Commission of Canada, Thunder Bay, Ontario, 15 December 2011, Statement Number: 2011-4200.

97. TRC, AVS, Bernice Jacks, Statement to the Truth and Reconciliation Commission of Canada, Victoria, British Columbia, 13 April 2012, Statement Number: 2011-3971.

98. TRC, AVS, Victoria Boucher-Grant, Statement to the Truth and Reconciliation Commission of Canada, Ottawa, Ontario, 5 February 2011, Statement Number: 01-ON-05FE11-004.

99. TRC, AVS, Elaine Durocher, Statement to the Truth and Reconciliation Commission of Canada, Winnipeg, Manitoba, 16 June 2010, Statement Number: 02-MB-16JU10-059.

100. TRC, AVS, Brian Rae, Statement to the Truth and Reconciliation Commission of Canada, Thunder Bay, Ontario, 14 July 2010, Statement Number: 2011-4198.

101. TRC, AVS, Julianna Alexander, Statement to the Truth and Reconciliation Commission of Canada, Enderby, British Columbia, 12 October 2011, Statement Number: 2011-3286.

102. TRC, AVS, Murray Crowe, Statement to the Truth and Reconciliation Commission of Canada, Sault Ste. Marie, Ontario, 1 July 2011, Statement Number: 2011-0306.

103. TRC, AVS, Wilbur Abrahams, Statement to the Truth and Reconciliation Commission of Canada, Terrace, British Columbia, 30 November 2011, Statement Number: 2011-3301.

104. TRC, AVS, John B. Custer, Statement to the Truth and Reconciliation Commission of Canada, Winnipeg, Manitoba, 19 June 2010, Statement Number: 02-MB-19JU10-057.

105. TRC, AVS, Elizabeth Tapiatic Chiskamish, Statement to the Truth and Reconciliation Commission of Canada, Chisasibi, Québec, 20 March 2013, Statement Number: 2011-3363. (Translated from Cree to English by Translation Bureau, Public Works and Government Services Canada.) †

106. TRC, AVS, Phyllis Webstad, Statement to the Truth and Reconciliation Commission of Canada, Williams Lake, British Columbia, 16 May 2013, Statement Number: SP111.

107. Monica Lamb-Yorski, "Orange Shirt Day Makes its Debut in Williams Lake Sept. 30," *Williams Lake Tribune*, 19 September 2013, http://www.wltribune.com/news/224499761.html.

108. TRC, AVS, Larry Beardy, Statement to the Truth and Reconciliation Commission of Canada, Thompson, Manitoba, 25 September 2012, Statement Number: SP082.

109. TRC, AVS, Ilene Nepoose, Statement to the Truth and Reconciliation Commission of Canada, Hobbema, Alberta, 25 July 2013, Statement Number: 2011-2380.

110. TRC, AVS, Nick Sibbeston, Statement to the Truth and Reconciliation Commission of Canada, Inuvik, Northwest Territories, 29 June 2011, Statement Number: NNE202.

111. TRC, AVS, Carmen Petiquay, Statement to the Truth and Reconciliation Commission of Canada, LaTuque, Québec, 5 March 2013, Statement Number: SP104.

112. TRC, AVS, Martin Nicholas, Statement to the Truth and Reconciliation Commission of Canada, Grand Rapids, Manitoba, 24 February 2010, Statement Number: 07-MB-24FB10-001.

113. TRC, AVS, Frances Tait, Statement to the Truth and Reconciliation Commission of Canada, Victoria, British Columbia, 13 April 2012, Statement Number: 2011-3974.

114. TRC, AVS, Dorothy Ross, Statement to the Truth and Reconciliation Commission of Canada, Thunder Bay, Ontario, 25 November 2010, Statement Number: 01-ON-24NOV10-014.

115. TRC, AVS, Lorna Morgan, Statement to the Truth and Reconciliation Commission of Canada, Winnipeg, Manitoba, 17 June 2010, Statement Number: 02-MB-16JU10-041.

116. TRC, AVS, Geraldine Bob, Statement to the Truth and Reconciliation Commission of Canada, Fort Simpson, Northwest Territories, 23 November 2011, Statement number: 2011-2685.

117. TRC, AVS, Stella August, Statement to the Truth and Reconciliation Commission of Canada, Winnipeg, Manitoba, 16 June 2010, Statement Number: 02-MB-16JU10-005.

118. TRC, AVS, William Herney, Statement to the Truth and Reconciliation Commission of Canada, Halifax, Nova Scotia, 29 October 2011, Statement Number: 2011-2923.

119. TRC, AVS, Margaret Plamondon, Statement to the Truth and Reconciliation Commission of Canada, Fort Smith, Northwest Territories, 6 May 2011, Statement Number: 2011-0387.

120. TRC, AVS, Joanne Morrison Methot, Statement to the Truth and Reconciliation Commission of Canada, Halifax, Nova Scotia, 28 October 2011, Statement Number: 2011-2875.

121. TRC, AVS, Shirley Ida Moore, Statement to the Truth and Reconciliation Commission of Canada, Winnipeg, Manitoba, 2 March 2011, Statement Number: 2011-0089.

122. TRC, AVS, Arthur Ron McKay, Statement to the Truth and Reconciliation Commission of Canada, Winnipeg, Manitoba, 18 June 2010, Statement Number: 02-MB-18JU10-044.

123. TRC, AVS, Margo Wylde, Statement to the Truth and Reconciliation Commission of Canada, Val d'Or, Québec, 5 February 2012, Statement Number: SP100.

124. TRC, AVS, William Antoine, Statement to the Truth and Reconciliation Commission of Canada, Little Current, Ontario, 12 May 2011, Statement Number: 2011-2002.

125. TRC, AVS, Peter Nakogee, Statement to the Truth and Reconciliation Commission of Canada, Timmins, Ontario, 9 November 2010, Statement Number: 01-ON-4-6NOV10-023. (Translated from Swampy Cree to English by Translation Bureau, Public Works and Government Services Canada.)

126. TRC, AVS, Marcel Guiboche, Statement to the Truth and Reconciliation Commission of Canada, Winnipeg, Manitoba, 19 June 2010, Statement Number: 02-MB-19JU10-034.

127. TRC, AVS, Calvin Myerion, Statement to the Truth and Reconciliation Commission of Canada, Winnipeg, Manitoba, 16 June 2010, Statement Number: 02-MB-16JU10-122.

128. TRC, AVS, Lily Bruce, Statement to the Truth and Reconciliation Commission of Canada, Alert Bay, British Columbia, 4 August 2011, Statement Number: 2011-3285.

129. TRC, AVS, Andrew Bull Calf, Statement to the Truth and Reconciliation Commission of Canada, Lethbridge, Alberta, 10 October 2013, Statement Number: 2011-0273.

130. TRC, AVS, Percy Thompson, Statement to the Truth and Reconciliation Commission of Canada, Hobbema, Alberta, 25 July 2013, Statement Number: SP125.

131. TRC, AVS, [Name redacted], Statement to the Truth and Reconciliation Commission of Canada, Deline, Northwest Territories, 2 March 2010, Statement Number: 07-NWT-02MR10-002.

132. TRC, AVS, Alfred Nolie, Statement to the Truth and Reconciliation Commission of Canada, Alert Bay, British Columbia, 20 October 2011, Statement Number: 2011-3293.

133. TRC, AVS, Martin Nicholas, Statement to the Truth and Reconciliation Commission of Canada, Grand Rapids, Manitoba, 24 February 2010, Statement Number: 07-MB-24FB10-001.

134. TRC, AVS, Meeka Alivaktuk (translated from Inuktitut), Statement to the Truth and Reconciliation Commission of Canada, Pangnirtung, Nunavut, 13 February 2012, Statement Number: SP045.

135. TRC, AVS, Emily Kematch, Statement to the Truth and Reconciliation Commission of Canada, Winnipeg, Manitoba, 18 June 2010, Statement Number: 02-MB-18JU10-063.

136. TRC, AVS, Greg Rainville, Statement to the Truth and Reconciliation Commission of Canada, Saskatoon, Saskatchewan, 22 June 2012, Statement Number: 2011-1752.

137. TRC, AVS, Robert Malcolm, Statement to the Truth and Reconciliation Commission of Canada, Winnipeg, Manitoba, 17 June 2010, Statement Number: 02-MB-16JU10-090.

138. TRC, AVS, Jacqueline Barney, Statement to the Truth and Reconciliation Commission of Canada, Val d'Or, Québec, 5 February 2012, Statement Number: SP100.

139. TRC, AVS, Dianne Bossum, Statement to the Truth and Reconciliation Commission of Canada, La Tuque, Québec, 6 March 2013, Statement Number: SP105.

140. TRC, AVS, Geraldine Shingoose, Statement to the Truth and Reconciliation Commission of Canada, Winnipeg, Manitoba, 19 June 2010, Statement Number: 02-MB-19JU10-033.

141. TRC, AVS, Dorothy Nolie, Statement to the Truth and Reconciliation Commission of Canada, Alert Bay, British Columbia, 20 October 2011, Statement Number: 2011-3294.

142. TRC, AVS, Leon Wyallon, Statement to the Truth and Reconciliation Commission of Canada, Behchoko, Northwest Territories, 15 April 2011, Statement Number: 2011-0244.

143. TRC, AVS, David Nevin, Statement to the Truth and Reconciliation Commission of Canada, Indian Brook, Nova Scotia, 12 October 2011, Statement Number: SP029.

144. TRC, AVS, Alan Knockwood, Statement to the Truth and Reconciliation Commission of Canada, Indian Brook, Nova Scotia, 12 October 2011, Statement Number: SP029.

145. TRC, AVS, Allen Kagak, Statement to the Truth and Reconciliation Commission of Canada, Inuvik, Northwest Territories, 29 June 2011, Statement Number: SC090.

146. TRC, AVS, Richard Kaiyogan, Statement to the Truth and Reconciliation Commission of Canada, Inuvik, Northwest Territories, 30 June 2011, Statement Number: SC091.

147. TRC, AVS, Sam Kautainuk (translated from Inuktitut), Statement to the Truth and Reconciliation Commission of Canada, Pond Inlet, Nunavut, 7 February 2012, Statement Number: SP044.

148. TRC, AVS, Pierrette Benjamin, Statement to the Truth and Reconciliation Commission of Canada, La Tuque, Québec, 6 March 2013, Statement Number: SP105.

149. TRC, AVS, Alphonsine McNeely, Statement to the Truth and Reconciliation Commission of Canada, Fort Good Hope, Northwest Territories, 13 July 2010, Statement Number: 01-NWT-JY10-002.

150. TRC, AVS, Ken A. Littledeer, Statement to the Truth and Reconciliation Commission of Canada, Thunder Bay, Ontario, 26 November 2010, Statement Number: 01-ON-24-NOV10-028.

151. TRC, AVS, William Herney, Statement to the Truth and Reconciliation Commission of Canada, Halifax, Nova Scotia, 29 October 2011, Statement Number: 2011-2923.

152. TRC, AVS, Mary Courchene, Statement to the Truth and Reconciliation Commission of Canada, Pine Creek First Nation, Manitoba, 28 November 2011, Statement Number: 2011-2515.

153. TRC, AVS, Lydia Ross, Statement to the Truth and Reconciliation Commission of Canada, Winnipeg, Manitoba, 16 June 2010, Statement Number: 02-MB-16JU10-029.

154. TRC, AVS, Monique Papatie, Statement to the Truth and Reconciliation Commission of Canada, Val d'Or, Québec, 6 February 2012, Statement Number: SP101.

155. TRC, AVS, Arthur Ron McKay, Statement to the Truth and Reconciliation Commission of Canada, Winnipeg, Manitoba, 18 June 2010, Statement Number: 02-MB-18Ju10-044.

156. TRC, AVS, Ronalee Lavallee, Statement to the Truth and Reconciliation Commission of Canada, Saskatoon, Saskatchewan, 24 June 2012, Statement Number: 2011-1776.

157. TRC, AVS, Mary Stoney, Statement to the Truth and Reconciliation Commission of Canada, Hobbema, Alberta, 24 July 2013, Statement Number: SP124.

158. TRC, AVS, Albert Fiddler, Statement to the Truth and Reconciliation Commission of Canada, Saskatoon, Saskatchewan, 24 June 2012, Statement Number: 2011-1760.

159. TRC, AVS, Alex Alikashuak, Statement to the Truth and Reconciliation Commission of Canada, Winnipeg, Manitoba, 16 June 2010, Statement Number: 02-MB-16JU10-137.

160. TRC, AVS, Ellen Smith, Statement to the Truth and Reconciliation Commission of Canada, Fort McPherson, Northwest Territories, 14 September 2011, Statement Number: 2011-0346.

161. TRC, AVS, Russell Bone, Statement to the Truth and Reconciliation Commission of Canada, Keeseekoowenin First Nation, Manitoba, 28 May 2010, Statement Number: S-KFN-MB-01-001.

162. TRC, AVS, Rose Dorothy Charlie, Statement to the Truth and Reconciliation Commission of Canada, Whitehorse, Yukon, 27 May 2011, Statement Number: 2011-1134.

163. TRC, AVS, Robert Joseph, Statement to the Truth and Reconciliation Commission of Canada, Winnipeg, Manitoba, 16 June 2010, Statement Number: SC093.

164. TRC, AVS, Paul Dixon, Statement to the Truth and Reconciliation Commission of Canada, Val d'Or, Québec, 6 February 2012, Statement Number: SP101.

165. TRC, AVS, John Kistabish, Statement to the Truth and Reconciliation Commission of Canada, 26 April 2013, Montreal, Québec, Statement Number: 2011-6135

166. TRC, AVS, Joline Huskey, Statement to the Truth and Reconciliation Commission of Canada, Behchoko, Northwest Territories, 15 April 2011, Statement Number: 2011-0231.

167. TRC, AVS, Bruce R. Dumont, Statement to the Truth and Reconciliation Commission of Canada, Batoche, Saskatchewan, 23 July 2010, Statement Number: 01-SK-18-25JY10-013.

168. TRC, AVS, Andrew Bull Calf, Statement to the Truth and Reconciliation Commission of Canada, Lethbridge, Alberta, 10 October 2013, Statement Number: 2011-0273.

169. TRC, AVS, Evelyn Kelman, Statement to the Truth and Reconciliation Commission of Canada, Lethbridge, Alberta, 10 October 2013, Statement Number: SP128.

170. TRC, AVS, Marilyn Buffalo, Statement to the Truth and Reconciliation Commission of Canada, Hobbema, Alberta, 25 July 2013, Statement Number: SP125.

171. TRC, AVS, Sarah McLeod, Statement to the Truth and Reconciliation Commission of Canada, Kamloops, British Columbia, 8 August 2009, Statement Number: 2011-5009.

172. TRC, AVS, Mary Olibuk Tatty, Statement to the Truth and Reconciliation Commission of Canada, Rankin Inlet, Nunavut, 21 March 2011, Statement Number: 2011-0156.

173. TRC, AVS, Thaddee Andre, Statement to the Truth and Reconciliation Commission of Canada, (Translated from French) Montreal, 25 April 2013, Québec, Statement Number: 2011-6068.

174. TRC, AVS, [Name redacted], Statement to the Truth and Reconciliation Commission of Canada, Winnipeg, Manitoba, 18 June 2010, Statement Number: 02-MB-18JU10-055.

175. TRC, AVS, Gordon James Pemmican, Statement to the Truth and Reconciliation Commission of Canada, Winnipeg, Manitoba, 18 June 2010, Statement Number: 02-MB-18JU10-069.

176. TRC, AVS, [Name redacted], Statement to the Truth and Reconciliation Commission of Canada, Gambier Island, British Columbia, 29 July 2011, Statement Number: 2011-3279.

177. TRC, AVS, Jeanette Basile Laloche, Statement to the Truth and Reconciliation Commission of Canada, (Translated from French) Montreal, Québec, 27 April 2013, Statement Number: 2011-6136.

178. Radunovich and Evans, "Bed Wetting," 1–2.

179. TRC, AVS, Albert Fiddler, Statement to the Truth and Reconciliation Commission of Canada, Saskatoon, Saskatchewan, 24 June 2012, Statement Number: 2011-1760.

180. TRC, AVS, Russell Bone, Statement to the Truth and Reconciliation Commission of Canada, Keeseekoowenin First Nation, Manitoba, 28 May 2010, Statement Number: S-KFN-MB-01-001.

181. TRC, AVS, [Name redacted], Statement to the Truth and Reconciliation Commission of Canada, Gambier Island, British Columbia, 29 July 2011, Statement Number: 2011-3279.

182. TRC, AVS, Helen Kakekayash, Statement to the Truth and Reconciliation Commission of Canada, Ottawa, Ontario, 5 February 2011, Statement Number: 01-ON-05FE11-002.

183. TRC, AVS, Alfred Nolie, Statement to the Truth and Reconciliation Commission of Canada, Alert Bay, British Columbia, 20 October 2011, Statement Number: 2011-3293.

184. TRC, AVS, Louise Large, Statement to the Truth and Reconciliation Commission of Canada, St. Paul, Alberta, 7 January 2011, Statement Number: 01-AB-06JA11-012.

185. TRC, AVS, Patrick James Hall, Statement to the Truth and Reconciliation Commission of Canada, Winnipeg, Manitoba, 21 December 2010, Statement Number: 03-001-10-036.

186. TRC, AVS, Josephine Eshkibok, Statement to the Truth and Reconciliation Commission of Canada, Little Current, Ontario, 13 May 2011, Statement Number: 2011-2014.

187. TRC, AVS, Wesley Keewatin, Statement to the Truth and Reconciliation Commission of Canada, Gambier Island, British Columbia, 28 July 2011, Statement Number: 2011-3276.

188. TRC, AVS, Wendy Lafond, Statement to the Truth and Reconciliation Commission of Canada, Bato-che, Saskatchewan, 24 July 2010, Statement Number: 01-SK-18-25JY10-015.

189. TRC, AVS, Don Willie, Statement to the Truth and Reconciliation Commission of Canada, Alert Bay, British Columbia, 3 August 2011, Statement Number: 2011-3284.

190. TRC, AVS, Frank Tomkins, Statement to the Truth and Reconciliation Commission of Canada, Bato-che, Saskatchewan, 21 July 2010, Statement Number: 01-SK-18-25JY10-009.

191. TRC, AVS, William Francis Paul, Statement to the Truth and Reconciliation Commission of Canada, Halifax, Nova Scotia, 28 October 2011, Statement Number: 2011-2873.

192. TRC, AVS, Joseph Ward, Statement to the Truth and Reconciliation Commission of Canada, Halifax, Nova Scotia, 28 October 2011, Statement Number: 2011-2872.

193. TRC, AVS, Mary Rose Julian, Statement to the Truth and Reconciliation Commission of Canada, Hal-ifax, Nova Scotia, 27 October 2011, Statement Number: 2011-2880.

194. TRC, AVS, Benjamin Joseph Lafford, Statement to the Truth and Reconciliation Commission of Can-ada, Eskasoni, Nova Scotia, 14 October 2011, Statement Number: SP030.

195. Radunovich and Evans, "Bed Wetting," 3.

196. TRC, AVS, Benjamin Joseph Lafford, Statement to the Truth and Reconciliation Commission of Can-ada, Eskasoni, Nova Scotia, 14 October 2011, Statement Number: SP030.

197. TRC, AVS, Joanne Morrison Methot, Statement to the Truth and Reconciliation Commission of Can-ada, Halifax, Nova Scotia, 28 October 2011, Statement Number: 2011-2875.

198. TRC, AVS, Ron Windsor, Statement to the Truth and Reconciliation Commission of Canada, Terrace, British Columbia, 1 December 2011, Statement Number: 2011-3307.

199. TRC, AVS, Nora Abou-Tibbett, Statement to the Truth and Reconciliation Commission of Canada, Watson Lake, Yukon, 25 May 2011, Statement Number: 2011-0205.

200. TRC, AVS, John B. Custer, Statement to the Truth and Reconciliation Commission of Canada, Winni-peg, Manitoba, 19 June 2010, Statement Number: 02-MB-19JU10-057.

201. TRC, AVS, Noel Knockwood, Statement to the Truth and Reconciliation Commission of Canada, Hal-ifax, Nova Scotia, 29 October 2011, Statement Number: 2011-2922.

202. TRC, AVS, Lydia Ross, Statement to the Truth and Reconciliation Commission of Canada, Winnipeg, Manitoba, 16 June 2010, Statement Number: 02-MB-16JU10-029.

203. TRC, AVS, Mel H. Buffalo, Statement to the Truth and Reconciliation Commission of Canada, Hobbema, Alberta, 24 July 2013, Statement Number: 2011-2535.

204. TRC, AVS, [Name redacted], Statement to the Truth and Reconciliation Commission of Canada, Prince Albert, Saskatchewan, 1 February 2012, Statement Number: 2011-3879. (Translated from Woodland Cree to English by Translation Bureau, Public Works and Government Services Canada.)

205. TRC, AVS, Daniel Andre, Statement to the Truth and Reconciliation Commission of Canada, White-horse, Yukon, 23 May 2011, Statement Number: 2011 0202.

206. TRC, AVS, Percy Tuesday, Statement to the Truth and Reconciliation Commission of Canada, Winni-peg, Manitoba,18 June 2010, Statement Number: 02-MB-18JU10-083.

207. TRC, AVS, Stella Bone, Statement to the Truth and Reconciliation Commission of Canada, Keesee-koowenin First Nation, Manitoba, 29 May 2010, Statement Number: S-KFN-MB-01-006.

208. TRC, AVS, Bernadette Nadjiwan, Statement to the Truth and Reconciliation Commission of Canada, Spanish, Ontario, 12 September 2009, Statement Number: 2011-5029.

209. TRC, AVS, David Charleson, Statement to the Truth and Reconciliation Commission of Canada, Der-oche, British Columbia, 20 January 2010, Statement Number: 2011-5043.

210. TRC, AVS, Louise Large, Statement to the Truth and Reconciliation Commission of Canada, St. Paul, Alberta, 7 January 2011, Statement Number: 01-AB-06JA11-012.

211. TRC, AVS, Ilene Nepoose, Statement to the Truth and Reconciliation Commission of Canada, Hobbema, Alberta, 25 July 2013, Statement Number: 2011-2380.

212. TRC, AVS, Larry Roger Listener, Statement to the Truth and Reconciliation Commission of Canada, 25 July 2013, Hobbema, Alberta, Statement Number: SP125.

213. TRC, AVS, Lydia Ross, Statement to the Truth and Reconciliation Commission of Canada, Winnipeg, Manitoba,16 June 2010, Statement Number: 02-MB-16JU10-029.

214. TRC, AVS, Vitaline Elsie Jenner, Statement to the Truth and Reconciliation Commission of Canada, Winnipeg, Manitoba, 16 June 2010, Statement Number: 02-MB-16JU10-131.

215. TRC, AVS, Shirley Waskewitch, Statement to the Truth and Reconciliation Commission of Canada, Saskatoon, Saskatchewan, 24 June 2012, Statement Number: 2011-3521.

216. TRC, AVS, Lydia Ross, Statement to the Truth and Reconciliation Commission of Canada, Winnipeg, Manitoba, 16 June 2010, Statement Number: 02-MB-16JU10-029.

217. TRC, AVS, Marlene Kayseas, Statement to the Truth and Reconciliation Commission of Canada, Regina, Saskatchewan, 16 January 2012, Statement Number: SP035.

218. TRC, AVS, Martha Minoose, Statement to the Truth and Reconciliation Commission of Canada, Lethbridge, Alberta, 10 October 2013, Statement Number: 2011-1748.

219. TRC, AVS, Stella Bone, Statement to the Truth and Reconciliation Commission of Canada, Keeseekoowenin First Nation, Manitoba, 29 May 2010, Statement Number: S-KFN-MB-01-006.

220. TRC, AVS, Bernice Jacks, Statement to the Truth and Reconciliation Commission of Canada, Victoria, British Columbia, 13 April 2012, Statement Number: 2011-3971.

221. TRC, AVS, Wilbur Abrahams, Statement to the Truth and Reconciliation Commission of Canada, Terrace, British Columbia, 30 November 2011, Statement Number: 2011-3301.

222. TRC, AVS, Antonette White, Statement to the Truth and Reconciliation Commission of Canada, Victoria, British Columbia, 13 April 2012, Statement Number: 2011-3984.

223. TRC, AVS, Kiatch Nahanni, Statement to the Truth and Reconciliation Commission of Canada, Fort Simpson, Northwest Territories, 23 November 2011, Statement Number: 2011-2684.

224. TRC, AVS, Ken A. Littledeer, Statement to the Truth and Reconciliation Commission of Canada, Thunder Bay, Ontario, 26 November 2010, Statement Number: 01-ON-24-NOV10-028.

225. TRC, AVS, Lorna Morgan, Statement to the Truth and Reconciliation Commission of Canada, Winnipeg, Manitoba, 17 June 2010, Statement Number: 02-MB-16JU10-041.

226. TRC, AVS, Daisy Diamond, Statement to the Truth and Reconciliation Commission of Canada, Winnipeg, Manitoba, 18 June 2010, Statement Number: SC110.

227. TRC, AVS, Florence Horassi, Statement to the Truth and Reconciliation Commission of Canada, Tulita, Northwest Territories, 10 May 2011, Statement Number: 2011-0394.

228. TRC, AVS, Simon Awashish, Statement to the Truth and Reconciliation Commission of Canada, La Tuque, Québec, 5 March 2013, Statement Number: SP104.

229. TRC, AVS, Dora Fraser, Statement to the Truth and Reconciliation Commission of Canada, Winnipeg, Manitoba, 19 June 2010, Statement Number: 02-MB-19JU10-012.

230. TRC, AVS, Ellen Okimaw, Statement to the Truth and Reconciliation Commission of Canada, Timmins, Ontario, 8 November 2010, Statement Number: 01-ON-4-6NOV10-022.

231. TRC, AVS, Woodie Elias, Statement to the Truth and Reconciliation Commission of Canada, Fort McPherson, Northwest Territories, 12 September 2012, Statement Number: 2011-0343.

232. TRC, AVS, Dorothy Nolie, Statement to the Truth and Reconciliation Commission of Canada, Alert Bay, British Columbia, 20 October 2011, Statement Number: 2011-3294.

233. TRC, AVS, Faron Fontaine, Statement to the Truth and Reconciliation Commission of Canada, Long Plain First Nation, Manitoba, 27 July 2010, Statement Number: 01-MB-26JY10-009.

234. TRC, AVS, Andrew Paul, Statement to the Truth and Reconciliation Commission of Canada, Paulatuk, Northwest Territories, 17 April 2012, Statement Number: SP067.

235. TRC, AVS, Nellie Trapper, Statement to the Truth and Reconciliation Commission of Canada, Winnipeg, Manitoba, 18 June 2010, Statement Number: 02-MB-16JU10-086.

236. TRC, AVS, Rick Gilbert, Statement to the Truth and Reconciliation Commission of Canada, Vancouver, British Columbia, 20 September 2013, Statement Number: 2011-2389.

237. TRC, AVS, Doris Young, Statement to the Truth and Reconciliation Commission of Canada, Saskatoon, Saskatchewan, 22 June 2012, Statement Number: 2011-3517.

238. TRC, AVS, Ken A. Littledeer, Statement to the Truth and Reconciliation Commission of Canada, Thunder Bay, Ontario, 26 November 2010, Statement Number: 01-ON-24-NOV10-028.

239. TRC, AVS, Don Willie, Statement to the Truth and Reconciliation Commission of Canada, Alert Bay, British Columbia, 3 August 2011, Statement Number: 2011-3284.

240. TRC, AVS, Ray Silver, Statement to the Truth and Reconciliation Commission of Canada, Mission, British Columbia, 17 May 2011, Statement Number: 2011-3467.

241. TRC, AVS, Mary Beatrice Talley, Statement to the Truth and Reconciliation Commission of Canada, High Level, Alberta, 3 July 2013, Statement Number: 2011-3197.

242. TRC, AVS, William Antoine, Statement to the Truth and Reconciliation Commission of Canada, Little Current, Ontario, 12 May 2011, Statement Number: 2011-2002.

243. TRC, AVS, Gerald McLeod, Statement to the Truth and Reconciliation Commission of Canada, Whitehorse, Yukon, 27 May 2011, Statement Number: 2011-1130.

244. TRC, AVS, Louise Large, Statement to the Truth and Reconciliation Commission of Canada, St. Paul, Alberta, 7 January 2011, Statement Number: 01-AB-06JA11-012.

245. TRC, AVS, Shirley Ida Moore, Statement to the Truth and Reconciliation Commission of Canada, Winnipeg, Manitoba, 2 March 2011, Statement Number: 2011-0089.

246. TRC, AVS, Chris Frenchman, Statement to the Truth and Reconciliation Commission of Canada, Hobbema, Alberta, 24 July 2013, Statement Number: SP124.

247. TRC, AVS, Mel H. Buffalo, Statement to the Truth and Reconciliation Commission of Canada, Hobbema, Alberta, 24 July 2013, Statement Number: SP124.

248. TRC, AVS, Darlene Thomas, Statement to the Truth and Reconciliation Commission of Canada, Vancouver, British Columbia, 19 September 2013, Statement Number: 2011-3200.

249. TRC, AVS, Connie McNab, Statement to the Truth and Reconciliation Commission of Canada, Fort Simpson, Northwest Territories, 23 November 2011, Statement Number: 2011-2715.

250. TRC, AVS, Bernard Catcheway, Statement to the Truth and Reconciliation Commission of Canada, Skownan First Nation, Manitoba, 12 October 2011, Statement Number: 2011-2510.

251. TRC, AVS, Diane Bossum, Statement to the Truth and Reconciliation Commission of Canada, La Tuque, Québec, 5 March 2013, Statement Number: 2011-5079.

252. TRC, AVS, Bernard Sutherland, Statement to the Truth and Reconciliation Commission of Canada, Fort Albany, Ontario, 29 January 2013, Statement Number: 2011-3180. (Translated from Cree to English by Translation Bureau, Public Works and Government Services Canada.)

253. TRC, AVS, Ethel Johnson, Statement to the Truth and Reconciliation Commission of Canada, Eskasoni First Nation, Nova Scotia, 14 October 2011, Statement Number: 2011-2680.

254. TRC, AVS, Mary Beatrice Talley, Statement to the Truth and Reconciliation Commission of Canada, High Level, Alberta, 3 July 2013, Statement Number: 2011-3197.

255. TRC, AVS, Victoria McIntosh, Statement to the Truth and Reconciliation Commission of Canada, Winnipeg, Manitoba, 16 June 2010, Statement Number: 02-MB-16JU10-123.

256. TRC, AVS, Stella Bone, Statement to the Truth and Reconciliation Commission of Canada, Keeseekoowenin First Nation, Manitoba, 29 May 2010, Statement Number: S-KFN-MB-01-006.

257. Canada, *Annual Report of the Department of Indian Affairs, 1947*, 216.

258. TRC, AVS, Alfred Nolie, Statement to the Truth and Reconciliation Commission of Canada, Alert Bay, British Columbia, 20 October 2011, Statement Number: 2011-3293.

259. TRC, AVS, Shirley M. Villeneuve, Statement to the Truth and Reconciliation Commission of Canada, Fort Simpson, Northwest Territories, 23 February 2011, Statement Number: 2011-2691.

260. TRC, AVS, Stella Bone, Statement to the Truth and Reconciliation Commission of Canada, Keeseekoowenin First Nation, Manitoba, 29 May 2010, Statement Number: S-KFN-MB-01-006.

261. TRC, AVS, Mel H. Buffalo, Statement to the Truth and Reconciliation Commission of Canada, Hobbema, Alberta, 24 July 2013, Statement Number: 2011-2535.

262. TRC, AVS, Daisy Hill, Statement to the Truth and Reconciliation Commission of Canada, Victoria, British Columbia, 13 April 2012, Statement Number: 2011-3967.

263. TRC, AVS, Julianna Alexander, Statement to the Truth and Reconciliation Commission of Canada, Enderby, British Columbia, 12 October 2011, Statement Number: 2011-3286.

264. TRC, AVS, Inez Dieter, Statement to the Truth and Reconciliation Commission of Canada, Regina, Saskatchewan, 16 January 2012, Statement Number: SP035.

265. TRC, AVS, Frances Tait, Statement to the Truth and Reconciliation Commission of Canada, Victoria, British Columbia, 13 April 2012, Statement Number: 2011-3974.

266. TRC, AVS, Hazel Bitternose, Statement to the Truth and Reconciliation Commission of Canada, Regina, Saskatchewan, 17 January 2012, Statement Number: SP036.

267. TRC, AVS, Gladys Prince, Statement to the Truth and Reconciliation Commission of Canada, Brandon, Manitoba, 13 October 2011, Statement Number: 2011-2498. (Translated from Ojibway to English by Translation Bureau, Public Works and Government Services Canada.)

268. TRC, AVS, Doris Judy McKay, Statement to the Truth and Reconciliation Commission of Canada, Rolling River First Nation, Manitoba, 23 November 2011, Statement Number: 2011-2514.

269. TRC, AVS, Betty Smith-Titus, Statement to the Truth and Reconciliation Commission of Canada, Whitehorse, Yukon, 27 May 2011, Statement Number: 2011-1132.

270. TRC, AVS, [Name redacted], Statement to the Truth and Reconciliation Commission of Canada, Key First Nation, Saskatchewan, 21 January 2012, Statement Number: SP039.

271. TRC, AVS, Mary Rose Julian, Statement to the Truth and Reconciliation Commission of Canada, Halifax, Nova Scotia, 27 October 2011, Statement Number: 2011-2880.

272. TRC, AVS, Ilene Nepoose, Statement to the Truth and Reconciliation Commission of Canada, Hobbema, Alberta, 25 July 2013, Statement Number: 2011-2380.

273. TRC, AVS, Campbell Papequash, Statement to the Truth and Reconciliation Commission of Canada, Key First Nation, Saskatchewan, 20 January 2012, Statement Number: SP038.

274. TRC, AVS, Ula Hotonami, Statement to the Truth and Reconciliation Commission of Canada, 5 January 2012, Winnipeg, Manitoba, Statement Number: 2011-2654.

275. TRC, AVS, Andrew Speck, Statement to the Truth and Reconciliation Commission of Canada, Victoria, British Columbia, 14 April 2012, Statement Number: 2011-3988.

276. TRC, AVS, Ellen Smith, Statement to the Truth and Reconciliation Commission of Canada, Fort McPherson, Northwest Territories, 14 September 2011, Statement Number: 2011-0346.

277. TRC, AVS, [Name redacted], Statement to the Truth and Reconciliation Commission of Canada, Eskasoni First Nation, Nova Scotia, 14 October 2011, Statement Number: 2011-2681.

278. TRC, AVS, Josephine Eshkibok, Statement to the Truth and Reconciliation Commission of Canada, Little Current, Ontario, 13 May 2011, Statement Number: 2011-2014.

279. TRC, AVS, Darlene Wilson, Statement to the Truth and Reconciliation Commission of Canada, Port Alberni, British Columbia, 13 March 2012, Statement Number: 2011-4065.

280. TRC, AVS, Geraldine Bob, Statement to the Truth and Reconciliation Commission of Canada, Fort Simpson, Northwest Territories, 23 November 2011, Statement Number: 2011-2685.

281. TRC, AVS, Rose Marie Prosper, Statement to the Truth and Reconciliation Commission of Canada, Halifax, Nova Scotia, 28 October 2011, Statement Number: 2011-2868.

282. TRC, AVS, Isabelle Whitford, Statement to the Truth and Reconciliation Commission of Canada, Keeseekoowenin First Nation, Manitoba, 28 May 2010, Statement Number: S-KFN-MB-01-004.

283. TRC, AVS, Emily Kematch, Statement to the Truth and Reconciliation Commission of Canada, Winnipeg, Manitoba, 18 June 2010, Statement Number: 02-MB-18JU10-063.

284. TRC, AVS, Shirley Ida Moore, Statement to the Truth and Reconciliation Commission of Canada, Winnipeg, Manitoba, 2 March 2011, Statement Number: 2011-0089.

285. TRC, AVS, Florence Horassi, Statement to the Truth and Reconciliation Commission of Canada, Tulita, Northwest Territories, 10 May 2011, Statement Number: 2011-0394.

286. TRC, AVS, Thomas Keesick, Statement to the Truth and Reconciliation Commission of Canada, Winnipeg, Manitoba, 16 June 2010, Statement Number: 02-MB-16JU10-156.

287. TRC, AVS, Rick Gilbert, Statement to the Truth and Reconciliation Commission of Canada, Vancouver, British Columbia, 20 September 2013, Statement Number: 2011-2389.

288. TRC, AVS, Roger Cromarty, Statement to the Truth and Reconciliation Commission of Canada, Winnipeg, Manitoba, 17 June 2010, Statement Number: 02-MB-16JU10-132.

289. TRC, AVS, Joanne Morrison Methot, Statement to the Truth and Reconciliation Commission of Canada, Halifax, Nova Scotia, 28 October 2011, Statement Number: 2011-2875.

290. TRC, AVS, Lizette Olson, Statement to the Truth and Reconciliation Commission of Canada, Prince Albert, Saskatchewan, 1 February 2012, Statement Number: 2011-3878. (Translated from Woodland Cree to English by Translation Bureau, Public Works and Government Services Canada.)

291. TRC, AVS, Violet Beaulieu, Statement to the Truth and Reconciliation Commission of Canada, Fort Resolution, Northwest Territories, 28 April 2011, Statement Number: 2011-0377.

292. TRC, AVS, Campbell Papequash, Statement to the Truth and Reconciliation Commission of Canada, Key First Nation, Saskatchewan, 20 January 2012, Statement Number: SP038.

293. TRC, AVS, Bernadette Fox, Statement to the Truth and Reconciliation Commission of Canada, Lethbridge, Alberta, 9 October 2013, Statement Number: SP127.

294. TRC, AVS, Noel Starblanket, Statement to the Truth and Reconciliation Commission of Canada, Regina, Saskatchewan, 16 January 2012, Statement Number: 2011-3314.

295. TRC, AVS, Antonette White, Statement to the Truth and Reconciliation Commission of Canada, Victoria, British Columbia, 13 April 2012, Statement Number: 2011-3984.

296. TRC, AVS, Geraldine Archie, Statement to the Truth and Reconciliation Commission of Canada, Winnipeg, Manitoba, 18 June 2010, Statement Number: SC110.

297. TRC, AVS, Roger Cromarty, Statement to the Truth and Reconciliation Commission of Canada, Winnipeg, Manitoba, 17 June 2010, Statement Number: 02-MB-16JU10-132.

298. TRC, AVS, Louise Large, Statement to the Truth and Reconciliation Commission of Canada, St. Paul, Alberta, 7 January 2011, Statement Number: 01-AB-06JA11-012.

299. TRC, AVS, Ronalee Lavallee, Statement to the Truth and Reconciliation Commission of Canada, Saskatoon, Saskatchewan, 24 June 2012, Statement Number: 2011-1776.

300. TRC, AVS, Geraldine Bob, Statement to the Truth and Reconciliation Commission of Canada, Fort Simpson, Northwest Territories, 23 November 2011, Statement Number: 2011-2685.

301. TRC, AVS, Rita Carpenter, Statement to the Truth and Reconciliation Commission of Canada, Tsiigehtchic, Northwest Territories, 8 September 2011, Statement Number: 2011-0339.

302. TRC, AVS, Victoria Boucher-Grant, Statement to the Truth and Reconciliation Commission of Canada, Ottawa, Ontario, 5 February 2011, Statement Number: 01-ON-05FE11-004.

303. TRC, AVS, Fred Brass, Statement to the Truth and Reconciliation Commission of Canada, Key First Nation, Saskatchewan, 21 January 2012, Statement Number: SP039.

304. TRC, AVS, Joseph Martin Larocque, Statement to the Truth and Reconciliation Commission of Canada, Saskatoon, Saskatchewan, 21 June 2012, Statement Number: 2011-4386.

305. TRC, AVS, Fred Kistabish, Statement to the Truth and Reconciliation Commission of Canada, Val d'Or, Québec, 6 February 2012, Statement Number: SP101.

306. TRC, AVS, Martha Minoose, Statement to the Truth and Reconciliation Commission of Canada, Lethbridge, Alberta, 10 October 2013, Statement Number: 2011-1748.

307. TRC, AVS, Vitaline Elsie Jenner, Statement to the Truth and Reconciliation Commission of Canada, Winnipeg, Manitoba, 16 June 2010, Statement Number: 02-MB-16JU10-131.

308. TRC, AVS, Frank Tomkins, Statement to the Truth and Reconciliation Commission of Canada, Batoche, Saskatchewan, 21 July 2010, Statement Number: 01-SK-18-25JY10-009.

309. TRC, AVS, Fred Brass, Statement to the Truth and Reconciliation Commission of Canada, Key First Nation, Saskatchewan, 21 January 2012, Statement Number: SP039.

310. TRC, AVS, Arthur Ron McKay, Statement to the Truth and Reconciliation Commission of Canada, Winnipeg, Manitoba, 18 June 2010, Statement Number: 02-MB-18JU10-044.

311. TRC, AVS, Ula Hotonami, Statement to the Truth and Reconciliation Commission of Canada, Winnipeg, Manitoba, 5 January 2012, Statement Number: 2011-2654.

312. TRC, AVS, Julianna Alexander, Statement to the Truth and Reconciliation Commission of Canada, Enderby, British Columbia, 12 October 2011, Statement Number: 2011-3286.

313. TRC, AVS, Mary Stoney, Statement to the Truth and Reconciliation Commission of Canada, Hobbema, Alberta, 24 July 2013, Statement Number: SP124.

314. TRC, AVS, Elizabeth Papatie, Statement to the Truth and Reconciliation Commission of Canada, Val d'Or, Québec, 6 February 2012, Statement Number: SP101.

315. TRC, AVS, Inez Dieter, Statement to the Truth and Reconciliation Commission of Canada, Regina, Saskatchewan, 16 January 2012, Statement Number: SP035.

316. TRC, AVS, Daniel Nanooch, Statement to the Truth and Reconciliation Commission of Canada, High Level, Alberta, 4 July 2013, Statement Number: 2011-1868.

317. TRC, AVS, Madeleine Dion Stout, Statement to the Truth and Reconciliation Commission of Canada, Winnipeg, Manitoba, 18 June 2010, Statement Number: 02-MB-18JU10-059.

318. TRC, AVS, Wilbur Abrahams, Statement to the Truth and Reconciliation Commission of Canada, Terrace, British Columbia, 30 November 2011, Statement Number: 2011-3301.

319. TRC, AVS, Bernice Jacks, Statement to the Truth and Reconciliation Commission of Canada, Victoria, British Columbia, 13 April 2012, Statement Number: 2011-3971.

320. TRC, AVS, Sheila Gunderson, Statement to the Truth and Reconciliation Commission of Canada, Fort Simpson, Northwest Territories, 23 November 2011, Statement Number: 2011-2687.

321. TRC, AVS, Helen Kakekayash, Statement to the Truth and Reconciliation Commission of Canada, Ottawa, Ontario, 5 February 2011, Statement Number: 01-ON-05FE11-002.

322. TRC, AVS, Peter Ross, Statement to the Truth and Reconciliation Commission of Canada, Tsiigehtchic, Northwest Territories, 8 September 2011, Statement Number: 2011-0340.

323. TRC, AVS, Margaret Simpson, Statement to the Truth and Reconciliation Commission of Canada, Winnipeg, Manitoba, 18 June 2010, Statement Number: 02-MB-18JU10-051.

324. TRC, AVS, Connie McNab, Statement to the Truth and Reconciliation Commission of Canada, Fort Simpson, Northwest Territories, 23 November 2011, Statement Number: 2011-2715.

325. TRC, AVS, Bernard Catcheway, Statement to the Truth and Reconciliation Commission of Canada, Skownan First Nation, Manitoba, 12 October 2011, Statement Number: 2011-2510.

326. TRC, AVS, Dorene Bernard, Statement to the Truth and Reconciliation Commission of Canada, Indian Brook, Nova Scotia, 12 October 2011, Statement Number: SP029.

327. TRC, AVS, Julianna Alexander, Statement to the Truth and Reconciliation Commission of Canada, Enderby, British Columbia, 12 October 2011, Statement Number: 2011-3286.

328. TRC, AVS, Elizabeth Good, Statement to the Truth and Reconciliation Commission of Canada, Mission, British Columbia, 18 May 2011, Statement Number: 2011-3469.

329. TRC, AVS, Joanne Morrison Methot, Statement to the Truth and Reconciliation Commission of Canada, Halifax, Nova Scotia, 28 October 2011, Statement Number: 2011-2875.

330. TRC, AVS, Beverley Anne Machelle, Statement to the Truth and Reconciliation Commission of Canada, Whitehorse, Yukon, 27 May 2011, Statement Number: 2011-1133.

331. TRC, AVS, Lena McKay, Statement to the Truth and Reconciliation Commission of Canada, Fort Resolution, Northwest Territories, 28 April 2011, Statement Number: 2011-0382.

332. TRC, AVS, Andy Norwegian, Statement to the Truth and Reconciliation Commission of Canada, Fort Simpson, Northwest Territories, 23 November 2011, Statement Number: SP033.

333. TRC, AVS, Ilene Nepoose, Statement to the Truth and Reconciliation Commission of Canada, Hobbema, Alberta, 25 July 2013, Statement Number: 2011-2380.

334. TRC, AVS, Isabelle Whitford, Statement to the Truth and Reconciliation Commission of Canada, Keeseekoowenin First Nation, Manitoba, 28 May 2010, Statement Number: S-KFN-MB-01-004.

335. TRC, AVS, John Edwards, Statement to the Truth and Reconciliation Commission of Canada, Inuvik, Northwest Territories, 5 August 2011, Statement Number: 2011-0328.

336. TRC, AVS, Donald Copenace, Statement to the Truth and Reconciliation Commission of Canada, Winnipeg, Manitoba, 17 June 2010, Statement Number: 02-MB-17JU10-062.

337. TRC, AVS, Violet Beaulieu, Statement to the Truth and Reconciliation Commission of Canada, Fort Resolution, Northwest Territories, 28 April 2011, Statement Number: 2011-0377.

338. TRC, AVS, Muriel Morrisseau, Statement to the Truth and Reconciliation Commission of Canada, Winnipeg, Manitoba, 18 June 2010, Statement Number: 02-MB-18JU10-057.

339. TRC, AVS, Vitaline Elsie Jenner, Statement to the Truth and Reconciliation Commission of Canada, Winnipeg, Manitoba, 16 June 2010, Statement Number: 02-MB-16JU10-131.

340. TRC, AVS, Alphonsine McNeely, Statement to the Truth and Reconciliation Commission of Canada, Fort Good Hope, Northwest Territories, 13 July 2010, Statement Number: 01-NWT-JY10-002.

341. TRC, AVS, [Name redacted], Statement to the Truth and Reconciliation Commission of Canada, Winnipeg, Manitoba, 18 June 2010, Statement Number: 02-MB-18JU10-062.

342. TRC, AVS, Gerald McLeod, Statement to the Truth and Reconciliation Commission of Canada, Whitehorse, Yukon, 27 May 2011, Statement Number: 2011-1130.

343. TRC, AVS, Nellie Ningewance, Statement to the Truth and Reconciliation Commission of Canada, Sault Ste. Marie, Ontario, 1 July 2011, Statement Number: 2011-0305.

344. TRC, AVS, Mary Courchene, Statement to the Truth and Reconciliation Commission of Canada, Pine Creek First Nation, Manitoba, 28 November 2011, Statement Number: 2011-2515.

345. TRC, AVS, Ben Sylliboy, Statement to the Truth and Reconciliation Commission of Canada, Eskasoni First Nation, Nova Scotia, 14 October 2011, Statement Number: SP030.

346. TRC, AVS, Loretta Mainville, Statement to the Truth and Reconciliation Commission of Canada, Winnipeg, Manitoba, 16 June 2010, Statement Number: 02-MB-16JU10-089.

347. TRC, AVS, Madeleine Dion Stout, Statement to the Truth and Reconciliation Commission of Canada, Winnipeg, Manitoba, 18 June 2010, Statement Number: 02-MB-18JU10-059.

348. TRC, AVS, Tina Duguay, Statement to the Truth and Reconciliation Commission of Canada, Kamloops, British Columbia, 9 August 2009, Statement Number: 2011-5002.

349. TRC, AVS, Leon Wyallon, Statement to the Truth and Reconciliation Commission of Canada, Behchoko, Northwest Territories, 15 April 2011, Statement Number: 2011-0244.

350. TRC, AVS, Doris Young, Statement to the Truth and Reconciliation Commission of Canada, Saskatoon, Saskatchewan, 22 June 2012, Statement Number: 2011-3517.

351. TRC, AVS, Josephine Eshkibok, Statement to the Truth and Reconciliation Commission of Canada, Little Current, Ontario, 13 May 2011, Statement Number: 2011-2014.

352. TRC, AVS, Doris Judy McKay, Statement to the Truth and Reconciliation Commission of Canada, Rolling River First Nation, Manitoba, 23 November 2011, Statement Number: 2011-2514.

353. TRC, AVS, Geraldine Shingoose, Statement to the Truth and Reconciliation Commission of Canada, Winnipeg, Manitoba, 19 June 2010, Statement Number: 02-MB-19JU10-033.

354. TRC, AVS, Ula Hotonami, Statement to the Truth and Reconciliation Commission of Canada, Winnipeg, Manitoba, 5 January 2012, Statement Number: 2011-2654.

355. TRC, AVS, Frances Tait, Statement to the Truth and Reconciliation Commission of Canada, Victoria, British Columbia, 13 April 2012, Statement Number: 2011-3974.

356. TRC, AVS, Don Willie, Statement to the Truth and Reconciliation Commission of Canada, Alert Bay, British Columbia, 3 August 2011, Statement Number: 2011-3284.

357. TRC, AVS, [Name redacted], Statement to the Truth and Reconciliation Commission of Canada, Little Current, Ontario, 13 May 2011, Statement Number: 2011-2012.

358. TRC, AVS, Wilbur Abrahams, Statement to the Truth and Reconciliation Commission of Canada, Terrace, British Columbia, 30 November 2011, Statement Number: 2011-3301.

359. TRC, AVS, Victoria Boucher-Grant, Statement to the Truth and Reconciliation Commission of Canada, Ottawa, Ontario, 5 February 2011, Statement Number: 01-ON-05FE11-004.

360. TRC, AVS, Ben Sylliboy, Statement to the Truth and Reconciliation Commission of Canada, Eskasoni, Nova Scotia, 14 October 2011, Statement Number: SP030.

361. TRC, AVS, Julianna Alexander, Statement to the Truth and Reconciliation Commission of Canada, Enderby, British Columbia, 12 October 2011, Statement Number: 2011-3286.

362. TRC, AVS, William Francis Paul, Statement to the Truth and Reconciliation Commission of Canada, Halifax, Nova Scotia, 28 October 2011, Statement Number: 2011-2873.

363. TRC, AVS, Darryl Siah, Statement to the Truth and Reconciliation Commission of Canada, St. Mary's Mission, British Columbia, 18 May 2011, Statement Number: 2011-3473.

364. TRC, AVS, Mary Teya, Statement to the Truth and Reconciliation Commission of Canada, Aklavik , Northwest Territories, 12 May 2011, Statement Number: SP019.

365. TRC, AVS, Kiatch Nahanni, Statement to the Truth and Reconciliation Commission of Canada, Fort Simpson, Northwest Territories, 23 November 2011, Statement Number: 2011-2684.

366. TRC, AVS, Rosie Kagak, Statement to the Truth and Reconciliation Commission of Canada, Inuvik, Northwest Territories, 29 June 2011, Statement Number: SC090.

367. TRC, AVS, Dorothy Hart, Statement to the Truth and Reconciliation Commission of Canada, Nelson House First Nation, Manitoba, 22 February 2012, Statement Number: 2011-2586.

368. TRC, AVS, Frederick Ernest Koe, Statement to the Truth and Reconciliation Commission of Canada, Inuvik, Northwest Territories, 30 June 2011, Statement Number: SC091.

369. TRC, AVS, Mollie Roy, Statement to the Truth and Reconciliation Commission of Canada, White-horse, Yukon, 26 May 2011, Statement Number: 2011-1129.

370. TRC, AVS, Florence Horassi, Statement to the Truth and Reconciliation Commission of Canada, Tulita, Northwest Territories, 10 May 2011, Statement Number: 2011-0394.

371. TRC, AVS, Agnes Moses, Statement to the Truth and Reconciliation Commission of Canada, Inuvik, Northwest Territories, 29 June 2011, Statement Number: SC090.

372. TRC, AVS, Cecilia Whitefield-Big George, Statement to the Truth and Reconciliation Commission of Canada, Winnipeg, Manitoba, 17 June 2010, Statement Number: 02-MB-17JU10-030.

373. TRC, AVS, Mary Courchene, Statement to the Truth and Reconciliation Commission of Canada, Pine Creek First Nation, Manitoba, 28 November 2011, Statement Number: 2011-2515.

374. TRC, AVS, Carmen Petiquay, Statement to the Truth and Reconciliation Commission of Canada, La Tuque, Québec, 5 March 2013, Statement Number: SP104.

375. TRC, AVS, Jennie Blackbird, Statement to the Truth and Reconciliation Commission of Canada, Muncey, Ontario, 16 September 2011, Statement Number: 2011-4188.

376. TRC, AVS, Vitaline Elsie Jenner, Statement to the Truth and Reconciliation Commission of Canada, Winnipeg, Manitoba, 16 June 2010, Statement Number: 02-MB-16JU10-131.

377. TRC, AVS, Albert Elias, Statement to the Truth and Reconciliation Commission of Canada, Inuvik, Northwest Territories, 1 July 2011, Statement Number: SC092.

378. TRC, AVS, Betsy Olson, Statement to the Truth and Reconciliation Commission of Canada, Saska-toon, Saskatchewan, 21 June 2012, Statement Number: 2011-4378.

379. TRC, AVS, Ellen Smith, Statement to the Truth and Reconciliation Commission of Canada, Fort McPherson, Northwest Territories, 14 September 2011, Statement Number: 2011-0346

380. TRC, AVS, Raphael Victor Paul, Statement to the Truth and Reconciliation Commission of Canada, Winnipeg, Manitoba, 19 June 2010, Statement Number: 02-MB-19JU10-051.

381. TRC, AVS, Frances Tait, Statement to the Truth and Reconciliation Commission of Canada, Victoria, British Columbia, 13 April 2012, Statement Number: 2011-3974.

382. TRC, AVS, Raymond Cutknife, Statement to the Truth and Reconciliation Commission of Canada, Hobbema, Alberta, 25 July 2013, Statement Number: SP125.

383. TRC, AVS, Timothy Henderson, Statement to the Truth and Reconciliation Commission of Canada, Winnipeg, Manitoba, 28 June 2011, Statement Number: 2011-0291.

384. TRC, AVS, William Herney, Statement to the Truth and Reconciliation Commission of Canada, Halifax, Nova Scotia, 29 October 2011, Statement Number: 2011-2923.

385. TRC, AVS, Shirley Waskewitch, Statement to the Truth and Reconciliation Commission of Canada, Saskatoon, Saskatchewan, 24 June 2012, Statement Number: 2011-3521.

386. TRC, AVS, Patrick Bruyere, Statement to the Truth and Reconciliation Commission of Canada, Winnipeg, Manitoba, 16 June 2010, Statement Number: 02-MB-16JU10-157.

387. TRC, AVS, Ernest Barkman, Statement to the Truth and Reconciliation Commission of Canada, Garden Hill First Nation, Manitoba, 30 March 2011, Statement Number: 2011-0123. (Translated from Oji-Cree to English by Translation Bureau, Public Works and Government Services Canada.)

388. TRC, AVS, Paul Dixon, Statement to the Truth and Reconciliation Commission of Canada, Val d'Or, Québec, 6 February 2012, Statement Number: SP101.

389. TRC, AVS, Rick Gilbert, Statement to the Truth and Reconciliation Commission of Canada, Vancouver, British Columbia, 20 September 2013, Statement Number: 2011-2389.

390. TRC, AVS, Bob Baxter, Statement to the Truth and Reconciliation Commission of Canada, Thunder Bay, Ontario, 24 November 2010, Statement Number: 01-ON-24NOV10-012.

391. TRC, AVS, Betsy Annahatak, Statement to the Truth and Reconciliation Commission of Canada, Halifax, Nova Scotia, 28 October 2011, Statement Number: 2011-2896.

392. TRC, AVS, Noel Knockwood, Statement to the Truth and Reconciliation Commission of Canada, Halifax, Nova Scotia, 29 October 2011, Statement Number: 2011-2922.

393. TRC, AVS, Nellie Ningewance, Statement to the Truth and Reconciliation Commission of Canada, Sault Ste. Marie, Ontario, 1 July 2011, Statement Number: 2011-0305.

394. TRC, AVS, Shirley Williams, Statement to the Truth and Reconciliation Commission of Canada, Spanish, Ontario, 12 September 2009, Statement Number: 2011-5040.

395. TRC, AVS, Daniel Andre, Statement to the Truth and Reconciliation Commission of Canada, Whitehorse, Yukon, 23 May 2011, Statement Number: 2011-0202.

396. TRC, AVS, Alan Knockwood, Statement to the Truth and Reconciliation Commission of Canada, Indian Brook, Nova Scotia, 12 October 2011, Statement Number: SP029.

397. TRC, AVS, Jeanne Paul, Statement to the Truth and Reconciliation Commission of Canada, Mission, British Columbia, 18 May 2011, Statement Number: 2011-3464.

398. TRC, AVS, Josiah Fiddler, Statement to the Truth and Reconciliation Commission of Canada, Winnipeg, Manitoba, 18 June 2010, Statement Number: SC111.

399. TRC, AVS, Nick Sibbeston, Statement to the Truth and Reconciliation Commission of Canada, Inuvik, Northwest Territories, 30 June 2011, Statement Number: NNE202.

400. TRC, AVS, Jack Anawak, Statement to the Truth and Reconciliation Commission of Canada, Inuvik, Northwest Territories, 30 June 2011, Statement Number: NNE202.

401. TRC, AVS, Murray Crowe, Statement to the Truth and Reconciliation Commission of Canada, Sault Ste. Marie, Ontario, 1 July 2011, Statement Number: 2011-0306.

402. TRC, AVS, Joanne Morrison Methot, Statement to the Truth and Reconciliation Commission of Canada, Halifax, Nova Scotia, 28 October 2011, Statement Number: 2011-2875.

403. TRC, AVS, Lydia Ross, Statement to the Truth and Reconciliation Commission of Canada, Winnipeg, Manitoba, 16 June 2010, Statement Number: 02-MB-16JU10-029.

404. TRC, AVS, Robert Malcolm, Statement to the Truth and Reconciliation Commission of Canada, Winnipeg, Manitoba, 17 June 2010, Statement Number: 02-MB-16JU10-090.

405. TRC, AVS, Clara Quisess, Statement to the Truth and Reconciliation Commission of Canada, Winnipeg, Manitoba, 17 June 2010, Statement Number: 02-MB-17JU10-032.

406. TRC, AVS, Florence Horassi, Statement to the Truth and Reconciliation Commission of Canada, Tulita, Northwest Territories, 10 May 2011, Statement Number: 2011-0394.

407. TRC, AVS, Stephen Kakfwi, Statement to the Truth and Reconciliation Commission of Canada, Inuvik, Northwest Territories, 30 June 2011, Statement Number: NNE202.

408. TRC, AVS, Victoria McIntosh, Statement to the Truth and Reconciliation Commission of Canada, Winnipeg, Manitoba, 16 June 2010, Statement Number: 02-MB-16JU10-123.

409. TRC, AVS, Megan Molaluk, Statement to the Truth and Reconciliation Commission of Canada, Inuvik, Northwest Territories, 29 June 2011, Statement Number: SC090.

410. TRC, AVS, Elizabeth Joyce Brass, Statement to the Truth and Reconciliation Commission of Canada, Winnipeg, Manitoba, 19 June 2010, Statement Number: 02-MB-19JU10-005.

411. TRC, AVS, Antonette White, Statement to the Truth and Reconciliation Commission of Canada, Victoria, British Columbia, 13 April 2012, Statement Number: 2011-3984.

412. TRC, AVS, Helen Harry, Statement to the Truth and Reconciliation Commission of Canada, Vancouver, British Columbia, 20 September 2013, Statement Number: 2011-3203.

413. TRC, AVS, Margaret Simpson, Statement to the Truth and Reconciliation Commission of Canada, Winnipeg, Manitoba, 18 June 2010, Statement Number: 02-MB-18JU10-051.

414. TRC, AVS, Ken A. Littledeer, Statement to the Truth and Reconciliation Commission of Canada, Thunder Bay, Ontario, 26 November 2010, Statement Number: 01-ON-24-NOV10-028.

415. TRC, AVS, Noel Knockwood, Statement to the Truth and Reconciliation Commission of Canada, Halifax, Nova Scotia, 29 October 2011, Statement Number: 2011-2922.

416. TRC, AVS, John B. Custer, Statement to the Truth and Reconciliation Commission of Canada, Winnipeg, Manitoba, 19 June 2010, Statement Number: 02-MB-19JU10-057.

417. TRC, AVS, Hazel Ewanchuk, Statement to the Truth and Reconciliation Commission of Canada, Winnipeg, Manitoba, 16 June 2010, Statement Number: 02-MB-16JU10-112.

418. TRC, AVS, Elaine Durocher, Statement to the Truth and Reconciliation Commission of Canada, Winnipeg, Manitoba, 16 June 2010, Statement Number: 02-MB-16JU10-059.

419. TRC, AVS, David Charleson, Statement to the Truth and Reconciliation Commission of Canada, Deroche, British Columbia, 20 January 2010, Statement Number: 2011-5043.

420. TRC, AVS, Isabelle Whitford, Statement to the Truth and Reconciliation Commission of Canada, Keeseekoowenin First Nation, Manitoba, 28 May 2010, Statement Number: S-KFN-MB-01-004.

421. TRC, AVS, Betsy Olson, Statement to the Truth and Reconciliation Commission of Canada, Saskatoon, Saskatchewan, 21 June 2012, Statement Number: 2011-4378.

422. TRC, AVS, Noel Knockwood, Statement to the Truth and Reconciliation Commission of Canada, Halifax, Nova Scotia, 29 October 2011, Statement Number: 2011 2922.

423. TRC, AVS, Mary Lou Iahtail, Statement to the Truth and Reconciliation Commission of Canada, Ottawa, Ontario, 5 February 2011, Statement Number: 01-ON-05FE11-005.

424. TRC, AVS, Leona Agawa, Statement to the Truth and Reconciliation Commission of Canada, Sault Ste. Marie, Ontario, 6 November 2010, Statement Number: 01-ON-4-6 NOV10-006.

425. TRC, AVS, Dorothy Ross, Statement to the Truth and Reconciliation Commission of Canada, Thunder Bay, Ontario, 25 November 2010, Statement Number: 01-ON-24NOV10-014.

426. TRC, AVS, Margaret Paulette, Statement to the Truth and Reconciliation Commission of Canada, Eskasoni, Nova Scotia, 14 October 2011, Statement Number: SP030.

427. TRC, AVS, Clara Munroe, Statement to the Truth and Reconciliation Commission of Canada, Key First Nation, Saskatchewan, 21 January 2012, Statement Number: SP039.

428. TRC, AVS, Mary Courchene, Statement to the Truth and Reconciliation Commission of Canada, Pine Creek First Nation, Manitoba, 28 November 2011, Statement Number: 2011-2515.

429. TRC, AVS, Flora Northwest, Statement to the Truth and Reconciliation Commission of Canada, Hobbema, Alberta , 24 July 2013, Statement Number: SP124.

430. TRC, AVS, Victoria McIntosh, Statement to the Truth and Reconciliation Commission of Canada, Winnipeg, Manitoba, 16 June 2010, Statement Number: 02-MB-16JU10-123.

431. TRC, AVS, Tina Duguay, Statement to the Truth and Reconciliation Commission of Canada, Kamloops, British Columbia, 9 August 2009, Statement Number: 2011-5002.

432. TRC, AVS, Walter Jones, Statement to the Truth and Reconciliation Commission of Canada, Victoria, British Columbia, 14 April 2012, Statement Number: 2011-4008.

433. TRC, AVS, Roger Cromarty, Statement to the Truth and Reconciliation Commission of Canada, Winnipeg, Manitoba, 17 June 2010, Statement Number: 02-MB-16JU10-132.

434. TRC, AVS, Lena Small, Statement to the Truth and Reconciliation Commission of Canada, Hobbema, Alberta, 24 July 2013, Statement Number: SP124.

435. TRC, AVS, Nora Abou-Tibbett, Statement to the Truth and Reconciliation Commission of Canada, Watson Lake, Yukon, 25 May 2011, Statement Number: 2011-0205.

436. TRC, AVS, Lorna Cochrane, Statement to the Truth and Reconciliation Commission of Canada, Winnipeg, Manitoba, 18 June 2010, Statement Number: SC110.

437. TRC, AVS, Pierre Papatie, Statement to the Truth and Reconciliation Commission of Canada, 23 June 2012, Saskatoon, Saskatchewan, Statement Number: 2011-1794.

438. TRC, AVS, Madeleine Dion Stout, Statement to the Truth and Reconciliation Commission of Canada, Winnipeg, Manitoba, 18 June 2010, Statement Number: 02-MB-18JU10-059.

439. TRC, AVS, Roddy Soosay, Statement to the Truth and Reconciliation Commission of Canada, Hobbema, Alberta, 25 July 2013, Statement Number: 2011-2379. For Halvar Jonson, see: The Alberta Teachers' Association, "Halvar Jonson—Best Possible Education Minister at a Very Difficult Time," http://www.teachers.ab.ca/Publications/ATA%20Magazine/Volume-93/Number-2/Pages/Halvar-Jonson.aspx.

440. TRC, AVS, Lawrence Wanakamik, Statement to the Truth and Reconciliation Commission of Canada, Thunder Bay, Ontario, 6 January 2011, Statement Number: 01-ON-06JA11-002.

441. TRC, AVS, Alice Quinney, Statement to the Truth and Reconciliation Commission of Canada, Winnipeg, Manitoba, 18 June 2010, Statement Number: 02-MB-18JU10-049.

442. TRC, AVS, Martha Loon, Statement to the Truth and Reconciliation Commission of Canada, Thunder Bay, Ontario, 25 November 2010, Statement Number: 01-ON-24NOV10-021.

443. TRC, AVS, Frederick Ernest Koe, Statement to the Truth and Reconciliation Commission of Canada, Inuvik, Northwest Territories, 30 June 2011, Statement Number: SC091.

444. TRC, AVS, Helen Hanson, Statement to the Truth and Reconciliation Commission of Canada, Deroche, British Columbia, 20 January 2010, Statement Number: 2011-5045.

445. TRC, AVS, Eli Carpenter, Statement to the Truth and Reconciliation Commission of Canada, Winnipeg, Manitoba, 17 June 2010, Statement Number: 02-MB-17JU10-018.

446. TRC, AVS, William Antoine, Statement to the Truth and Reconciliation Commission of Canada, Little Current, Ontario, 12 May 2011, Statement Number: 2011-2002.

447. TRC, AVS, Madeleine Dion Stout, Statement to the Truth and Reconciliation Commission of Canada, Winnipeg, Manitoba, 18 June 2010, Statement Number: 02-MB-18JU10-059.

448. Holder, "Teaching Left-Handers to Write," Handedness Research Institute, http://handedness.org/ action/leftwrite.html (accessed 16 January 2014); Siebner, Limmer, Peinemann, et al., "Long-term Consequences," 2816.

449. Lewis, "Psychological Approach," 499.

450. TRC, AVS, William Antoine, Statement to the Truth and Reconciliation Commission of Canada, Little Current, Ontario, 12 May 2011, Statement Number: 2011-2002.

451. TRC, AVS, Louise Large, Statement to the Truth and Reconciliation Commission of Canada, St. Paul, Alberta, 7 January 2011, Statement Number: 01-AB-06JA11-012.

452. TRC, AVS, Archie Hyacinthe, Statement to the Truth and Reconciliation Commission of Canada, Kenora, Ontario, 15 March 2011, Statement Number: 2011-0279.

453. TRC, AVS, Doris Young, Statement to the Truth and Reconciliation Commission of Canada, Saskatoon, Saskatchewan, 22 June 2012, Statement Number: 2011-3517.

454. TRC, AVS, Margaret Plamondon, Statement to the Truth and Reconciliation Commission of Canada, Fort Smith, Northwest Territories, 6 May 2011, Statement Number: 2011-0387.

455. TRC, AVS, Dorothy Ross, Statement to the Truth and Reconciliation Commission of Canada, Thunder Bay, Ontario, 25 November 2010, Statement Number: 01-ON-24NOV10-014.

456. TRC, AVS, Shirley Leon, Statement to the Truth and Reconciliation Commission of Canada, Deroche, British Columbia, 19 January 2010, Statement Number: 2011-5048.

457. TRC, AVS, Martina Therese Fisher, Statement to the Truth and Reconciliation Commission of Canada, Bloodvein First Nation, Manitoba, 26 January 2012, Statement Number: 2011-2564.

458. TRC, AVS, Emily Kematch, Statement to the Truth and Reconciliation Commission of Canada, Winnipeg, Manitoba, 18 June 2010, Statement Number: 02-MB-18JU10-063.

459. TRC, AVS, Richard Hall, Statement to the Truth and Reconciliation Commission of Canada, Vancouver, British Columbia, 18 September 2013, Statement Number: 2011-1852.

460. TRC, AVS, Annie Wesley, Statement to the Truth and Reconciliation Commission of Canada, Thunder Bay, Ontario, 25 November 2010, Statement Number: 01-ON-24NOV10-034.

461. TRC, AVS, Ken Lacquette, Statement to the Truth and Reconciliation Commission of Canada, Winnipeg, Manitoba, 18 June 2010, Statement Number: 02-MB-18JU10-052.

462. TRC, AVS, Anthony Wilson, Statement to the Truth and Reconciliation Commission of Canada, Terrace, British Columbia, 30 November 2011, Statement Number: 2011-3303.

463. TRC, AVS, Shirley Brass, Statement to the Truth and Reconciliation Commission of Canada, Key First Nation, Saskatchewan, 22 January 2012, Statement Number: SP040.

464. TRC, AVS, Arthur Ron McKay, Statement to the Truth and Reconciliation Commission of Canada, Winnipeg, Manitoba, 18 June 2010, Statement Number: 02-MB-18JU10-044.

465. TRC, AVS, Ivan George, Statement to the Truth and Reconciliation Commission of Canada, Mission, British Columbia, 18 May 2011, Statement Number: 2011-3472.

466. TRC, AVS, Muriel Morrisseau, Statement to the Truth and Reconciliation Commission of Canada, Winnipeg, Manitoba, 18 June 2010, Statement Number: 02-MB-18JU10-057.

467. TRC, AVS, Josie Angeconeb, Statement to the Truth and Reconciliation Commission of Canada, Winnipeg, Manitoba, 18 June 2010, Statement Number: SC110.

468. TRC, AVS, William Garson, Statement to the Truth and Reconciliation Commission of Canada, Split Lake, Manitoba, 24 March 2011, Statement Number: 2011-0122.

469. TRC, AVS, Walter Jones, Statement to the Truth and Reconciliation Commission of Canada, Victoria, British Columbia, 14 April 2012, Statement Number: 2011-4008.

470. TRC, AVS, Marguerite Wabano, Statement to the Truth and Reconciliation Commission of Canada, Moosonee, Ontario, 28 February 2013, Statement Number: 2011-4491 (Translated from Swampy Cree by Wintranslation, 2015_073_1).

471. TRC, AVS, Isaac Daniels, Statement to the Truth and Reconciliation Commission of Canada, Saskatoon, Saskatchewan, 22 June 2012, Statement Number: 2011-1779.

472. TRC, AVS, Dora Necan, Statement to the Truth and Reconciliation Commission of Canada, Ignace, Ontario, 3 June 2011, Statement Number: 2011-1503.

473. TRC, AVS, Nellie Cournoyea, Statement to the Truth and Reconciliation Commission of Canada, Inuvik, Northwest Territories, 28 June 2011, Statement Number: NNE105.

474. TRC, AVS, Lawrence Waquan, Statement to the Truth and Reconciliation Commission of Canada, Winnipeg, Manitoba, 18 June 2010, Statement Number: SC111.

475. TRC, AVS, Roy Denny, Statement to the Truth and Reconciliation Commission of Canada, Eskasoni, Nova Scotia, 14 October 2011, Statement Number: 2011-2678.

476. TRC, AVS, Richard Morrison, Statement to the Truth and Reconciliation Commission of Canada, Winnipeg, Manitoba, 17 June 2010, Statement Number: 02-MB-17JU10-080.

477. TRC, AVS, Beverley Anne Machelle, Statement to the Truth and Reconciliation Commission of Canada, Whitehorse, Yukon, 27 May 2011, Statement Number: 2011-1133.

478. TRC, AVS, Doug Beardy, Statement to the Truth and Reconciliation Commission of Canada, Thunder Bay, Ontario, 14 December 2011, Statement Number: 2011-4197.

479. TRC, AVS, Isabelle Whitford, Statement to the Truth and Reconciliation Commission of Canada, Keeseekoowenin First Nation, Manitoba, 28 May 2010, Statement Number: S-KFN-MB-01-004.

480. TRC, AVS, Rachel Chakasim, Statement to the Truth and Reconciliation Commission of Canada, Timmins, Ontario, 9 November 2010, Statement Number: 01-ON-4-6NOV10-019.

481. TRC, AVS, Ricky Kakekagumick, Statement to the Truth and Reconciliation Commission of Canada, Thunder Bay, Ontario, 15 December 2011, Statement Number: 2011-4200.

482. TRC, AVS, Dorothy Jane Beaulieu, Statement to the Truth and Reconciliation Commission of Canada, Fort Resolution, Northwest Territories, 28 April 2011, Statement Number: 2011-0379.

483. TRC, AVS, Stella Marie Tookate, Statement to the Truth and Reconciliation Commission of Canada, Timmins, Ontario, 9 November 2010, Statement Number: 01-ON-8-10NOV10-003.

484. TRC, AVS, Fred Brass, Statement to the Truth and Reconciliation Commission of Canada, Key First Nation, Saskatchewan, 21 January 2012, Statement Number: SP039.

485. TRC, AVS, Geraldine Bob, Statement to the Truth and Reconciliation Commission of Canada, Fort Simpson, Northwest Territories, 23 November 2011, Statement Number: 2011-2685.

486. TRC, AVS, Joanne Morrison Methot, Statement to the Truth and Reconciliation Commission of Canada, Halifax, Nova Scotia, 28 October 2011, Statement Number: 2011-2875.

487. TRC, AVS, Alfred Nolie, Statement to the Truth and Reconciliation Commission of Canada, Alert Bay, British Columbia, 20 October 2011, Statement Number: 2011-3293.

488. TRC, AVS, Ron Windsor, Statement to the Truth and Reconciliation Commission of Canada, Kitamaat Village, British Columbia, 1 December 2011, Statement Number: 2011-3307.

489. TRC, AVS, Ken A. Littledeer, Statement to the Truth and Reconciliation Commission of Canada, Thunder Bay, Ontario, 26 November 2010, Statement Number: 01-ON-24-NOV10-028.

490. TRC, AVS, Doug Beardy, Statement to the Truth and Reconciliation Commission of Canada, Thunder Bay, Ontario, 14 December 2011, Statement Number: 2011-4197.

491. TRC, AVS, Frances Tait, Statement to the Truth and Reconciliation Commission of Canada, Victoria, British Columbia, 13 April 2012, Statement Number: 2011-3974.

492. TRC, AVS, Alphonsine McNeely, Statement to the Truth and Reconciliation Commission of Canada, Fort Good Hope, Northwest Territories, 13 July 2010, Statement Number: 01-NWT-JY10-002.

493. TRC, AVS, Mervin Mirasty, Statement to the Truth and Reconciliation Commission of Canada, Saskatoon, Saskatchewan, 21 June 2012, Statement Number: 2011-4391.

494. TRC, AVS, Diana Lariviere, Statement to the Truth and Reconciliation Commission of Canada, Little Current, Ontario, 13 May 2011, Statement Number: 2011-2011.

495. TRC, AVS, Lynda Pahpasay McDonald, Statement to the Truth and Reconciliation Commission of Canada, Winnipeg, Manitoba, 16 June 2010, Statement Number: 02-MB-16JU10-130.

496. TRC, AVS, Wesley Keewatin, Statement to the Truth and Reconciliation Commission of Canada, Gambier Island, British Columbia, 28 July 2011, Statement Number: 2011-3276.

497. TRC, AVS, Inez Dieter, Statement to the Truth and Reconciliation Commission of Canada, Regina, Saskatchewan, 16 January 2012, Statement Number: SP035. For potential of hearing loss resulting from slaps to ears, see: Rehman, Hamid, Sangoo, et al., "Pattern of Hearing Loss," 124.

498. TRC, AVS, Delores Adolph, Statement to the Truth and Reconciliation Commission of Canada, Mission, British Columbia, 19 May 2011, Statement Number: 2011-3458.

499. TRC, AVS, Dorothy Ross, Statement to the Truth and Reconciliation Commission of Canada, Thunder Bay, Ontario, 25 November 2010, Statement Number: 01-ON-24NOV10-014.

500. TRC, AVS, Archie Hyacinthe, Statement to the Truth and Reconciliation Commission of Canada, Kenora, Ontario, 15 March 2011, Statement Number: 2011-0279.

501. TRC, AVS, Joseph Wabano, Statement to the Truth and Reconciliation Commission of Canada, Fort Albany, Ontario, 29 January 2013, Statement Number: SP099.

502. TRC, AVS, Edmund Metatawabin, Statement to the Truth and Reconciliation Commission of Canada, Fort Albany, Ontario, 28 January 2013, Statement Number: SP098. For details on chair, see: Metatawabin, Up Ghost River, 63, 79, 80, 222.

503. TRC, AVS, Simeon Nakoochee, Statement to the Truth and Reconciliation Commission of Canada, Fort Albany, Ontario, 28 January 2013, Statement Number: 2011-4316.

504. TRC, AVS, Jonas Grandjambe, Statement to the Truth and Reconciliation Commission of Canada, Fort Good Hope, Northwest Territories, 15 July 2010, Statement Number: 01-NWT-JY10-024.

505. TRC, AVS, Margaret Plamondon, Statement to the Truth and Reconciliation Commission of Canada, Fort Smith, Northwest Territories, 6 May 2011, Statement Number: 2011-0387.

506. TRC, AVS, Noel Starblanket, Statement to the Truth and Reconciliation Commission of Canada, Regina, Saskatchewan, 16 January 2012, Statement Number: 2011-0314.

507. TRC, AVS, Adam Highway, Statement to the Truth and Reconciliation Commission of Canada, Pelican Narrows, Saskatchewan, 14 February 2012, Statement Number: 2011-1781. (Translated from Woodland Cree to English by Translation Bureau, Public Works and Government Services Canada.)

508. TRC, AVS, Earl Clarke, Statement to the Truth and Reconciliation Commission of Canada, Poundmaker First Nation, Saskatchewan, 30 June 2010, Statement Number: 01-SK-JU10-002.

509. TRC, AVS, Ernest Barkman, Statement to the Truth and Reconciliation Commission of Canada, Garden Hill First Nation, Manitoba, 30 March 2011, Statement Number: 2011-0123. (Translated from Oji-Cree to English by Translation Bureau, Public Works and Government Services Canada.)

510. TRC, AVS, Shirley Ida Moore, Statement to the Truth and Reconciliation Commission of Canada, Winnipeg, Manitoba, 2 March 2011, Statement Number: 2011-0089.

511. TRC, AVS, Gerald McLeod, Statement to the Truth and Reconciliation Commission of Canada, Whitehorse, Yukon, 27 May 2011, Statement Number: 2011-1130.

512. TRC, AVS, Eli Carpenter, Statement to the Truth and Reconciliation Commission of Canada, Winnipeg, Manitoba, 17 June 2010, Statement Number: 02-MB-17JU10-018.

513. TRC, AVS, Mary Vivier, Statement to the Truth and Reconciliation Commission of Canada, Winnipeg, Manitoba, 18 June 2010, Statement Number: 02-MB-18JU10-082.

514. TRC, AVS, Daniel Andre, Statement to the Truth and Reconciliation Commission of Canada, Whitehorse, Yukon, 23 May 2011, Statement Number: 2011-0202.

515. TRC, AVS, Nellie Ningewance, Statement to the Truth and Reconciliation Commission of Canada, Sault Ste. Marie, 1 July 2011, Statement Number: 2011-0305.

516. TRC, AVS, William Antoine, Statement to the Truth and Reconciliation Commission of Canada, Little Current, Ontario, 12 May 2011, Statement Number: 2011-2002.

517. TRC, AVS, Lawrence Wanakamik, Statement to the Truth and Reconciliation Commission of Canada, Thunder Bay, Ontario, 6 January 2011, Statement Number: 01-ON-06JA11-002.

518. TRC, AVS, Eva Simpson, Statement to the Truth and Reconciliation Commission of Canada, Norway House First Nation, Manitoba, 10 May 2011, Statement Number: 2011-0290.

519. TRC, AVS, J. G. Michel Sutherland, Statement to the Truth and Reconciliation Commission of Canada, Fort Albany, Ontario, 29 January 2013, Statement Number: SP099.

520. TRC, AVS, Doris Young, Statement to the Truth and Reconciliation Commission of Canada, Saskatoon, Saskatchewan, 22 June 2012, Statement Number: 2011-3517.

521. TRC, AVS, Violet Beaulieu, Statement to the Truth and Reconciliation Commission of Canada, Fort Resolution, Northwest Territories, 28 April 2011, Statement Number: 2011-0377.

522. TRC, AVS, Dorothy Ross, Statement to the Truth and Reconciliation Commission of Canada, Thunder Bay, Ontario, 25 November 2010, Statement Number: 01-ON-24NOV10-014.

523. TRC, AVS, Clara Munroe, Statement to the Truth and Reconciliation Commission of Canada, Key First Nation, Saskatchewan, 21 January 2012, Statement Number: SP039.

524. TRC, AVS, Tina Duguay, Statement to the Truth and Reconciliation Commission of Canada, Kamloops, British Columbia, 9 August 2009, Statement Number: 2011-5002.

525. TRC, AVS, Percy Tuesday, Statement to the Truth and Reconciliation Commission of Canada, Winnipeg, Manitoba, 18 June 2010, Statement Number: 02-MB-18JU10-083.

526. TRC, AVS, Joseph Ward, Statement to the Truth and Reconciliation Commission of Canada, Halifax, Nova Scotia, 28 October 2011, Statement Number: 2011-2872.

527. TRC, AVS, Noel Knockwood, Statement to the Truth and Reconciliation Commission of Canada, Halifax, Nova Scotia, 29 October 2011, Statement Number: 2011-2922.

528. TRC, AVS, Faron Fontaine, Statement to the Truth and Reconciliation Commission of Canada, Long Plain First Nation, Manitoba, 27 July 2010, Statement Number: 01-MB-26JY10-009.

529. TRC, AVS, Lena McKay, Statement to the Truth and Reconciliation Commission of Canada, Fort Resolution, Northwest Territories, 28 April 2011, Statement Number: 2011-0382.

530. TRC, AVS, Eugene Tetreault, Statement to the Truth and Reconciliation Commission of Canada, Williams Lake, British Columbia, 20 December 2010, Statement Number: 01-BC-20DE10-001.

531. TRC, AVS, Ula Hotonami, Statement to the Truth and Reconciliation Commission of Canada, Winnipeg, Manitoba, 5 January 2012, Statement Number: 2011-2654.

532. TRC, AVS, Roger Cromarty, Statement to the Truth and Reconciliation Commission of Canada, Winnipeg, Manitoba, 17 June 2010, Statement Number: 02-MB-16JU10-132.

533. TRC, AVS, Roy Johnson, Statement to the Truth and Reconciliation Commission of Canada, Dawson City, Yukon, 24 May 2011, Statement Number: 2011-0203.

534. TRC, AVS, Mollie Roy, Statement to the Truth and Reconciliation Commission of Canada, Whitehorse, Yukon, 26 May 2011, Statement Number: 2011-1129.

535. TRC, AVS, Larry Beardy, Statement to the Truth and Reconciliation Commission of Canada, Thompson, Manitoba, 25 September 2012, Statement Number: SP082.

536. *Indian Residential Schools Settlement Agreement*, 8 May 2006, Schedule N, "Mandate for the Truth and Reconciliation Commission [of Canada]," 3, http://www.residentialschoolsettlement.ca/SCHEDULE_N.pdf (accessed 14 March 2015).

537. TRC, AVS, Jean Pierre Bellemare, Statement to the Truth and Reconciliation Commission of Canada, La Tuque, Québec, 5 March 2013, Statement Number: SP104.

538. TRC, AVS, Andrew Yellowback, Statement to the Truth and Reconciliation Commission of Canada, Kamloops, British Columbia, 9 August 2009, Statement Number: 2011-5015.

539. See, for example: TRC, AVS, Mary Lou Iahtail, Statement to the Truth and Reconciliation Commission of Canada, Ottawa, Ontario, 5 February 2011, Statement Number: 01-ON-05FE11-005.

540. See, for example: TRC, AVS, [Name redacted], Statement to the Truth and Reconciliation Commission of Canada, Winnipeg, Manitoba, 18 June 2010, Statement Number: 02-MB-18JU10-055; TRC, AVS, Myrna Kaminawaish, Statement to the Truth and Reconciliation Commission of Canada, Thunder Bay, Ontario, 7 January 2011, Statement Number: 01-ON-06JA11-004; TRC, AVS, Percy Tuesday, Statement to the Truth and Reconciliation Commission of Canada, Winnipeg, Manitoba, 18 June 2010, Statement Number: 02-MB-18JU10-083; TRC, AVS, Isaac Daniels, Statement to the Truth and Reconciliation Commission of Canada, Saskatoon, Saskatchewan, 22 June 2012, Statement Number: 2011-1779.

541. TRC, AVS, Sheila Gunderson, Statement to the Truth and Reconciliation Commission of Canada, Fort Simpson, Northwest Territories, 23 November 2011, Statement Number: 2011-2687.

542. See, for example: TRC, AVS, [Name redacted], Statement to the Truth and Reconciliation Commission of Canada, Winnipeg, Manitoba, 18 June 2010, Statement Number: 02-MB-18JU10-055; TRC, AVS, Leona Bird, Statement to the Truth and Reconciliation Commission of Canada, Saskatoon, Saskatchewan, 21 June 2012, Statement Number: 2011-4415; TRC, AVS, Barbara Ann Pahpasay Skead, Statement to the Truth and Reconciliation Commission of Canada, Winnipeg, Manitoba, 17 June 2010, Statement Number: 02-MB-16JU10-159.

543. TRC, AVS, Stella Marie Tookate, Statement to the Truth and Reconciliation Commission of Canada, Timmins, Ontario, 9 November 2010, Statement Number: 01-ON-8-10NOV10-003.

544. TRC, AVS, Josephine Sutherland, Statement to the Truth and Reconciliation Commission of Canada, Timmins, Ontario, 8 November 2010, Statement Number: 01-ON4-6NOV10-013.

545. TRC, AVS, [Name redacted], Statement to the Truth and Reconciliation Commission of Canada, Gambier Island, British Columbia, 29 July 2011, Statement Number: 2011-3279.

546. TRC, AVS, Marie Therese Kistabish, Statement to the Truth and Reconciliation Commission of Canada, Val d'Or, Québec, 6 February 2012, Statement Number: SP101.

547. TRC, AVS, Richard Morrison, Statement to the Truth and Reconciliation Commission of Canada, Winnipeg, Manitoba, 17 June 2010, Statement Number: 02-MB-17JU10-080.

548. TRC, AVS, Raynie Tuckanow, Statement to the Truth and Reconciliation Commission of Canada, Regina, Saskatchewan, 17 January 2012, Statement Number: SP036.

549. TRC, AVS, Leonard Peter Alexcee, Statement to the Truth and Reconciliation Commission of Canada, Vancouver, British Columbia, 18 September 2013, Statement Number: 2011-3228.

550. TRC, AVS, Mary Vivier, Statement to the Truth and Reconciliation Commission of Canada, Winnipeg, Manitoba, 18 June 2010, Statement Number: 02-MB-18JU10-082.

551. TRC, AVS, Donna Antoine, Statement to the Truth and Reconciliation Commission of Canada, Enderby, British Columbia, 13 October 2011, Statement Number: 2011-3287.

552. TRC, AVS, Helen Harry, Statement to the Truth and Reconciliation Commission of Canada, Vancouver, British Columbia, 20 September 2013, Statement Number: 2011-3203.

553. TRC, AVS, Vitaline Elsie Jenner, Statement to the Truth and Reconciliation Commission of Canada, Winnipeg, Manitoba, 16 June 2010, Statement Number: 02-MB-16JU10-131.

554. TRC, AVS, Louisa Papatie, Statement to the Truth and Reconciliation Commission of Canada, Val d'Or, Québec, 6 February 2012, Statement Number: SP101.

555. TRC, AVS, Ricky Kakekagumick, Statement to the Truth and Reconciliation Commission of Canada, Thunder Bay, Ontario, 15 December 2011, Statement Number: 2011-4200.

556. TRC, AVS, Bernard Catcheway, Statement to the Truth and Reconciliation Commission of Canada, Skownan First Nation, Manitoba, 12 October 2011, Statement Number: 2011-2510.

557. TRC, AVS, Doris Judy McKay, Statement to the Truth and Reconciliation Commission of Canada, Rolling River First Nation, Manitoba, 23 November 2011, Statement Number: 2011-2514.

558. TRC, AVS, Mervin Mirasty, Statement to the Truth and Reconciliation Commission of Canada, Saskatoon, Saskatchewan, 21 June 2012, Statement Number: 2011-4391.

559. TRC, AVS, Flora Northwest, Statement to the Truth and Reconciliation Commission of Canada, Hobbema, Alberta, 24 July 2013, Statement Number: SP124.

560. TRC, AVS, Aaron Leon, Statement to the Truth and Reconciliation Commission of Canada, Mission, British Columbia, 19 May 2011, Statement Number: 2011-3460.

561. TRC, AVS, Richard Hall, Statement to the Truth and Reconciliation Commission of Canada, Vancouver, British Columbia, 18 September 2013, Statement Number: 2011-1852.

562. TRC, AVS, Frances Tait, Statement to the Truth and Reconciliation Commission of Canada, Victoria, British Columbia, 13 April 2012, Statement Number: 2011-3974.

563. TRC, AVS, Timothy Henderson, Statement to the Truth and Reconciliation Commission of Canada, Winnipeg, Manitoba, 28 June 2011, Statement Number: 2011-0291.

564. TRC, AVS, Nellie Ningewance, Statement to the Truth and Reconciliation Commission of Canada, Sault Ste. Marie, Ontario, 1 July 2011, Statement Number: 2011-0305.

565. TRC, AVS, Marlene Kayseas, Statement to the Truth and Reconciliation Commission of Canada, Regina, Saskatchewan, 16 January 2012, Statement Number: SP035.

566. TRC, AVS, Andrew Captain, Statement to the Truth and Reconciliation Commission of Canada, Winnipeg, Manitoba, 18 June 2010, Statement Number: SC111.

567. TRC, AVS, [Name redacted], Statement to the Truth and Reconciliation Commission of Canada, Little Current, Ontario, 13 May 2011, Statement Number: 2011-2012.

568. TRC, AVS, Fred Brass, Statement to the Truth and Reconciliation Commission of Canada, Key First Nation, Saskatchewan, 21 January 2012, Statement Number: SP039.

569. TRC, AVS, Elaine Durocher, Statement to the Truth and Reconciliation Commission of Canada, Winnipeg, Manitoba, 16 June 2010, Statement Number: 02-MB-16JU10-059.

570. TRC, AVS, John B. Custer, Statement to the Truth and Reconciliation Commission of Canada, Winnipeg, Manitoba, 19 June 2010, Statement Number: 02-MB-19JU10-057.

571. TRC, AVS, Louise Large, Statement to the Truth and Reconciliation Commission of Canada, St. Paul, Alberta, 7 January 2011, Statement Number: 01-AB-06JA11-012.

572. TRC, AVS, Ben Pratt, Statement to the Truth and Reconciliation Commission of Canada, Regina, Saskatchewan, 18 January 2012, Statement Number: 2011-3318.

573. TRC, AVS, Percy Isaac, Statement to the Truth and Reconciliation Commission of Canada, Regina, Saskatchewan, 16 January 2012, Statement Number: SP035.

574. Mandryk, "Uneasy Neighbours," 210.

575. TRC, AVS, Eric Robinson, Statement to the Truth and Reconciliation Commission of Canada, Winnipeg, Manitoba, 16 June 2010, Statement Number: SC093.

576. TRC, AVS, Clara Quisess, Statement to the Truth and Reconciliation Commission of Canada, Winnipeg, Manitoba, 17 June 2010, Statement Number: 02-MB-17JU10-032.

577. TRC, AVS, Lynda Pahpasay McDonald, Statement to the Truth and Reconciliation Commission of Canada, Winnipeg, Manitoba, 16 June 2010, Statement Number: 02-MB-16JU10-130.

578. TRC, AVS, Helen Harry, Statement to the Truth and Reconciliation Commission of Canada, Vancouver, British Columbia, 20 September 2013, Statement Number: 2011-3203.

579. TRC, AVS, Larry Roger Listener, Statement to the Truth and Reconciliation Commission of Canada, Hobbema, Alberta, 25 July 2013, Statement Number: SP125.

580. TRC, AVS, Mary Vivier, Statement to the Truth and Reconciliation Commission of Canada, Winnipeg, Manitoba, 18 June 2010, Statement Number: SC110.

581. Elisabeth Ashini, Statement to the Truth and Reconciliation Commission of Canada, (Translated from French) Montreal, Québec, 27 April 2013, Statement Number: 2011-6139.

582. TRC, AVS, Norman Courchene, Statement to the Truth and Reconciliation Commission of Canada, Winnipeg, Manitoba, 16 June 2010, Statement Number: 02-MB-16JU10-065.

583. TRC, AVS, Amelia Galligos-Thomas, Statement to the Truth and Reconciliation Commission of Canada, Victoria, British Columbia, 13 April 2012, Statement Number: 2011-3975.

584. TRC, AVS, Ivan George, Statement to the Truth and Reconciliation Commission of Canada, Mission, British Columbia, 18 May 2011, Statement Number: 2011-3472.

585. TRC, AVS, Dorothy Jane Beaulieu, Statement to the Truth and Reconciliation Commission of Canada, Fort Resolution, Northwest Territories, 28 April 2011, Statement Number: 2011-0379.

586. TRC, AVS, Lorna Morgan, Statement to the Truth and Reconciliation Commission of Canada, Winnipeg, Manitoba, 17 June 2010, Statement Number: 02-MB-16JU10-041.

587. TRC, AVS, Ben Pratt, Statement to the Truth and Reconciliation Commission of Canada, Regina, Saskatchewan, 18 January 2012, Statement Number: 2011-3318.

588. TRC, AVS, Michael Muskego, Statement to the Truth and Reconciliation Commission of Canada, Winnipeg, Manitoba, 18 June 2010, Statement Number: 02-MB-18JU10-045.

589. TRC, AVS, Josephine Sutherland, Statement to the Truth and Reconciliation Commission of Canada, Timmins, Ontario, 8 November 2010, Statement Number: 01-ON4-6NOV10-013.

590. TRC, AVS, Jimmy Cunningham, Statement to the Truth and Reconciliation Commission of Canada, Edmonton, Alberta, 30 March 2014, Statement Number: SP207.

591. TRC, AVS, Violet Rupp Cook, Statement to the Truth and Reconciliation Commission of Canada, Bloodvein First Nation, Manitoba, 25 January 2012, Statement Number: 2011-2565.

592. TRC, AVS, Elizabeth Good, Statement to the Truth and Reconciliation Commission of Canada, Mission, British Columbia, 18 May 2011, Statement Number: 2011-3469.

593. TRC, AVS, Hazel Mary Anderson, Statement to the Truth and Reconciliation Commission of Canada, Winnipeg, Manitoba, 18 June 2010, Statement Number: 02-MB-18JU10-034.

594. TRC, AVS, Peter Ross, Statement to the Truth and Reconciliation Commission of Canada, Tsiige-htchic, Northwest Territories, 8 September 2011, Statement Number: 2011-0340.

595. TRC, AVS, Hazel Mary Anderson, Statement to the Truth and Reconciliation Commission of Canada, Winnipeg, Manitoba, 18 June 2010, Statement Number: 02-MB-18JU10-034.

596. TRC, AVS, Wayne Reindeer, Statement to the Truth and Reconciliation Commission of Canada, Hobbema, Alberta, 25 July 2013, Statement Number: SP125.

597. TRC, AVS, Ken A. Littledeer, Statement to the Truth and Reconciliation Commission of Canada, Thunder Bay, Ontario, 26 November 2010, Statement Number: 01-ON-24-NOV10-028.

598. TRC, AVS, Sphenia Jones, Statement to the Truth and Reconciliation Commission of Canada, Terrace, British Columbia, 29 November 2011, Statement Number: 2011-3300.

599. TRC, AVS, Lawrence Waquan, Statement to the Truth and Reconciliation Commission of Canada, Winnipeg, Manitoba, 18 June 2010, Statement Number: SC111.

600. TRC, AVS, Mel H. Buffalo, Statement to the Truth and Reconciliation Commission of Canada, Hobbema, Alberta, 24 July 2013, Statement Number: SP124.

601. TRC, AVS, William Garson, Statement to the Truth and Reconciliation Commission of Canada, Split Lake First Nation, Manitoba, 24 March 2011, Statement Number: 2011-0122.

602. TRC, AVS, Percy Thompson, Statement to the Truth and Reconciliation Commission of Canada, Hobbema, Alberta, 25 July 2013, Statement Number: SP125.

603. TRC, AVS, Alice Ruperthouse, Statement to the Truth and Reconciliation Commission of Canada, Val d'Or, Québec, 5 February 2012, Statement Number: SP100.

604. TRC, AVS, Albert Elias, Statement to the Truth and Reconciliation Commission of Canada, Inuvik, Northwest Territories, 1 July 2011, Statement Number: SC092.

605. TRC, AVS, Denis Morrison, Statement to the Truth and Reconciliation Commission of Canada, Winnipeg, Manitoba, 17 June 2010, Statement Number: 02-MB-17JU10-028.

606. TRC, AVS, Timothy Henderson, Statement to the Truth and Reconciliation Commission of Canada, Winnipeg, Manitoba, 18 June 2010, Statement Number: 02-MB-18JU10-048.

607. TRC, AVS, Joseph Maud, Statement to the Truth and Reconciliation Commission of Canada, Winnipeg, Manitoba, 19 June 2010, Statement Number: 02-MB-18JU10-081.

608. TRC, AVS, Bob Baxter, Statement to the Truth and Reconciliation Commission of Canada, Thunder Bay, Ontario, 24 November 2010, Statement Number: 01-ON-24NOV10-012.

609. TRC, AVS, Clara Quisess, Statement to the Truth and Reconciliation Commission of Canada, Winnipeg, Manitoba, 17 June 2010, Statement Number: 02-MB-17JU10-032.

610. TRC, AVS, Louisa Birote, Statement to the Truth and Reconciliation Commission of Canada, La Tuque, Québec, 5 March 2013, Statement Number: SP104.

611. TRC, AVS, David Charleson, Statement to the Truth and Reconciliation Commission of Canada, Deroche, British Columbia, 20 January 2010, Statement Number: 2011-5043.

612. TRC, AVS, Victoria McIntosh, Statement to the Truth and Reconciliation Commission of Canada, Winnipeg, Manitoba, 16 June 2010, Statement Number: 02-MB-16JU10-123.

613. TRC, AVS, [Name redacted], Statement to the Truth and Reconciliation Commission of Canada, Winnipeg, Manitoba, 18 June 2010, Statement Number: 02-MB-18JU10-062.

614. TRC, AVS, Leona Bird, Statement to the Truth and Reconciliation Commission of Canada, Saskatoon, Saskatchewan, 21 June 2012, Statement Number: 2011-4415.

615. TRC, AVS, Louise Large, Statement to the Truth and Reconciliation Commission of Canada, St. Paul, Alberta, 7 January 2011, Statement Number: 01-AB-06JA11-012.

616. TRC, AVS, Don Willie, Statement to the Truth and Reconciliation Commission of Canada, Alert Bay, British Columbia, 3 August 2011, Statement Number: 2011-3284.

617. TRC, AVS, Mary Stoney, Statement to the Truth and Reconciliation Commission of Canada, Hobbema, Alberta, 24 July 2013, Statement Number: SP124.

618. TRC, AVS, Geraldine Shingoose, Statement to the Truth and Reconciliation Commission of Canada, Winnipeg, Manitoba, 19 June 2010, Statement Number: 02-MB-19JU10-033.

619. TRC, AVS, Eva Bad Eagle, Statement to the Truth and Reconciliation Commission of Canada, Lethbridge, Alberta, 9 October 2013, Statement Number: SP127.

620. TRC, AVS, Janet Murray, Statement to the Truth and Reconciliation Commission of Canada, Prince Albert, Saskatchewan, 1 February 2012, Statement Number: 2011-3881. (Translated from Woodland Cree to English by Translation Bureau, Public Works and Government Services Canada.)

621. TRC, AVS, Daniel Nanooch, Statement to the Truth and Reconciliation Commission of Canada, High Level, Alberta, 4 July 2013, Statement Number: 2011-1868.

622. TRC, AVS, Eva Bad Eagle, Statement to the Truth and Reconciliation Commission of Canada, Lethbridge, Alberta, 9 October 2013, Statement Number: SP127.

623. TRC, AVS, Gordon Keewatin, Statement to the Truth and Reconciliation Commission of Canada, Regina, Saskatchewan, 18 August 2010, Statement Number: 01-SK-18AU10-003.

624. TRC, AVS, Mary Rose Julian, Statement to the Truth and Reconciliation Commission of Canada, Halifax, Nova Scotia, 27 October 2011, Statement Number: 2011-2880.

625. TRC, AVS, Harvey Behn, Statement to the Truth and Reconciliation Commission of Canada, Watson Lake, Yukon, 25 May 2011, Statement Number: SP021.

626. TRC, AVS, Roger Cromarty, Statement to the Truth and Reconciliation Commission of Canada, Winnipeg, Manitoba, 17 June 2010, Statement Number: 02-MB-16JU10-132.

627. TRC, AVS, Louise Large, Statement to the Truth and Reconciliation Commission of Canada, St. Paul, Alberta, 7 January 2011, Statement Number: 01-AB-06JA11-012.

628. TRC, AVS, Nellie Trapper, Statement to the Truth and Reconciliation Commission of Canada, Winnipeg, Manitoba, 18 June 2010, Statement Number: 02-MB-16JU10-086.

629. TRC, AVS, Angus Havioyak, Statement to the Truth and Reconciliation Commission of Canada, Kugluktuk, Nunavut, 13 April 2011, Statement Number: 2011-0518.

630. TRC, AVS, Allen Kanayok, Statement to the Truth and Reconciliation Commission of Canada, Cambridge Bay, Nunavut, 11 April 2011, Statement Number: 2011-0176.

631. TRC, AVS, Les Carpenter, Statement to the Truth and Reconciliation Commission of Canada, Inuvik, Northwest Territories, 30 June 2011, Statement Number: NNE202.

632. TRC, AVS, Paul Andrew, Statement to the Truth and Reconciliation Commission of Canada, Inuvik, Northwest Territories, 30 June 2011, Statement Number: NNE202.

633. TRC, AVS, Alphonsine McNeely, Statement to the Truth and Reconciliation Commission of Canada, Fort Good Hope, Northwest Territories, 13 July 2010, Statement Number: 01-NWT-JY10-002.

634. TRC, AVS, Edwin F. Jebb, Statement to the Truth and Reconciliation Commission of Canada, Opaskwayak Cree First Nation, Manitoba, 17 January 2012, Statement Number: 2011-0295.

635. TRC, AVS, Martina Therese Fisher, Statement to the Truth and Reconciliation Commission of Canada, Bloodvein First Nation, Manitoba, 26 January 2012, Statement Number: 2011-2564.

636. TRC, AVS, Noel Starblanket, Statement to the Truth and Reconciliation Commission of Canada, Regina, Saskatchewan, 16 January 2012, Statement Number: 2011-3314.

637. TRC, AVS, Dorothy Ross, Statement to the Truth and Reconciliation Commission of Canada, Thunder Bay, Ontario, 25 November 2010, Statement Number: 01-ON-24NOV10-014.

638. TRC, AVS, Lydia Ross, Statement to the Truth and Reconciliation Commission of Canada, Winnipeg, Manitoba, 16 June 2010, Statement Number: 02-MB-16JU10-029.

639. TRC, AVS, Isaac Daniels, Statement to the Truth and Reconciliation Commission of Canada, Saskatoon, Saskatchewan, 22 June 2012, Statement Number: 2011-1779.

640. TRC, AVS, Gordon Keewatin, Statement to the Truth and Reconciliation Commission of Canada, Regina, Saskatchewan, 18 August 2010, Statement Number: 01-SK-18AU10-003.

641. TRC, AVS, Albert Fiddler, Statement to the Truth and Reconciliation Commission of Canada, Saskatoon, Saskatchewan, 24 June 2012, Statement Number: 2011-1760.

642. See, for example: TRC, AVS, Albert Fiddler, Statement to the Truth and Reconciliation Commission of Canada, Saskatoon, Saskatchewan, 24 June 2012, Statement Number: 2011-1760; TRC, AVS, Farrel Francis, Statement to the Truth and Reconciliation Commission of Canada, Winnipeg, Manitoba, 18 June 2010, Statement Number: 02-MB-18JU10-032; TRC, AVS, Betsy Olson, Statement to the Truth and Reconciliation Commission of Canada, Saskatoon, Saskatchewan, 21 June 2012, Statement Number: 2011-4378; TRC, AVS, Leanne Sleigh, Statement to the Truth and Reconciliation Commission of Canada, Winnipeg, Manitoba, 16 June 2010, Statement Number: SC093; TRC, AVS, Ronalee Lavallee, Statement to the Truth and Reconciliation Commission of Canada, Saskatoon, Saskatchewan, 24 June 2012, Statement Number: 2011-1776; TRC, AVS, Archie Hyacinthe, Statement to the Truth and Reconciliation Commission of Canada, Kenora, Ontario, 15 March 2011, Statement Number: 2011-0279; TRC, AVS, Roy Johnson, Statement to the Truth and Reconciliation Commission of Canada, Dawson City, Yukon, 24 May 2011, Statement Number: 2011-0203; TRC, AVS, Henry Bob, Statement to the Truth and Reconciliation Commission of Canada, Terrace, British Columbia, 30 November 2011, Statement Number: 2011-3305.

643. See, for example: TRC, AVS, Ruth Chapman, Statement to the Truth and Reconciliation Commission of Canada, Winnipeg, Manitoba, 16 June 2010, Statement Number: 02-MB-16JU10-118; TRC, AVS, Gordon James Pemmican, Statement to the Truth and Reconciliation Commission of Canada, Winnipeg, Manitoba, 18 June 2010, Statement Number: 02-MB-18JU10-0069; TRC, AVS, Mary Vivier, Statement to the Truth and Reconciliation Commission of Canada, Winnipeg, Manitoba, 18 June 2010, Statement Number: 02-MB-18JU10-082; TRC, AVS, Roy Johnson, Statement to the Truth and Reconciliation Commission of Canada, Dawson City, Yukon, 24 May 2011, Statement Number: 2011-0203; TRC, AVS, Ken Lacquette, Statement to the Truth and Reconciliation Commission of Canada, Winnipeg, Manitoba, 18 June 2010, Statement Number: 02-MB-18JU10-052.

644. TRC, AVS, Agnes Moses, Statement to the Truth and Reconciliation Commission of Canada, Inuvik, Northwest Territories, 29 June 2011, Statement Number: SC090.

645. TRC, AVS, Don Willie, Statement to the Truth and Reconciliation Commission of Canada, Alert Bay, British Columbia, 3 August 2011, Statement Number: 2011-3284.

646. TRC, AVS, Ilene Nepoose, Statement to the Truth and Reconciliation Commission of Canada, Hobbema, Alberta, 25 July 2013, Statement Number: 2011-2380.

647. TRC, AVS, Alphonsine McNeely, Statement to the Truth and Reconciliation Commission of Canada, Fort Good Hope, Northwest Territories, 13 July 2010, Statement Number: 01-NWT-JY10-002.

648. TRC, AVS, Wesley Keewatin, Statement to the Truth and Reconciliation Commission of Canada, Gambier Island, British Columbia, 28 July 2011, Statement Number: 2011-3276.

649. TRC, AVS, Gladys Prince, Statement to the Truth and Reconciliation Commission of Canada, Brandon, Manitoba, 13 October 2011, Statement Number: 2011-2498. (Translated from Ojibway to English by Translation Bureau, Public Works and Government Services Canada.)

650. TRC, AVS, Gordon James Pemmican, Statement to the Truth and Reconciliation Commission of Canada, Winnipeg, Manitoba, 18 June 2010, Statement Number: 02-MB-18JU10-0069.

651. TRC, AVS, Gordon James Pemmican, Statement to the Truth and Reconciliation Commission of Canada, Winnipeg, Manitoba, 17 June 2010, Statement Number: SC108.

652. TRC, AVS, Bernard Catcheway, Statement to the Truth and Reconciliation Commission of Canada, Skownan First Nation, Manitoba, 12 October 2011, Statement Number: 2011-2510.

653. See, for example: TRC, AVS, Roy Johnson, Statement to the Truth and Reconciliation Commission of Canada, Dawson City, Yukon, 24 May 2011, Statement Number: 2011-0203; TRC, AVS, Millie Anderson, Statement to the Truth and Reconciliation Commission of Canada, Regina, Saskatchewan, 18 August 2010, Statement Number: 01-SK-18AU10-002.

654. TRC, AVS, Henry Bob, Statement to the Truth and Reconciliation Commission of Canada, Terrace, British Columbia, 30 November 2011, Statement Number: 2011-3305.

655. TRC, AVS, Alphonsine McNeely, Statement to the Truth and Reconciliation Commission of Canada, Fort Good Hope, Northwest Territories, 13 July 2010, Statement Number: 01-NWT-JY10-002.

656. TRC, AVS, Mabel Brown, Statement to the Truth and Reconciliation Commission of Canada, Inuvik, Northwest Territories, 28 September 2011, Statement Number: 2011-0325.

657. TRC, AVS, [Name redacted], Statement to the Truth and Reconciliation Commission of Canada, Fort Simpson, Northwest Territories, 23 November 2011, Statement Number: 2011-2689.

658. TRC, AVS, Greg Murdock, Statement to the Truth and Reconciliation Commission of Canada, Winnipeg, Manitoba, 18 June 2010, Statement Number: SC111.

659. See, for example: TRC, AVS, Bernard Catcheway, Statement to the Truth and Reconciliation Commission of Canada, Skownan First Nation, Manitoba, 12 October 2011, Statement Number: 2011-2510; TRC, AVS, Doris Judy McKay, Statement to the Truth and Reconciliation Commission of Canada, Rolling River First Nation, Manitoba, 23 November 2011, Statement Number: 2011-2514

660. TRC, AVS, Robert Malcolm, Statement to the Truth and Reconciliation Commission of Canada, Winnipeg, Manitoba, 17 June 2010, Statement Number: 02-MB-16JU10-090.

661. TRC, AVS, Georgina Harry, Statement to the Truth and Reconciliation Commission of Canada, Mission, British Columbia, 19 May 2011, Statement Number: 2011-3459.

662. TRC, AVS, Roger Cromarty, Statement to the Truth and Reconciliation Commission of Canada, Winnipeg, Manitoba, 17 June 2010, Statement Number: 02-MB-16JU10-132.

663. TRC, AVS, Lydia Ross, Statement to the Truth and Reconciliation Commission of Canada, Winnipeg, Manitoba, 16 June 2010, Statement Number: 02-MB-16JU10-029.

664. TRC, AVS, Sarah Cleary, Statement to the Truth and Reconciliation Commission of Canada, Tulita, Northwest Territories, 10 May 2011, Statement Number: SP018.

665. TRC, AVS, Marie Brown, Statement to the Truth and Reconciliation Commission of Canada, Saskatoon, Saskatchewan, 21 June 2012, Statement Number: 2011-4421.

666. TRC, AVS, Martha Minoose, Statement to the Truth and Reconciliation Commission of Canada, Lethbridge, Alberta, 10 October 2013, Statement Number: 2011-1748.

667. TRC, AVS, Shirley Waskewitch, Statement to the Truth and Reconciliation Commission of Canada, Saskatoon, Saskatchewan, 24 June 2012, Statement Number: 2011-3521.

668. TRC, AVS, Vitaline Elsie Jenner, Statement to the Truth and Reconciliation Commission of Canada, Winnipeg, Manitoba, 16 June 2010, Statement Number: 02-MB-16JU10-131.

669. TRC, AVS, Forrest Kendi, Statement to the Truth and Reconciliation Commission of Canada, Inuvik, Northwest Territories, 1 July 2011, Statement Number: SC092.

670. TRC, AVS, Greg Rainville, Statement to the Truth and Reconciliation Commission of Canada, Saskatoon, Saskatchewan, 22 June 2012, Statement Number: 2011-1752.

671. TRC, AVS, Ray Silver, Statement to the Truth and Reconciliation Commission of Canada, Mission, British Columbia, 17 May 2011, Statement Number: 2011-3467.

672. TRC, AVS, Mary Coon-Come, Statement to the Truth and Reconciliation Commission of Canada, La Tuque, Québec, 6 March 2013, Statement Number: SP105.

673. TRC, AVS, Alex Alikashuak, Statement to the Truth and Reconciliation Commission of Canada, Winnipeg, Manitoba, 16 June 2010, Statement Number: 02-MB-16JU10-137. For Paulosie Meeko's name, see: *Winnipeg Free Press*, "Mauled by Polar Bear, Youth Dies," 18 November 1968.

674. TRC, AVS, [Name redacted], Statement to the Truth and Reconciliation Commission of Canada, Deline, Northwest Territories, 2 March 2010, Statement Number: 07-NWT-02MR1-002.

675. TRC, AVS, Stella August, Statement to the Truth and Reconciliation Commission of Canada, Winnipeg, Manitoba, 16 June 2010, Statement Number: 02-MB-16JU10-005.

676. TRC, AVS, Marjorie Ovayuak, Statement to the Truth and Reconciliation Commission of Canada, Tuktoyaktuk, Northwest Territories, 19 September 2011, Statement Number: 2011-0351.

677. TRC, AVS, Gerald McLeod, Statement to the Truth and Reconciliation Commission of Canada, Whitehorse, Yukon, 27 May 2011, Statement Number: 2011-1130.

678. TRC, AVS, Clara Quisess, Statement to the Truth and Reconciliation Commission of Canada, Winnipeg, Manitoba, 17 June 2010, Statement Number: 02-MB-17JU10-032.

679. TRC, AVS, Paul Johnup, Statement to the Truth and Reconciliation Commission of Canada, Winnipeg, Manitoba, 16 June 2010, Statement Number: 02-MB-16JU10-147.

680. TRC, AVS, Monique Papatie, Statement to the Truth and Reconciliation Commission of Canada, Val d'Or, Québec, 6 February 2012, Statement Number: SP101.

681. TRC, AVS, Lillian Kennedy, Statement to the Truth and Reconciliation Commission of Canada, Bloodvein First Nation, Manitoba, 25 January 2012, Statement Number: 2011-2563.

682. TRC, AVS, Jennie Thomas, Statement to the Truth and Reconciliation Commission of Canada, Victoria, British Columbia, 14 April 2012, Statement Number: 2011-3992.

683. TRC, AVS, Shirley Ida Moore, Statement to the Truth and Reconciliation Commission of Canada, Winnipeg, Manitoba, 2 March 2011, Statement Number: 2011-0089.

684. TRC, AVS, Geraldine Shingoose, Statement to the Truth and Reconciliation Commission of Canada, Winnipeg, Manitoba, 19 June 2010, Statement Number: 02-MB-19JU10-033.

685. TRC, AVS, Jeanne Rioux, Statement to the Truth and Reconciliation Commission of Canada, Vancouver, British Columbia, 18 September 2013, Statement Number: 2011-3206.

686. TRC, AVS, Martha Minoose, Statement to the Truth and Reconciliation Commission of Canada, Lethbridge, Alberta, 10 October 2013, Statement Number: 2011-1748.

687. TRC, AVS, Alphonsine McNeely, Statement to the Truth and Reconciliation Commission of Canada, Fort Good Hope, Northwest Territories, 13 July 2010, Statement Number: 01-NWT-JY10-002.

688. TRC, AVS, David Charleson, Statement to the Truth and Reconciliation Commission of Canada, Deroche, British Columbia, 20 January 2010, Statement Number: 2011-5043.

689. TRC, AVS, William Antoine, Statement to the Truth and Reconciliation Commission of Canada, Little Current, Ontario, 12 May 2011, Statement Number: 2011-2002.

690. TRC, AVS, Donald Copenace, Statement to the Truth and Reconciliation Commission of Canada, Winnipeg, Manitoba, 17 June 2010, Statement Number: 02-MB-17JU10-062.

691. TRC, AVS, Amelia Galligos-Thomas, Statement to the Truth and Reconciliation Commission of Canada, Victoria, British Columbia, 13 April 2012, Statement Number: 2011-3975.

692. TRC, AVS, Robert Malcolm, Statement to the Truth and Reconciliation Commission of Canada, Winnipeg, Manitoba, 17 June 2010, Statement Number: 02-MB-16JU10-090.

693. TRC, AVS, Mary Rose Julian, Statement to the Truth and Reconciliation Commission of Canada, Halifax, Nova Scotia, 27 October 2011, Statement Number: 2011-2880.

694. TRC, AVS, Percy Tuesday, Statement to the Truth and Reconciliation Commission of Canada, Winnipeg, Manitoba, 18 June 2010, Statement Number: 02-MB-18JU10-083.

695. TRC, AVS, Christina Kimball, Statement to the Truth and Reconciliation Commission of Canada, Winnipeg, Manitoba, 17 January 2011, Statement Number: 03-001-10-020.

696. TRC, AVS, Noel Starblanket, Statement to the Truth and Reconciliation Commission of Canada, Regina, Saskatchewan, 16 January 2012, Statement Number: 2011-3314.

697. TRC, AVS, Geraldine Shingoose, Statement to the Truth and Reconciliation Commission of Canada, Winnipeg, Manitoba, 19 June 2010, Statement Number: 02-MB-19JU10-033.

698. TRC, AVS, Paul Andrew, Statement to the Truth and Reconciliation Commission of Canada, Inuvik, Northwest Territories, 30 June 2011, Statement Number: NNE202.

699. TRC, AVS, John Kistabish, Statement to the Truth and Reconciliation Commission of Canada, 26 April 2013, Montreal, Québec, Statement Number: 2011-6135

700. TRC, AVS, Pierre Papatie, Statement to the Truth and Reconciliation Commission of Canada, 23 June 2012, Saskatoon, Saskatchewan, Statement Number: 2011-1794.

701. TRC, AVS, Aaron Leon, Statement to the Truth and Reconciliation Commission of Canada, Mission, British Columbia, 19 May 2011, Statement Number: 2011-3460.

702. TRC, AVS, Alice Quinney, Statement to the Truth and Reconciliation Commission of Canada, Winnipeg, Manitoba, 18 June 2010, Statement Number: 02-MB-18JU10-049.

703. TRC, AVS, Mel H. Buffalo, Statement to the Truth and Reconciliation Commission of Canada, Hobbema, Alberta, 24 July 2013, Statement Number: 2011-2535.

704. TRC, AVS, Albert Fiddler, Statement to the Truth and Reconciliation Commission of Canada, Saskatoon, Saskatchewan, 24 June 2012, Statement Number: 2011-1760.

705. TRC, AVS, Orval Commanda, Statement to the Truth and Reconciliation Commission of Canada, Spanish, Ontario, 13 September 2009, Statement Number: 2011-5022.

706. TRC, AVS, William Antoine, Statement to the Truth and Reconciliation Commission of Canada, Little Current, Ontario, 12 May 2011, Statement Number: 2011-2002.

707. TRC, AVS, Joseph Maud, Statement to the Truth and Reconciliation Commission of Canada, Winnipeg, Manitoba, 19 June 2010, Statement Number: 02-MB-18JU10-081.

708. Bruyere, "Introduction" to Robinson, *Frontrunners,* 4–5.

709. TRC, AVS, Patrick Bruyere, Statement to the Truth and Reconciliation Commission of Canada, Winnipeg, Manitoba, 16 June 2010, Statement Number: 02-MB-16JU10-157.

710. Robinson, *Frontrunners*; Robinson, Lewis, and Jarvis, *Niigaanibatowaad FrontRunners: a play in two acts*, National Film Board of Canada, 2007.

711. Sired, "Frontrunners," University of Calgary, On Campus, http://www.ucalgary.ca/news/uofcpublications/oncampus/biweekly/sept28-07/frontrunners.
712. TRC, AVS, Roddy Soosay, Statement to the Truth and Reconciliation Commission of Canada, Hobbema, Alberta, 25 July 2013, Statement Number: 2011-2379.
713. Marks, *They Call Me Chief*, 34.
714. TRC, NRA, INAC – Departmental Library – Ottawa, "Saskatchewan Midget Hockey Champions," Indian Record, volume 12, number 5, May 1949. [SMD-002829] Sasakamoose played with the Chicago Blackhawks in the 1952–53 season. Bill Robinson, who was born on the Sandy Lake Reserve in Saskatchewan but did not have Status under the *Indian Act*, played with the New York Rangers the year before. Marks, *They Call Me Chief*, 31.
715. TRC, AVS, Fred Sasakamoose, Statement to the Truth and Reconciliation Commission of Canada, Prince Albert, Saskatchewan, 2 February 2012, Statement Number: SP043.
716. Marks, *They Call Me Chief*, 35.
717. TRC, AVS, Fred Sasakamoose, Statement to the Truth and Reconciliation Commission of Canada, Prince Albert, Saskatchewan, 2 February 2012, Statement Number: SP043.
718. Haig-Brown, *Resistance and Renewal*, 77.
719. TRC, AVS, Jean Margaret Brown, Statement to the Truth and Reconciliation Commission of Canada, Enderby, British Columbia, 13 October 2011, Statement Number: 2011-3290.
720. TRC, AVS, Wilbur Abrahams, Statement to the Truth and Reconciliation Commission of Canada, Terrace, British Columbia, 30 November 2011, Statement Number: 2011-3301.
721. U'Mista Cultural Society, "Speck, Henry—U'dzistalis," http://www.umista.org/giftshop/item.php?item=448 (accessed 9 August 2013).
722. TRC, AVS, Don Willie, Statement to the Truth and Reconciliation Commission of Canada, Alert Bay, British Columbia, 3 August 2011, Statement Number: 2011-3284.
723. TRC, AVS, Michael Cheena, Statement to the Truth and Reconciliation Commission of Canada, Halifax, Nova Scotia, 27 October 2011, Statement Number: SC074.
724. TRC, AVS, Earl Clarke, Statement to the Truth and Reconciliation Commission of Canada, Poundmaker First Nation, Saskatchewan, 30 June 2010, Statement Number: 01-SK-JU10-002.
725. TRC, AVS, Ray Silver, Statement to the Truth and Reconciliation Commission of Canada, Mission, British Columbia, 17 May 2011, Statement Number: 2011-3467.
726. TRC, AVS, Thomas Keesick, Statement to the Truth and Reconciliation Commission of Canada, Winnipeg, Manitoba, 16 June 2010, Statement Number: 02-MB-16JU10-156.
727. TRC, AVS, Noel Knockwood, Statement to the Truth and Reconciliation Commission of Canada, Halifax, Nova Scotia, 29 October 2011, Statement Number: 2011-2922.
728. TRC, AVS, Alan Knockwood, Statement to the Truth and Reconciliation Commission of Canada, Indian Brook, Nova Scotia, 12 October 2011, Statement Number: SP029.
729. TRC, AVS, Larry Roger Listener, Statement to the Truth and Reconciliation Commission of Canada, Hobbema, Alberta, 25 July 2013, Statement Number: SP125.
730. TRC, AVS, Greg Rainville, Statement to the Truth and Reconciliation Commission of Canada, Saskatoon, Saskatchewan, 22 June 2012, Statement Number: 2011-1752.
731. TRC, AVS, Ronalee Lavallee, Statement to the Truth and Reconciliation Commission of Canada, Saskatoon, Saskatchewan, 24 June 2012, Statement Number: 2011-1776.
732. TRC, AVS, Velma Jackson, Statement to the Truth and Reconciliation Commission of Canada, St. Paul, Alberta, 06 January 2011, Statement Number: 01-AB-06JA11-003.

733. TRC, AVS, Amber K. K. Pelletier, Statement to the Truth and Reconciliation Commission of Canada, Saskatoon, Saskatchewan, 24 June 2012, Statement Number: 2011-1773.

734. TRC, AVS, Roy Denny, Statement to the Truth and Reconciliation Commission of Canada, Eskasoni, Nova Scotia, 14 October 2011, Statement Number: 2011-2678.

735. TRC, AVS, Rebecca Many Grey Horses, Statement to the Truth and Reconciliation Commission of Canada, Lethbridge, Alberta, 9 October 2013, Statement Number: SP127.

736. TRC, AVS, Lena McKay, Statement to the Truth and Reconciliation Commission of Canada, Fort Resolution, Northwest Territories, 28 April 2011, Statement Number: 2011-0382.

737. TRC, AVS, Roy Johnson, Statement to the Truth and Reconciliation Commission of Canada, Dawson City, Yukon, 24 May 2011, Statement Number: 2011-0203.

738. TRC, AVS, William Francis Paul, Statement to the Truth and Reconciliation Commission of Canada, Halifax, Nova Scotia, 28 October 2011, Statement Number: 2011-2873.

739. TRC, AVS, Rose Marie Prosper, Statement to the Truth and Reconciliation Commission of Canada, Halifax, Nova Scotia, 28 October 2011, Statement Number: 2011-2868.

740. TRC, AVS, Dorene Bernard, Statement to the Truth and Reconciliation Commission of Canada, Indian Brook, Nova Scotia, 12 October 2011, Statement Number: SP029.